Parental & Caregiver Involvement in South African Education

Edited by

Zahraa McDonald | Adam Cooper
Ashnie Mahadew | Noxolo Xaba

HSRC PRESS

Published by HSRC Press
Private Bag X9182, Cape Town, 8000, South Africa
www.hsrcpress.ac.za

First published 2025

ISBN (soft cover) 978-0-7969-2698-2

© 2025 Human Sciences Research Council

Copy edited by Megan Hall
Proofread by Alison Paulin
Typeset by Lauren Pillay
Cover design by Riaan Wilmans
Index by Jacoba Ferreira
Printed and bound by Tandym Print
Distributed in Africa by Blue Weaver

Tel: +27 (021) 701 4477; Fax Local: (021) 701 7302
www.blueweaver.co.za

Distributed worldwide (except central and southern Africa)
by Lynne Rienner Publishers, Inc.
Tel: +1 303-444-6684; Fax: +1 303-444-0824; Email: cservice@rienner.com
www.rienner.com

Suggested citation: McDonald, Z., Cooper, A., Mahadew, A. & Xaba, N. (eds) (2025). *Parental and Caregiver Involvement in South African Education*. Cape Town: HSRC Press.

To parents and caregivers everywhere who strive to support their children as best they can.

Contents

Acronyms and Abbreviations

ALM	asset living measurement
ALS	Alladin Learning Solutions
ALW	Active Learning Workshop
ANNSSF	Amended National Norms and Standards for School Funding
DBE	Department of Basic Education
DoE	Department of Education
ECCE	early childhood care and education
ECD	early childhood development
EDR	educational design research
EGMA	Early Grade Mathematics Assessment
EGRS	Early Grade Reading Study
ELP	early learning programme
JET	JET Education Services
HODs	heads of department
LPPS	Little People Preschool
MCC	Magic Classroom Collective
NPDF	National Policy Development Framework
NECT	National Education Collaboration Trust
NGO	non-governmental organisation
NNSSF	National Norms and Standards for School Funding
NPO	non-profit organisation
NYS	National Youth Service
Reos	Reos Partners
SA Schools Act	South African Schools Act No. 84 of 1996
SASAS	South African Social Attitudes Survey
SGB	school governing body
SMT	school management team
TIME	Together in My Education
UNESCO	United Nations Educational, Scientific and Cultural Organisation
UNICEF	United Nations Children's Fund
WCED	Western Cape Education Department

List of Tables

List of Figures

List of Boxes

Acknowledgements

Children and edited books are the same in an important aspect: both take a village to raise.

The village would have nothing to raise if parents or caregivers did not conceive and support that child first. In the case of this book, that critical conceptual role was played by JET Education Services (James Keevy) and Reos Partners (Colleen Magner), who identified a gap that could be filled by an edited book that brought together research and practice on parent and caregiver involvement in education. Without the incubation and support of JET and Reos, this book would never have made it to publication. Our appreciation for their dedication runs deep.

Our sincere appreciation is extended to the parents/caregivers, teachers and communities who participated in the research studies reported in this book as well. Similarly, all financial support for research and interventions are acknowledged with gratitude.

To the authors who persevered through each arduous step of the journey to publication – without your contributions, this book would not be possible.

Our gratitude to Maureen Mosselson from JET for her expert editing and patient formatting of the manuscript. Metja Pale, Mark Forsberg and Lucille Smith are also acknowledged and appreciated for their part in editing chapters at various stages in the process. At the end, the support of Alli Gerths from Peace Corps contributed to us getting over the finish line.

We also thank the anonymous reviewers who provided valuable insights to strengthen this book.

Finally, we acknowledge the contribution of the HSRC Press, in particular Mthunzi Nxawe, Anthea Oosthuizen, and Shouneez Khan, for making this dream a reality.

Thank you.
The Editors

Foreword

Few of us would dispute the fact that the involvement of parents and caregivers in their children's learning and development, whether at home or at school, plays an important role in improved educational outcomes. Unfortunately, parental or caregiver involvement in children's education is commonly viewed as a stand-alone issue, disconnected from other structural and systemic issues that these caregivers and their children may be facing, such as poverty, unemployment, nutritional deficits, sexual and gender-based violence, and the intersection of race, since many lower-income parents are Black. The reality in South Africa sadly reflects this disjointedness. As the authors in this book will convincingly show, there are few systemic examples, other than school governing bodies, where parents and caregivers are legitimate partners in the education of their children (Gibbs, Sahin & Mapatwana 2021).

Early in 2021, Reos Partners (Reos) and JET Education Services (JET) embarked on a process to start unlocking this potential lever of parental and caregiver involvement in education, seeing it as an opportunity to significantly improve educational outcomes. Bringing together JET – with its tried-and-tested education ecosystems and collective impact convening ability – and Reos – with its years of experience in helping people to work together across differences to achieve system change – created a combination that could better understand the parental and caregiver landscape, and then address the gaps. The early stages of this process involved an invitation to the ecosystem role players to participate in a collaboration,[1] as well as a public webinar engagement in May 2021 with the title 'Collaborating for influence: The untapped potential of parental involvement in the education of children'. Melanie Ehren's work on accountability and trust (Ehren and Baxter 2021; Ehren, Baxter & Paterson 2018) provided an important point of reference.

It soon became clear to both partners that the area of parental and caregiver involvement in education in South Africa was not well coordinated, even though many NGOs, and even some universities, were actively working in it. From the perspective of parents and caregivers, it was clear that many do not feel that they are adequately able to support their children with their learning activities, either because of their own low levels of literacy or a lack of confidence. Others either do not know that they have a role to play in their children's education, or do not feel it is their responsibility. The perspective from government was equally conservative. While all parties agreed on the importance of understanding and benefiting from engaging parents and caregivers, not much evidence could be found that this was being done in a coordinated manner.

The initial call to action from JET and Reos for the various stakeholders to come together yielded limited results, prompting a return to planning. The pivot subsequently identified by JET and Reos, learning from the earlier attempts, was to start with mapping the current activities together with research related to the South African context. Comprehensive searches for published articles in this area led to a rather modest list of only 11 local academics, and around 9 established researchers that work in the area internationally and were relevant to the South African context. The South African academics were approached in late 2021, and, slowly but surely, the group started to expand as additional papers and authors were identified. This process eventually led to a more structured engagement with the authors.

Over the next 24 months, the editors worked with the group of authors to complete the 14 chapters that make up this book. Support from the HSRC to conduct the blind review of the chapters and subsequently in publishing the book was much appreciated. In our view, this book is a critical contribution to understanding and improving parental and caregiver involvement in education in South Africa. Each chapter presents a compelling case that parental and caregiver involvement in children's learning and development, whether at home or at school, plays a catalytic role in improved educational outcomes.

We are confident this publication has effectively realised its intended objective and will provide a pivotal framework for subsequent endeavours to encourage parental/caregiver participation in children's educational journeys. This book now sets in place an important cornerstone from which the involvement of parents and caregivers in their children's learning and development will be approached. As a concrete next step, each of the case studies will be further investigated through the appointment of a rural coordinator for parent and caregiver involvement. The initial phase of this work will entail close collaboration with the specific chapter authors and various local stakeholders in the KwaZulu-Natal, Western Cape, Northern Cape, and Mpumalanga provinces. We are appreciative of the support from the United States Peace Corps through which a volunteer will spend most of 2025 in moving this work ahead, with oversight and support from JET and Reos.

We acknowledge and appreciate the hard work of the editors, authors, and reviewers over the last two and more years. Thank you in particular to Zahraa McDonald, now based at the University of Johannesburg, Adam Cooper from the Human Sciences Research Council, Ashnie Mahadew from the University of Kwazulu-Natal, and Noxolo Xaba, previously at JET but now at the South African College of Applied Psychology in Pretoria, for coordinating the process with care and finesse. We also acknowledge the early work by Aynur Gul Sahin while on an internship at JET from the University of Pennsylvania and now at the Organisation for Economic Co-operation and Development, who helped us to get the ball rolling in 2021. Thanks also to Maureen Mosselson, Metja Pale, Mark Forsberg, and Lucille Smith for the initial editing of many drafts of the chapters that make up this book.

We have no doubt that the book brings together cutting-edge research and thought leadership from across South Africa to outline how to better involve caregivers in children's education journeys, which could ultimately improve both outcomes and livelihoods. We hope this book will seed the many more initiatives needed to strengthen this effort.

James Keevy (JET) and Colleen Magner (Reos): July 2025

Notes

1   JET Education Services & Reos Partners (2021) Parental involvement for school improvement: A South African perspective. *JET Bulletin* 3: 1–10. Accessed June 2025, https://www.jet.org.za/news/news/jet-exchanges-3-2021-parental-involvement

References

Ehren MCM & Baxter J (Eds) (2021) *Trust, accountability, and capacity in education system reform: Global perspectives in comparative education.* London: Routledge

Ehren M, Baxter J & Paterson A (2018) *Trust, capacity and accountability as conditions for education system improveement.* Johannesburg: JET Education Services

Gibbs C, Sahin A & Mapatwana A (2021) *Parental involvement for school improvement: A South African perspective.* JET Exchanges 2021(3). Johannesburg: JET Education Services. Accessed July 2025, https://www.jet.org.za/resources/jet-exchange_parental-involvement-for-school-improvement_final.pdf

Introduction

Adam Cooper, Zahraa McDonald, Ashnie Mahadew, and Noxolo Xaba

This book is an edited collection of chapters that focus on parent and caregiver involvement in South African schools, bringing together research and practice. The authors explore research, experiences, and lessons about parental and caregiver involvement across the education system, from early childhood development to basic education. The chapters move across times, places, and themes, raising questions for the future of educational research on parent and caregiver involvement in South African schools. While there is a strong emphasis on educational research, there is also concern for interventions and prospective futures more broadly. The book is therefore relevant for researchers, practitioners, and policymakers.

The book's focus on parents and caregivers means that education is conceived as a field that includes schools, homes, and communities, proposing that education operates as an ecosystem, rather than in an isolated setting. This challenges academics and students of education, as well as practitioners and policymakers, to think about their practices, methodologies, and assumptions in relation to a range of spaces that extend beyond the classroom. Our approach represents a bold relational orientation to educational research, challenging scholars to reflect upon and reconceptualise the spaces they assume are relevant to schooling.

This focus on parent/caregiver involvement in the wider schooling ecosystem means that the book brings together research on South African schooling that has generally either focused on 1) "identity and the contexts of schooling", and 2) the academic performance of learners. Parent and caregiver involvement in their children's education unites these usually separate concerns because this topic has clear implications for improving the quality of teaching and learning in schools and it highlights the social aspects inherent in education. As such, the chapters examine parents'/caregivers' involvement in education as a social phenomenon with implications, including (but not restricted to) children's performance at school. This approach poses serious questions for the dominant narrative in South Africa educational research and policy, one that assumes South African learners perform poorly because of 'in-school factors' and that the 'school can be targeted as it is a poverty trap' (Allais, Cooper & Shalem 2019: 110; see also Fataar 2015; Fataar 2016). An in-school focus ignores, almost wholesale, the fact that education is a social system connected to other parts of society, such as families and communities.

The narrative of the classroom as an insulated container of learning was severely challenged during the COVID-19 pandemic, which catalysed educational change; teachers and parents/caregivers had to adjust at full tilt to a new teaching and learning process, which included home-schooling and role change for both parents and teachers. Parents and caregivers had to take on the responsibilities of teachers by teaching their children with the support of teachers. Learners endured considerable trauma and stress at home and at school, with a positive collaboration/working relation between the teacher and parents aiding their holistic development. The pandemic clearly showed that, when primary caregivers collaborate with the school, greater potential exists to support children's learning and development.

Benefits included strengthened relations between the school and parents/caregivers; positive parental attitudes towards teachers and the school; improved learner performance in adaptive and social skills; an improved school climate; increased parental satisfaction with the school; and overall school improvement. The COVID-19 pandemic therefore challenged researchers to acknowledge connections between homes and schools, but it also placed the stresses education systems face in historical context, highlighting the intersectional nature of crises in contexts like South Africa.

But debates about the role of parent/caregiver involvement in education and how social factors shape performance did not begin with the COVID-19 pandemic. These concerns have been present in international research on parent involvement, which gained prominence from the 1970s onwards, as global shifts in education governance decentralised authority to local and school levels. International research initially lauded parent participation for its role in cultivating stable school communities, academic success, and student self-motivation (Henderson 1981). This work was later challenged by scholars interested in how political, cultural, and economic differences influenced the nature of parent participation among minorities, immigrants, and the historically excluded (Crozier 2001; Tinkler 2002; Quiocho & Daoud 2006; Kim 2009). Differences in language, culture, and communication practices between parents and teachers; the effect of barriers such as language, employment or education level on parental involvement; and potential strategies to build inclusivity in diverse school contexts all shape parent participation in schools.

While the international literature argues that having a parent interested in academic progress is beneficial to a child's learning and academic achievement (Đurišić & Bunijevac 2017; Topor et al. 2010) and that when parents and educators are "on the same page", it is easy to reinforce appropriate messages (Hill, Witherspoon & Bartz 2018), the bigger questions are "how" and "under what social conditions" parental participation can have this effect. Models of parental participation and cultivating whole-school communities, such as Hoover-Dempsey (Hoover-Dempsey & Sandler 1997; Hoover-Dempsey et al. 2005) or the school–family–community partnerships model of stakeholder relations by Epstein (1995, 2018), therefore require careful consideration of the historical and contextual conditions that enable participation and on what/whose terms. The variation in how researchers and scholars conceptualise parent participation can largely be attributed to these social and political forces, as the South African example so vividly demonstrates.

In post-apartheid South Africa, social forces clearly shaped the extent and nature of parental/caregiver participation through the form desegregation took, governance being devolved to School Governing Bodies, and the establishment of a wealth quintile system to differentiate between no-fee and fee-paying schools. Parents have adapted to the democratisation of school governance through school choice and participation in school governance, but their involvement in education is mediated by inequality, perceptions of community, decency, and class status, as well as the nature of the school environment (Smit & Liebenberg 2003; Nojaja 2009; Makgopa & Mokhele 2013; Munje & Mncube 2018). There are deep historical and political currents at work across these factors that continue to impact on the experiences of teachers, parents/caregivers, learners, and school communities. Scholars such as Nojaja (2009) and Munje and Mncube (2018) have therefore further developed or adapted models of parental participation specific to disadvantaged school contexts, dovetailing with ongoing global work around the fostering of multi-stakeholder partnerships in education.

This local and international contextualisation forms the backdrop for the way in which we have conceptualised this book, which is divided into three sections. The first section frames parental and caregiver involvement in South African education using a social justice approach to the topic: an approach that has guided the book's orientation overall. The second section unpacks, in more detail, the specific contexts of parental and caregiver involvement in education – the spaces where the battles for social justice play out. The final section looks at specific interventions in parental and caregiver involvement in education, exploring how a more just education system might be achieved. The logic of the book is therefore to begin by unpacking what it means for social and political forces to shape parent involvement, before going on to how these forces shape specific contexts, and what can be done to intervene on the ground.

Section A: Framing

The first section contains three chapters, each of which engages with the interaction or lack thereof between home and society. Chapter 1 examines the role afforded to parents and caregivers in South African education policy. The chapter illustrates that, in South Africa, education policy provides for parental and caregiver involvement in school. Zahraa McDonald, Lungelo Mthembu-Salter, and Noxolo Xaba analyse education policy with a social-justice lens and contend that economic inequalities mediate the rights and obligations afforded to parental and caregiver involvement in education. However, with regard to school governance and learning support, there is no recognition in education policy that socio-economic inequality could influence parental and caregiver involvement. The argument presented by the authors in the first chapter is that education policy discourse assumes level playing fields for parental and caregiver involvement in school governance and learning.

Chapter 2 continues the theme of Chapter 1. Bakang Mputle argues that parental and caregiver involvement can in fact not be equalised unless the socio-economic context is equalised. Until there is an equitable distribution within the socio-economic context, the author contends, parental and caregiver involvement cannot be conceived of in a one-dimensional manner; rather, each context will call upon differing interpretations and capabilities. If this is so and if parental and caregiver involvement is consequential for learning outcomes, where does this leave learners whose parents or caregivers are limited in the manner in which they are able to become involved in their children's education?

The last chapter in this section, Chapter 3, extends the argument in Chapter 1, analysing early childhood policy from a social justice perspective. Lydia-Anne Plaatjies argues that parental and caregiver involvement ought to commence at the point of policy development by including parental and caregiver voices when there is still maximum opportunity for impact. The chapter raises the crucial and pertinent questions: 'Where and when does parental and caregiver involvement start and end?' and 'If parents and caregivers are to be involved in policy making and development, which parents and caregivers act as representatives?'

Together the chapters in the first section view parental and caregiver involvement in education through a social justice lens, looking at policy, history, socio-economic limitations, and issues of representation.

Section B: Contexts

The second section contains five chapters focused on national, school-level, and family contexts.

Chapter 4 by Tarryn de Kock and Adam Cooper reports on the first nationally representative study of South African caregivers: a survey that delved into parents' and caregivers' perceptions of education quality and their self-reported involvement in schools. A sample of primary caregivers was drawn and the research conducted as a module of the South African Social Attitudes Survey. Fieldworkers went to a set of carefully chosen dwellings countrywide, which formed part of 500 Primary Sampling Units – geographical areas that collectively formed a nationally representative sample of 1 600 primary caregivers. The study helped to create a detailed picture of who South African parents/caregivers are, their financial and living conditions, and how they choose schools for their children. From the research, a comprehensive understanding was gained of how parents assess education quality, what they know about their child's school, and the ways in which they interact with these institutions.

Findings from the study indicated that parents/caregivers generally believe that educators, including school leadership, are performing well, particularly that the school provides comprehensive pastoral care for children, helping parents meet their children's daily needs of nutrition, clothing, and psycho-social support. Despite this, most parents admitted to knowing little about the daily workings of their child's school.

While the survey provides a springboard to understand these issues, the authors point to the absence of a nuanced culturally and sociologically informed understanding of the ways in which parent and caregiver involvement is enhanced or hindered, one that takes heed of the fact that parents are historically located actors whose practices are shaped by their own experiences, circumstances, and capacities. Parents or caregivers in South Africa are an extremely diverse group across race, class, age, geography, and culture, and this diversity needs to be at the forefront of understandings and possibilities for parent involvement. As social actors, parents wield different forms and amounts of power and resources, which needs to be considered in interventions.

Ashnie Mahadew's Chapter 5, on creating an inclusive learning environment in early childhood care and education (ECCE), focuses on enhancing partnerships with families in the years preceding formal schooling. Grounded in interpretivism, this chapter reports on semi-structured interviews carried out with a group of ECCE educators, a centre supervisor, a field monitor, and a research student at an ECCE centre in a low-income township. The core argument of the chapter emphasises that building partnerships with families goes deeper than involvement, and should enable families to increase their knowledge of children's needs and allow educators to acquire a deeper understanding of the family's culture and diversity. The chapter makes an important contribution to authentic inclusion in ECCE where families' voices of trauma and hope, in the form of challenges and interventions, are rarely heard. Due to the critical need for quality education in the early years, and the recognition of the value of family partnerships in education, positive ripple effects from this stage may be created throughout the years of formal schooling.

Bongani Nhlanhla Mkhize and Kerishka Govender's Chapter 6 explores the role of school principals in fostering parental/caregiver involvement, since leadership practices are pivotal to a school promoting parents as active members of the educational community. Their chapter used Phoenix, a low-income, predominantly Indian community in KwaZulu-Natal, for the research. The context shaped the findings and discussion, as the research site presented particular challenges to schools in generating parent involvement. This context was further complicated by the July 2021 unrest, which increased tensions between Indian people in Phoenix and people in neighbouring African townships, thereby negatively affecting parent involvement.

Of the three schools that participated in the research, one of the principals described positive experiences of parent involvement, while the other two had predominantly negative experiences. These positive or negative experiences were shaped by three main themes, namely communication with parents and caregivers, creating a welcoming and inviting environment for them, and building the leadership capacities of members of school governing bodies.

The school that achieved a more positive culture of parent/caregiver involvement described adopting a two-way approach to communication with parents. Two-way communication invites parents to become immersed in the school context and to take an active interest in their children's education. It induces mutual understanding between parents and educators and encourages both groups to develop a deeper understanding of children's needs. The school that created a positive culture of parent involvement also demonstrated a more thorough induction of parents into their role as school governing body members. A key challenge for principals in the study was developing the ability to adjust their leadership styles and practices in the light of local conditions, and to use technology, for example WhatsApp messages, to promote parent involvement.

Andrew Paterson, Melanie Ehren, and Zaahedah Vally's Chapter 7 describes the presence and workings of blame in South African schools, arguing that a reciprocal culture of blame exists between parents/caregivers and educators, with parents and caregivers perceiving educators as poorly trained, and educators perceiving parents and caregivers as uninterested. The chapter unpacks the role and function of blame as it operates between primary school educators and parents/caregivers. Examples of blame in schools are described in South Africa and elsewhere, and the concept of a blame cycle is introduced to explain how blame operates through feedback and reinforcement loops. A situation where groups blame one another impacts on trust and accountability, making it difficult for parents/caregivers and educators to work in partnership to improve children's education. The authors contend that schools and parents/caregivers struggle to take ownership of children's education, believing their efforts are futile due to the uncontrollable actions of the other group. The widespread existence of blame and blaming is underpinned by narratives where both groups abdicate responsibility, rather than promoting collaboration.

In a paired autobiographical reflection, Thembeka Myende and Phumlani Myende write in Chapter 8 about being Black middle-class parents and the challenges they experience in contemporary South Africa. While Thembeka Myende attended a quintile 5 school and was raised in a relatively affluent family, with a migrant mother who worked as a nurse in the United Kingdom, Phumlani Myende attended quintile 1 schools in rural KwaZulu-Natal.

In their reflection on contemporary Black middle-class parenting life, the authors grapple with the gap between their own pedagogical resources and those of their child's school, the appropriate roles for themselves and the school, the benefits and costs of "outsourcing" childcare to aftercare support and domestic help, and the unequally gendered dimensions of childcare that seem difficult to eradicate.

Frustratingly, the quantity and timing of homework required by the school did not form part of an intentional strategy for cognitive and intellectual development, they argue, but was, instead, linked to the school's belief that learners and parents/caregivers should not be idle. This created difficulties for a family in which both parents were working. In these and other ways the school intentionally or unintentionally reproduced gendered and middle-class norms through their practices and their expectations of parents/caregivers. While reflecting with anxiety on whether they were contributing sufficiently to their child's education, this married couple found solace in the fact that their child developed independent agency. Myende and Myende found ways to contribute substantially to their child's education while being full-time working professionals, something which they felt regularly went unacknowledged by their child's school.

The section offers rich perspectives on parental and caregiver engagement at multiple levels of the education system. The chapters highlight interactions in various contexts from school to home, across which parental and caregiver involvement is enacted. Moreover, this section shows how internal dynamics in individual contexts, including school and home, are dynamic and constantly shifting.

Section C: Intervening

This third section contains five chapters that describe, report on, and analyse specific interventions.

In Chapter 9, Kimberley Porteus, Nicky Roberts, and Nobuntu Mazeka examine parental/caregiver involvement in the rural South African context during COVID-19. The chapter is an exploratory study based on Educational Design Research, in which grade two parents/caregivers were given weekly homework workbooks for mathematics to help with reduced class time as a result of COVID-19 lockdowns, which particularly affected rural areas. The intervention case study took place across 13 rural primary schools in the Eastern Cape. The chapter contributes to understanding the impact of COVID-19 on education, as well as the role of project implementation in producing a positive impact on parental involvement.

Chapter 10, by Craig Gibbs and Kimberleigh Bodley, offers insights into rural school parental and caregiver engagement in literacy and numeracy in the Foundation Phase. The Alladin Learning Solutions case study programme was run across three South African provinces with a mixture of rural and semi-urban settings. The programme used parents/caregivers trained as peer educators to teach other parents about key parental involvement issues. Findings debunk the myth that educational learning only takes place in the school. The chapter contributes to strategies of involving parents/caregivers in rural settings for children aged between four and seven years.

Ximena Gonzalez and Khanyisa Mkhabele's Chapter 11 focuses on the aRe Bapaleng Programme, which was designed to enhance the capacity of parents or primary caregivers of young children in marginalised communities to support their children better. The authors report on their experiences and review the programme, which was facilitated through face-to-face workshops. The chapter highlights how the programme provided a platform for parents and caregivers to share their stories of trauma and hope.

Chapter 12 also engages with the topic of universal access to high-quality early childhood development (ECD) in South Africa. Magali von Blottnitz and Shelley O'Carroll focus on Together in My Education (TIME), a home learning programme for children in Grade R and Grade 1 and their families that intends to equip parents and caregivers to make up for the missed learning opportunities resulting from school closures, rotational timetabling, and the severe disruption of the ECD sector during the COVID-19 crisis. Adopting a qualitative approach, the authors narrate two case studies of teachers and caregivers. The chapter highlights how the trauma experienced by two very different schools and two families created barriers to sustained engagement between them. By highlighting how TIME extended education beyond the school walls, reshaping the social contract between schools and their communities and expanding the notion of the educator, the authors make a valuable contribution to research on parent and caregiver involvement in the Foundation Phase.

Adele Mooi and Abigail Dreyer, the authors of Chapter 13, focus on the Pathways Programme adopted by Little People Preschool and Community Development, where parental/caregiver involvement has contributed to the programme's successful delivery. Using a hermeneutic circle analysis, the authors argue that key components of text and context reveal new understandings of ECD policies. The chapter highlights a disjuncture or "voice gap" between those who are receivers of ECD services and policymakers. The voices of primary caregivers and mothers of young children are silenced. The strategies and actions presented provide a framework for how schools can connect with, engage, and sustain parent engagement in preschool activities through collaborative efforts to foster healthy development.

The chapters in the final section showcase five interventions that focus on how parental and caregiver involvement might enhance learning outcomes. The interventions examined were implemented in the ECD sector and primary schools, where change is most urgently needed.

Concluding chapter

In the concluding chapter, Colleen Magner and Mpinane Mahlatji draw out the vital lessons from all the chapters in the book in line with the approach called Systemic Collaboration. They argue for the adoption of a Systemic Collaborative approach to parental and caregiver involvement, based on the multiple contexts and varying roles parents and caregivers are expected to play in relation to others in education institutions.

By beginning with the politics of parent/caregiver involvement as a social justice issue, showing how this plays out in inter-connected contexts, and, finally, demonstrating how we might begin to intervene for a more equitable society, we hope that the three sections of the book transcend theory and practice to produce both an insightful and useful contribution to this topic.

Note

In this book we use the terms `parents' and `caregivers' interchangeably. While we acknowledge that they are not the same thing, South Africa's tumultuous history, which includes apartheid segregation, migrant labour and the HIV/AIDS pandemic, has resulted in a wide variety of household formations and caregiving arrangements. The nuclear family is far from the norm. Our intention in using these terms interchangeably is therefore to affirm and recognise the various people who care for South African children and become involved in their education, acknowledging them as relevant to these debates.

References

Allais S, Cooper A, & Shalem Y (2019) Rupturing or reinforcing inequality? The role of education in South Africa today. *Transformation: Critical Perspectives on Southern Africa* 101(1): 105-126

Crozier G (2001) Excluded parents: The deracialisation of parental involvement. *Race, Ethnicity and Education* 4(4): 329–341

Đurišić M & Bunijevac M (2017) Parental involvement as an important factor for successful education. *Center for Educational Policy Studies Journal* 7(3): 137–153

Epstein JL (1995) School/family/community partnerships. *Phi Delta Kappan* 76(9): 701–712

Epstein JL (2018) *School family and community partnerships: Preparing educators and improving schools.* New York: Routledge

Fataar A (2015) *Engaging schooling subjectivities across post-apartheid urban spaces.* Stellenbosch: African SUN Media

Fataar A (2016) Towards a humanising pedagogy through an engagement with the social-subjective in educational theorising in South Africa. *Educational Research for Social Change* 5(1): 10–21

Henderson A (1981) *Parent participation–student achievement: The evidence grows.* NCCE Occasional Papers, Columbia, MD

Hill NE, Witherspoon DP & Bartz D (2018) Parental involvement in education during middle school: Perspectives of ethnically diverse parents, teachers, and students. *The Journal of Educational Research* 111(1), 12–27

Hoover-Dempsey KV & Sandler HM (1997) Why do parents become involved in their children's education? *Review of Educational Research* 67(1): 3–42

Hoover-Dempsey KV, Walker MT, Sandler HM, Whetsel D, Green CL et al. (2005) Why do parents become involved? Research findings and implications. *The Elementary School Journal* 106/2:105–130

Kim, Y (2009) Minority parental involvement and school barriers: Moving the focus away from deficiencies of parents. *Educational Research Review* 4(2): 80–102

Makgopa M & Mokhele M (2013) Teachers' perceptions on parental involvement: A case study of two South African schools. *Journal of Educational and Social Research* 3(3): 219–226

Munje PN & Mncube V (2018) The lack of parent involvement as hindrance in selected public primary schools in South Africa: The voices of educators. *Perspectives in Education* 36(1): 80–93. Accessed April 2025, https://journals.ufs.ac.za/index.php/pie/article/view/3585/3374

Nojaja JM (2009) A model for parent involvement in disadvantaged South African schools. PhD dissertation, North-West University. Accessed April 2025, https://repository.nwu.ac.za/items/bc3425f4-7889-465f-b9e0-85632624e922

Quiocho AM & Daoud AM (2006) Dispelling myths about Latino parent participation in schools. *The Educational Forum* 70(3): 255–267

Smit AG & Liebenberg L (2003) Understanding the dynamics of parent involvement in schooling within the poverty context. *South African Journal of Education* 23(1): 1–5

Topor DR, Keane SP, Shelton TL & Calkins SD (2010) Parent involvement and student academic performance: A multiple mediational analysis. *Journal of Prevention & Intervention in the Community* 38(3): 183–197

Tinkler B (2002) A review of literature on Hispanic/Latino parent involvement in K–12 Education. Accessed April 2025, https://files.eric.ed.gov/fulltext/ED469134.pdf

Section

Framing

In line with the aims of this book, the opening section takes a social justice approach to parent and caregiver involvement in schools. This approach focuses on parity of participation and whether groups are able to interact in ways that are fair, meaning that one group is not dominated or exploited and that the interests of both groups are equitably served. Parent and caregiver involvement in schools is about the interaction between, on the one side, parents and caregivers, and, on the other side, school personnel and the wider institution of the school. When groups like parents and teachers interact, power relations mediated by class, race, gender, language, urban–rural divides, and many other aspects of identity shape how these interactions play out and whether one group dominates the other, with implications for social justice.

According to Nancy Fraser (1998, 2000, as cited in Chapter 1), parity of participation, which promotes social justice, depends on two related factors or conditions. First, resources must be adequately distributed so that people can participate independently and "with voice". Second, the institutionalised norms and values that underpin and shape participation should treat people equally and enable opportunities for all of those involved. Full participation in social processes is often restricted through institutionalised rules for engagement.

In this first section, McDonald, Mthembu-Salter, and Xaba argue in Chapter 1 that the unequal distribution of resources, the first of Fraser's two conditions, does not allow for parity of participation in South African schools, thereby inhibiting social justice.

Chapters 2 and 3 primarily engage with the second of Fraser's two conditions, showing how macro-level forces related to policy and ideology have a profound effect on the institutionalised norms and values that underpin and shape participation. In Chapter 3, Plaatjies shows that legislation around Early Childhood Development (ECD) policy overtly excludes parent voices from all aspects of ECD work, creating a particular set of institutionalised norms that restrict parent involvement in everyday interactions with educational institutions.

These material and policy-related aspects of parental involvement, which inhibit social justice, need to be understood as playing out in particular ideological and discursive regimes, shaping the kinds of parent involvement practices that become possible in schools. In Chapter 2, Mputle looks at how various discursive regimes, in both the United Kingdom and South Africa, shape the kinds of parent involvement practices that emerge. Mputle shows that these practices are not fixed and that broader ideological forces, such as neoliberalism, have a profound effect on the ways in which parent involvement is understood, valued, and judged.

1 *A Social Justice Perspective on Parental and Caregiver Involvement in Education Policy*

Zahraa McDonald, Lungelo Mthembu-Salter, and Noxolo Xaba

Introduction

Parental and caregiver involvement in education is generally conceptualised as activities and interactions between parents and caregivers on the one hand, and schools on the other. For example, Smith states that 'parental involvement is seen as an integration of home and school' (2006: 44). As such, parents and caregivers are expected to participate in the life of the school as well as to support children's learning from school at home (Smith 2006; Wilder 2014; Yang et al. 2023). This engagement with their children's learning begins from the earliest days of teaching a child to speak, to walk, and to interact with others. This is (sometimes slowly) transferred to schools as staff take over as the educators, and, as is often the case, allow parents and caregivers a share in a process staff see as rightly theirs (Goodall & Montgomery 2014). In the main then, parental and caregiver involvement in education is understood as activities and interactions involving parents' and caregivers' participation in endeavours that support their children's schooling and their learning at school.

An expanded definition of "parent" is used in this chapter to include not only those individuals who are raising their own children, but also those who are raising the children of family members (Brown & Beckett 2007). Caregivers are therefore included in the conception of parental involvement in the absence of parents, or where parents have passed away (Davis & Lambie 2005). From birth until children reach the age of sixteen, 85% of their waking life is spent at home and is thus strongly influenced by the family, making the parent the child's primary educator (Van Wyk & Lemmer 2009). Parents are considered their children's primary educators because of the socialisation that takes place before the school attending age (Maluleke 2014).

With this definition of parental involvement in mind, schools have a responsibility to enable parental and caregiver participation, because parents as a group are not equally empowered. School personnel should provide parents and caregivers with the information they need to be fully involved in their children's education: 'developing effective partnerships with families requires all school personnel to create a school environment that is accessible, inviting, and welcoming to caregivers' (Davis & Lambie 2005: 144). Such caregiver participation in school activities could include volunteer work, classroom visits, and interactions with class teachers (Jaiswal 2017). While, in principle, parents should be able to play active roles in shaping schools and have an impact on them by participating in teacher–parent organisations and electing board members and school officials, in practice, 'researchers agree that rates of parental involvement are lower in low-income communities than in higher income schools' (Smith 2006: 44). The reality is therefore that parent participation is low in most schools, and the participation of minority groups and low-income families is even lower (Bloch & Tabachnick 1993).

Assumptions about the reasons for this are that parents from low-income backgrounds are often not available due to high job demands that may lead to them being less involved (Smith 2006) or that they are isolated from the school culture (Delgado-Gaitan 1991). Such research, however, does not necessarily define "low income" or "less involved" or how these compare with rates of parental involvement at higher-income schools.

Irrespective of the definitions for low or high income, the notion that parental and caregiver participation, and thus involvement, is affected by income suggests that the distribution of resources among parents and caregivers is consequential for their participation in their children's school life. In turn, the notion that fairness in society relates to how income is distributed is associated with the concept of social justice (Mncube 2007).

In this chapter, we examine the manner in which discourses associated with parental and caregiver involvement in South African schooling engage with income distribution, with the aim of contributing to debates about an appreciation for achieving social justice through parental and caregiver involvement in education. Discourses from literature and policy are analysed from the perspective of Nancy Fraser's propositions of social justice, which assert that when individuals are misrecognised and misrepresented under conditions of maldistribution, the result is an unequal parity of participation. As a remedy, recognition, representation, and redistribution are required for parity of participation (Fraser 1995, 2000, 2005). The authors found that discourses of parental and caregiver involvement in education misrecognise the capabilities of parents and caregivers to participate in schooling based on misrepresentation and maldistribution of resources. In particular, the tiered schooling system, a feature of South African education since its inception and formalised in policy since the nineteenth century, has fed into discourses that have misrecognised the capabilities of parents and caregivers to participate in schooling. The chapter ends with implications for the current quintile system and for the proliferation of independent schools in relation to the recognition and representation of parents and caregivers in education.

Conceptualising social justice in education

While social justice has been defined in many ways, there is general agreement that it is a desirable and worthy goal. For Shriberg, social justice is 'associated with the idea that all individuals and groups must be treated with fairness and respect and that all are entitled to the resources and benefits that the school has to offer' (2008: 455). Social justice is traditionally a 'theory focusing on the distribution of income and other sources needed by human beings' (Mncube 2007: 130), which is used to explain fairness and unfairness in a society.

A social justice approach 'can provide a fuller rationale for a policy focus on education quality ... or by the existing human rights approach with its emphasis on the role of the state in guaranteeing basic rights' (Tikly & Barrett 2011: 3–4). A focus on addressing injustice in and through education, especially in contexts of economic inequalities, is often at the root of tensions and violence (Sayed & Ahmed 2015). Social justice is thus a necessary and important perspective to include in debates about education.

To the extent that social justice is affected by the distribution of resources, Fraser's conception of social justice offers valuable insights and tools to interrogate discourses associated with parental and caregiver involvement in education or participation in schooling. Her conceptualisation of social justice as full recognition, in contrast to misrecognition inferring injustice (2000), provides a basis for drawing out implications of social interactions. Injustice emanates from structural inequalities engendered by maldistribution, misrecognition, and misrepresentation. On the contrary, social and transformative justice is underpinned by redistribution, recognition, and representation (Fraser 1995, 2005). The concept of social justice therefore offers an explanatory framework for understanding the consequences of how discourses and material resources might impact on distribution, recognition, and representation.

Fraser, from a critical feminist perspective, asserts that in order to reach 'parity of participation' for all men and women in society, regardless of sex and sexual orientation, class, ethnicity, geographical location, and so forth, it is not enough to assume only the economic solution of redistribution. Rather, equal importance should be given to socio-cultural remedies for better recognition and political representation to ensure 'participation on par with others, as full partners in social interaction' (2005: 73). She asserts that there needs to be an acknowledgment of the varying needs, societal positions, and decision-making power: 'The root of the injustice, as well as its core, will be socio-economic maldistribution, while any attendant cultural injustices will derive ultimately from that economic root' (Fraser 1995: 75). Fraser, however, also considers the injustices of distribution and recognition to be intertwined, even though the root is maldistribution (1995). Similarly, 'it is also argued that social justice refers to notions of how everyone should be treated in a society that is believed to be good' (Mncube 2007: 131).

In line with this framing, the manner in which parents and caregivers are able to participate in schools can be examined in relation to how they are recognised in discourses associated with parental and caregiver involvement in education. Moreover, the extent to which and the manner in which recognition is tied to income distribution would provide critical insights for the appreciation of achieving social justice through parental and caregiver involvement in education.

South Africa is a prime example of such maldistribution in education. The public education system in South Africa is a bifurcated one, in which there is one set of schools for a multiracial elite, and another set of schools for an impoverished Black majority. Such bifurcation reproduces inequalities across intersections of race and class in terms of learning outcomes and access to the labour market, cementing past injustices (Sayed & Soudien 2005; Sayed & Motala 2012; Spaull 2013). As the country's national Department of Basic Education (DBE) comments, 'the quality of education for Black children is still largely poor, meaning employment, earning potential, and career mobility is reduced for these learners' (2015: 28). When one is misrecognised, one is 'denied the status of a full partner in social interaction' (Fraser 1998: 3). Social justice (in Fraser's conceptualisation) will not be achieved if individuals are misrecognised who either cannot participate or find it very difficult to participate in school-related activities because of a maldistribution of income. If that maldistribution of income simultaneously locks the community into a particular understanding of the world that is defined in terms of income distribution, to what extent is society able to transcend that? Discourses related to policy and research might lock communities into such conceptualisations.

Recognition 'is a remedy for injustice' (Fraser 1998: 5). Recognition, according to Hegel, refers to 'an ideal reciprocal relationship between subjects' (cited in Fraser 2000: 109). One becomes an individual subject in the process of recognising and being recognised (Fraser 2000). Achieving justice by recognition depends on how the misrecognition is occurring. Recognition is therefore not generic but context specific, in

Fraser's perspective. For her, recognition is as fundamental as economic redistribution to social justice. To ensure participation on par with others, equal importance should be attached to guaranteeing socio-cultural remedies of recognition as full partners in social interaction (Fraser 1998). For Fraser, recognition in the context of justice entails that everyone has an equal right to pursue social esteem under fair conditions of equal opportunity. Such conditions do not exist when, for example, institutionalised patterns of interpretation pervasively downgrade femininity, "non-whiteness", homosexuality, and everything culturally associated with them (1998: 4). If and when these institutionalised patterns of cultural value constitute actors as peers, capable of participating on par with one another in social life, then we can speak of reciprocal recognition and status equality (2000: 113).

When actors are constructed as invisible and less than full partners, this is misrecognition and status subordination (Fraser 2000). This chapter will examine the manner in which discourses associated with parental and caregiver involvement afford recognition in accordance with income distribution or do not recognise how income distribution might impact propensities to participate. The politics of recognition seeks a difference-friendly world 'where assimilation to majority or dominant cultural norms is no longer the price of equal respect' (Fraser 1998: 1). Fraser contends that it is unjust that some individuals and groups are denied the status of full partners in social interaction simply as a consequence of institutionalised patterns of cultural value in whose construction they have not equally participated, and which disparage their distinctive characteristics, or the distinctive characteristics assigned to them (1998: 3).

Misrecognition is the denial of recognition by others and distorts one's relationship to oneself and others (Fraser 2000). Misrecognition is therefore 'a status injury' or 'status inequality' (Fraser 2005). When one is misrecognised, one is 'denied the status of a full partner in social interaction' (Fraser 1998: 3). A consequence of misrecognition is that it denies affected individuals and groups the chance of participation on par with others (Fraser 1998). In other words, 'institutionalised hierarchies of cultural value … deny them the requisite standing' (Fraser 2005: 5). Being associated with a group that is misrecognised distorts one's sense of self. As a result of repeated encounters with the stigmatising gaze of a culturally dominant other, the members of disesteemed groups internalise negative self-images and are prevented from developing a healthy cultural identity of their own (Fraser 2000).

Policy discourses of income distribution related to parental and caregiver involvement in education

This section examines the discourses related to income distribution and parental and caregiver involvement in education policy in South Africa. As such, the definition of parental involvement, as well as a description of its contextual interactions in children's education, are considered.

South African education policy recognises that parents' responsibilities extend beyond educating their children at home to ensuring their children's right to education is also accessed. Chapter 2 of the South African Schools Act (SA Schools Act) stipulates that every parent must cause every learner for whom he or she is responsible to attend a school from the first school day of the year in which the learner reaches the age of seven until the last school day of the year in which the learner reaches fifteen years or grade nine, whichever occurs first (Republic of South Africa 1996).

Parents are required to share the responsibility of education with the state (Department of Education (DoE) 1997). This is confirmed by the DBE and the National Education Collaboration Trust (NECT) (2016a). The SA Schools Act sought to provide for a uniform system for organising, governing, and funding schools. The governance and funding of public and independent (private) schools alike are legislated by this Act, which affords all stakeholders the mandate to participate in the governance and management of the school.

Broad-based participation in decision-making processes were considered essential for the democratic movement as well as for social change according to the SA Schools Act, which devolved significant powers to school governing bodies (SGBs) as a mechanism for broad-based participation of members of school communities (Sayed, Kanjee & Nkomo 2013). SGBs comprise the school principal together with elected representatives of parents, educators, non-teaching staff, and (in secondary schools) learners (Republic of South Africa 1996). SGBs may also co-opt non-voting members.

Parents have a majority stake in SGBs. Therefore, there is required to be one more parent than the total of other voting members on the SGB (Republic of South Africa 1996). Thus, parents constitute 60% of the SGB, in which the chairperson is also a parent (Mbokodi & Singh 2011). Mosoge and Van der Westhuizen (1997) contend that the SA Schools Act mandated principals, teachers, parents, learners, and all community members with the task of changing traditionally authoritarian institutions into democratic centres where everyone could actively participate in the decision-making processes.

These statutory provisions afford parents control over school governance. The basic functions of all SGBs, as laid down by the SA Schools Act, include developing and adopting a constitution and a mission statement for the school; adopting a code of conduct for learners at the school; determining an admissions policy for the school; administering and controlling the school's property; raising additional income to supplement state funds (including the charging of school fees subject to the approval of parents); and other fundraising activities. The SA Schools Act regulates how parents may be exempted from paying school fees, which are otherwise compulsory once approved at a meeting of parents (Republic of South Africa 1996). In addition to basic SGB functions described in Section 21, SGBs can apply to the head of department (at the provincial department of education) to be allocated any of the following additional functions: maintaining and improving the school's property, buildings and grounds; determining the extramural curriculum for the school and the choice of subject options; purchasing textbooks, educational materials or equipment for the school; and paying for services to the school. Thus, while the SA Schools Act does not distinguish between the rights or responsibilities of parents on the basis of their financial background, it allows for parents and caregivers to provide for schools based on their financial capacity. By implication, the devolution of power to schools located in areas where racial segregation persisted lead Sayed and Ahmed (2009) to suggest that the National Party argued for educational decentralisation post-1994 because decentralisation allowed those who could pay greater control of schooling within the context of fee-paying versus non-fee-paying schooling.

The manner in which SGBs have been enacted in schools within different socio-economic contexts has, however, been acknowledged in literature. In other words, income distribution has been found to impact the operations of SGBs. For Mncube, 'school governance is used to highlight the way in which social justice does or does not manifest itself in governing bodies by looking at the involvement of parents and students in school structures' (2007: 131). Two types of exclusion have been defined: internal exclusion, where individuals are part of debates and decision-making but also excluded from them, for instance as a result of language barriers; and external exclusion, where individuals are excluded from debates and decision-making processes (Mncube 2007).

After the SA Schools Act (Republic of South Africa 1996), the government introduced the National Norms and Standards for School Funding (NNSSF) (DoE 1998) to address inequalities in the funding of schools within the education system by regulating funding allocations to schools (Sayed et al. 2020). The NNSSF provided a legal basis for school funding by classifying schools into wealth quintiles and subsidising them accordingly (Mestry 2014). This set in place pro-poor norms for expenditure by schools on municipal services such as water and electricity, stationery, and learning support materials. The formula for provincial schooling budgets resulted in 30% of the budget going to the poorest 20% of schools, while the least poor 20% receive 5% of the resources via a quintile-ranking mechanism to address equity in schools (DoE 1998). Poor schools ranked from quintiles 1 to 3 were declared no-fee schools (from 2007 for quintiles 1 and 2, and from 2009 for quintile 3) and were allocated a higher state subsidy than the affluent schools that were ranked in quintiles 4 and 5. However, this policy did not succeed in its equity intentions as designed (Sayed et al. 2020). In 2006, amendments to the norms for funding were introduced to effect further changes to school funding with the Amended National Norms and Standards for School Funding (ANNSSF) (DoE 2006). The ANNSSF noted and acknowledged the creation of a two-tier system as an unintended outcome of the SA Schools Act and ANNSSF:

> Ironically, given the emphasis on redress and equity, the funding provisions of the Act (SA Schools Act) appear to have worked thus far to the advantage of public schools patronised by middle-class and wealthy parents. The apartheid regime favoured such communities with high-quality facilities, equipment and resources. Vigorous fundraising by parent bodies, including commercial sponsorships and fee income, have enabled many such schools to add to their facilities, equipment and learning resources, and expand their range of cultural and sporting activities. Since 1995, when such schools have been required to down-size their staff establishments, many have been able to recruit additional staff on governing body contracts, paid from the school fund. (DoE 2006: 10)

The lists of no-fee schools are determined provincially by the provincial education departments, using a standard national procedure (Mestry 2014). Each school is assigned a poverty score using data from the community in which the school is located (DoE 2006). The three poverty indicators utilised for this purpose are income, unemployment rate, and level of education of the community, which are weighted to assign a poverty score for the community and school. At first, schools were allocated to a quintile 'according to the physical condition, facilities, and the relative poverty of the community around the school' but later in 2003, household income of the surrounding community was taken into account (Mestry 2014: 856). In 2008, this shifted to take account of the income dependency ratio or unemployment rate, and level of education or literacy rate of the school's surrounding community or geographical catchment area (Mestry 2014).

The school allocation is developed using five considerations. These include: the rights of learners; the minimum basic package to ensure quality education; prices of goods and services; national distribution of income difference and poverty; and finally, the state budget (DoE 2006). The document specifies what items are covered by this allocation, the majority of which fall into what can be termed running costs (such as stationery, maintenance, and services like electricity), with learning support materials (such as textbooks) being the only item more directly related to learning. The amendments to the way in which a school's quintile was calculated affected non-teaching allocations rather than addressing the inequality in teacher inputs and personnel spending. Schools lacking additional resources (such as qualified teachers) are not able to use these funds to meet such needs, despite being forced to compete within what appears to be a quasi-market (some schools being able to charge fees and others not) governed by parental choice (Woolman & Fleisch 2006). However, schools that receive income from school fees have the autonomy to hire additional teachers and, according to Sayed et al. (2017), it stands to reason that some schools have access to significantly more private resources than other schools, given the basis of determination (that is, income dependency ratio and education level of the school catchment). The policy does not account for the cumulative effect on schools in all quintiles (Sayed et al. 2017) that the unequal private parental or caregiver income has. A public official interviewed in 2015 described the South African education system as comprising 'two school systems':

> A system that is the former white Model C schools and they are becoming more integrated so they are not white anymore. So it's the former upper level State-funded schools who are now partly State- and private-funded because they charge … fairly high fees … so that's the one part of the system, let's call it the former Model C schools, and then you've got … State urban and rural (Black) schools … They talk about a bi-modal distribution, you know, so there's the ex-Model Cs and then there's the others. (Sayed et al. 2017: 103)

At fee-paying schools, parents who are not able to afford fees can apply for fee exemptions. The proportion of parental income to school fees is determined by a set formula that schools need to utilise upon receiving a written application from a parent. Exemptions, in theory, permit even the poor to attend rich or fee-charging schools (DoE 2006). Given the regulations and procedures related to school fees and fee exemptions, education policy in South Africa acknowledges unequal income distribution amongst parents of learners.

There is, however, no explicit recognition within policy that the unequal distribution of income can impact on parents' participation in school governance. According to the DBE and NECT, parental involvement is the continuous and intentional efforts of parents to participate in their children's education in ways that encompass multiple dimensions (2016b).

Parents and caregivers are also responsible for moulding and affecting their children's attitudes, demeanours, and routines, including those related to schooling (2016b).

The DBE and NECT (2016a) propose six focus areas of engagement to facilitate school–parent–community involvement: communicating, parenting, learning at home, volunteering, decision-making, and partnering with the community. Communicating refers to communication between the parents, school, and the community. The communication should be in relation to a particular outcome, such as learner achievement. Parenting then refers to helping parents or families establish a home environment that supports children as learners. Parenting can be improved by helping parents with their parenting skills; for instance, helping parents to understand children's developmental stages and identifying appropriate strategies for reacting to them. Learning at home refers to collaborating with parents to support the creation of suitable learning environments at home. Volunteering, which involves establishing a school volunteer programme, may be a challenge to most parents due to time, yet it is a good way of inviting parents' participation. Lastly, partnering with the community involves identifying resources from the community and integrating these towards promoting a shared vision for the school (2016a: 11). Decision-making within the context of schooling is thus envisioned by the DBE and NECT as an inclusive process involving parents and communities associated with a school. This could be via the SGB or other committees as well as via a variety of events (DBE & NECT 2016a).

The principles of the School–Parent–Community Engagement Framework are: participation as equal partners; evidence-based building on successful initiatives; being flexible and having respect for diversity; and being contextually appropriate (DBE & NECT 2016a). If the principles are applied, the recognition of income distribution ought to enter into how parental and caregiver involvement is enacted. Notwithstanding the six focus areas of engagement, the DBE and NECT acknowledge that 'poverty and its effects' as well as 'cultural and socio-economic isolation' are two factors that result in a lack of interest and barrier to parental involvement (2016a: 7). Thus, diversity amongst parents is recognised, including economic diversity, which implies differences in income distribution of parents. But the framework does not address unequal income distribution as an overt feature of developing interventions. Another potential tacit recognition of unequal income distribution is evident from one indicator related to improved communication associated with teachers and school management that refers to 'single-parent, dual income, and less formally educated families' (DBE & NECT 2016a: 20). In sum, while equal partnership is an explicit principle, the word 'unequal' does not appear in the framework, and unequal income distribution is not recognised as a factor in developing interventions or measuring their success.

Discussion and implications

This chapter has found that unequal income distribution amongst parents is recognised to the extent that there is a statutory mandate based on specific criteria linked to the income of surrounding communities that some schools can charge fees and others are non-fee paying. In addition, parents who are not able to pay school fees have recourse to exemptions. The relevant legislation and policies promulgated between 1996 and 2009 in South Africa also make provision for parents to participate in the governance of schools via SGBs. No remedies for differentiation in regard to parents' and caregivers' capability to participate in such governance structures are, however, discernible in policy discourse.

Policy documents from 2016 provide frameworks for broader-based participation, not limited to the SGB only. Those policy documents are based on equal participation and context-specific interventions that recognise diversity. Despite this recognition of a broad range of difference, the explicit recognition of unequal income distribution – and hence the exact effect it could have on representation – is absent from the policy discourse. Thus, even though the unequal distribution of parent and caregiver income is recognised in policy, the effect it has on parent and caregiver participation has not entered into the policy discourse, except subtly. In the absence of the explicit definition of the problem, remedies and specific features of interventions are unlikely to emerge.

The lack of parental and caregiver involvement is consequential for learning outcomes, and unequal income distribution has nuanced implications for reducing parental and caregiver involvement. Each of these are discussed below in order to offer recommendations for how policy discourse might shift the dial in more explicit and overt ways.

Research has found that when parents and caregivers participate in their children's education, education outcomes improve. Examples abound in the literature, with some of them noted here as verification. According to the research findings of the US Department of Education, 'children's success in reading comprehension is directly related to the availability of reading materials in the home. Children need positive encouragement in the form of praise and reward effect' (2000: 7). Parent volunteering also helps schools to perform well in cultural activities, as parents assist educators with skills needed in different activities (Hoberg 1999). This is all evidenced by a report conducted by the National School Public Relations Association (2006) and drawing on research by Comer (1986) and Gillum (1977), which showed that enhanced parental involvement leads to better academic performance, better school attendance, and improved behaviour of children at home and in school. To bring it back to the South African context, high school children whose parents are actively involved with their schooling have a higher rate of matriculation than those whose parents are passively involved. Moreover, children whose parents are involved in their schooling have higher aspirations for obtaining a bachelor's degree (Barnard 2004; Trusty 1999). Rumberger et al. (1990) have also found that parents of students who dropped out rarely attended their children's school functions or assisted their children with completing their homework. In addition, these parents were the least likely to punish their children for getting poor results. Furthermore, On Target Family Involvement explains that research on K–12 schools has linked parental involvement to educational outcomes, including increased achievement in test results, a decrease in the dropout rate, improved attendance, improved learner behaviour, improved teacher–parent relations, greater commitment to schoolwork, and improved attitudes towards school (Topor et al. 2010). Additionally, when parents are involved, they ensure that the learner spends more time on homework. This results in a decrease in the learner failing to complete homework (Van Wyk & Lemmer 2009). Parents assisting their children with homework and study programmes as well as discussing schoolwork with them contributes to their achievement (DePlanty, Coulter-Kern & Duchane 2007; Mestry & Grobler 2007).

The earlier in a child's life the parents become involved, the greater the effects will be on the child's educational progress. The effectiveness of this approach has been shown through various childhood education programmes, such as Head Start. According to a study conducted by Reutzel and Cooter (1996), positive effects were shown to increase when choices were provided to parents. The schools that offered a variety of ways for parents to get involved had an increased effect on student achievement. Giving parents various methods or activities to involve them in their children's lives increased the willingness and ability of parents to become involved. This increase in parental involvement has been shown to have a consistent, positive relationship with students' achievement and development at school (Tan, Lyu & Peng 2020).

Therefore, when schools and families work together to support learning, children tend to do better in school, stay in school for longer, and like school more. As a result, educators benefit when they receive support and appreciation from parents (Van Wyk 2010).

Another major factor in the positive impacts of parent–school involvement is that learners have higher expectations for their future if their parents are involved. Learners put in more effort, attention, and concentration, and are more interested in learning (Gonzalez-DeHass, Willems & Holbein 2005; Tan, Lyu & Peng 2020). Parents' attitudes towards education, their involvement, and expectations are therefore positively related to learners' educational aspirations (Garg et al. 2002; Nichols et al. 2010). Parents thus set limits, encourage learners, and remind them of the significance of education (Gonzalez-DeHass, Willems & Holbein 2005). Parents who get involved in their children's education convey the importance of education and that their child's endeavours matter (Rivera 2010). This is through parental conceptions of 'probable' futures (see Harrison & Waller 2018: 919), encapsulated in their academic expectations. However, the extent to which parents are capable of doing so depends on the nature of the income they receive. Upper middle class parents were typically found to be engaged in school activities and were influential in school decision-making, while working class parents took on a more supportive role in respect of their involvement with their children's school (Lareau 1987). Low or lower income can also be an indicator of further factors that are shown to limit parental and caregiver involvement in education, such as lower levels of literacy, or language skills that do not match those of the school's language of communication (Mncube 2007).

In South Africa, race can also intersect with income distribution as Black parents are more likely to have lower incomes. Mncube states that 'black African parents are reluctant and are not so keen to participate as much as they are supposed to' (2007: 137). It has also been argued that Black parents may not be able to adapt in a school that is dominated by white teaching staff, and 'some white parents might be irritated/exasperated by the presence of Black and Indian children in their school and decide to sit back' (Mncube 2007: 137). This is said to be indicative of 'sabotage to prove that racial integration was never meant to be' (Mncube 2007: 137).

Further consequences or effects of the intersections with income distribution are also experienced. For instance, Oyserman, Brickman and Rhodes (2007) report on how economic and other factors (such as language barriers) can increase parents' stress and reduce the time they have available to be involved with school. These factors limit social justice related to parental and caregiver involvement in their children's education because they limit equal participation.

Schools can be intimidating for many parents of learners. In poor communities in particular, there is an imbalance in power relations between parents and school staff. Parents often feel ill-equipped to engage with teachers and school management about the performance of their children and the school as a whole (Constantino, Cui & Faltis 1995: 19).

Some parents continue to understand parental involvement from the apartheid perspective when schools were governed differently. The apartheid regime created perceptions of what parental involvement should look like, even after democracy (Matshe 2014). The apathy of parents towards involvement in children's education in rural areas is largely due to the legacies of apartheid, when people of different races experienced the education system differently. Black people's participation in political decisions was disregarded, and the same was true for educational matters (Matshe 2014). Parents from low-income and previously disadvantaged populations experienced cultural exclusion in schools through communication and the formal nature of schools (Maluleke 2014). Bashini (1998, cited in Mestry and Grobler 2007) asserts that the lack of parental participation in education does not necessarily indicate a lack of interest but often stems from other issues such as poverty, single-parenthood, an inability to speak English, the impact of HIV and/or Aids, and socio-cultural exclusion. Singh, Mbokodi, and Msila assert that socio-economic status plays a role in parental involvement for reasons other than those that have been mentioned. Evidence for this statement was sought through the study over two years of historically disadvantaged secondary schools, including 24 parents of learners. Seventy per cent of the children were in households where they were expected to perform various domestic chores that took up a lot of their time (2004).

Another reason for a lack of parent–school involvement can be seen in parents' memories of their own failure at school. Such parents will not have much desire to return to a place that reminds them of their own failures (Brink & Chandler 1993).

Additionally, and unfortunately, many parents hold two or three jobs in order to cope with economic realities, and work schedules may often prevent these parents from attending meetings and other events at the school (Onikama, Hammond & Koki 1998). Conversely, parents of higher socio-economic status were found to be more involved in such school activities, including the volunteering that goes with them (Tan, Lyu & Peng 2020) These factors, coupled with the fact that many parents view the school and its teachers as being competent to deal with their children (Singh, Mbokodi & Msila 2004; Wherry 2009) and therefore do not see the education of their child as their own responsibility (Desforges & Abouchaar 2003), mean that parental involvement is rather low on the whole.

In some South African contexts, fathers who are physically absent from their children's lives are still considered by the school to be present because they provide for the financial needs of the children. The fact that these fathers are physically absent is likely to result in the single mother finding parent–school involvement that much harder, having to attend to a whole host of other parental commitments, such as ensuring there is food on the table (Salami & Okeke 2018). Such single parents therefore have less support than married parents and less help in monitoring their children (Amoateng et al. 2004). However, in a study conducted by Singh, Mbokodi and Msila (2004), mothers or female guardians attended school meetings and displayed more interest (presumably, than fathers or male guardians) in the children's learning progress in 80% of homes.

Conclusion

In conclusion, there is sufficient evidence that parental and caregiver involvement in education enhances learners' capabilities to succeed at learning outcomes. Moreover, there are laws that advocate and make provision for parental and caregiver involvement in South Africa, such as the SA Schools Act. As a legislated right, parents and caregivers are free to participate in the schooling of their children. Indeed, they are obligated to ensure their children are educated up to their fifteenth year. However, contextual realities in South African society mitigate this right and obligation. In particular, economic inequality is a single barrier yet one that intersects with a range of additional factors – such as literacy gaps, lack of time, and stress – that limit parental and caregiver participation in schooling and children's education. South African policy recognises income inequality in society by affording parents and caregivers remedies in instances where they are unable to afford school fees. Policy discourses, however, do not explicitly provide recourse for parental and caregiver participation beyond the non-payment of school fees.

Explicit directives, guidelines, or procedures are absent from the policy discourse for matters relating to school governance, learning, and parental involvement in the development of children's reading skill. As such, policy discourse does not foster social justice from the perspective of providing parents and caregivers with equal opportunities to participate in school activities. Considering the range of factors that might either intersect with or result from income inequality, it is recommended that such policy discourse should be generated considering the capabilities that impact involvement and that intersect with income distribution.

References

Amoateng AY, Richter AY, Makiwane M & Rama S (2004) *Describing the Structure and Needs of Families in South Africa: Towards the Development of a National Policy Framework for Families*. A Report Commissioned by the Department of Social Development. Pretoria: Child Youth and Family Development, Human Sciences Research Council

Barnard WM (2004) Parent involvement in elementary school and educational attainment. *Children and Youth Services Review* 26(1): 39–62

Bloch MN & Tabachnick BR (1993) Improving parent involvement as school reform: Rhetoric or reality? In NP Greenman (Ed.) *Changing schools: Recapturing the past or inventing the future?* Albany: State University of New York Press

Brink C & Chandler K (1993) Teach the parent, reach the child: Denver program improves home environment for kids. *Vocational Education Journal* 68(5): 26–48

Brown LH & Beckett KS (2007) Parent involvement in an alternative school for students at risk of educational failure. *Education and Urban Society* 39(4): 498–523

Comer JP (1986) Parent participation in the schools. *The Phi Delta Kappan* 67(6): 442–446

Constantino R, Cui L & Faltis C (1995) Chinese parental involvement: Reaching new levels. *Equity & Excellence in Education* 28(2): 46–50

Davis KM & Lambie GW (2005) Family engagement: A collaborative approach for middle school counselors. *Professional School Counseling* 9(2): 1096–2409

DBE (Department of Basic Education) (2015) Annual Report. Pretoria: DBE

DBE & NECT (National Education Collaboration Trust) (2016a) *School–parent–community engagement framework.* Centurion: NECT

DBE & NECT (2016b) *Practical guidelines: How parents can contribute meaningfully to the success of their children in schools.* Centurion: NECT

Delgado-Gaitan C (1991) Involving parents in the schools: A process of empowerment. *American Journal of Education* 100(1): 20–46

DePlanty J, Coulter-Kern R & Duchane KA (2007) Perceptions of parent involvement in academic achievement. *The Journal of Educational Research* 100(6): 361–368

Desforges C & Abouchaar A (2003) *The Impact of Parental Involvement, Parental Support and Family Education on Pupil Achievements and Adjustment: A Literature Review.* Report No. 433. Accessed April 2025, https://www.nationalnumeracy.org.uk/sites/default/files/documents/impact_of_parental_involvement/the_impact_of_parental_involvement.pdf

DoE (Department of Education) (1997) *Curriculum 2005: Lifelong learning for the 21st century.* Pretoria: DoE

DoE (1998) *Traditional and new learning environments.* Pretoria: DoE

DoE (2006) South African Schools Act, 1996 (Act no. 84 of 1996): Amended national norms and standards for school funding. (Notice 869) *Government Gazette* 494(29179): 1–56, 31 August

Fraser N (1995) From redistribution to recognition? Dilemmas of a 'post-socialist age'. *New Left Review* 212: 68–93

Fraser N (1998) *Social justice in the age of identity politics: Redistribution, recognition, participation.* WZB Discussion Paper No. FS I 98–108, Wissenschaftszentrum Berlin für Sozialforschung (WZB), Berlin

Fraser N (2000) Rethinking recognition. *New Left Review* 3: 107–120

Fraser N (2005) Reframing justice in a globalising world. *New Left Review* (36): 69–88

Garg R, Kauppi C, Lewko J & Urajnik D (2002) A structural model of educational aspirations. *Journal of Career Development* 29(2): 87–108

Gillum R (1977) The effects of parental involvement on student achievement in three Michigan performance contracting programs. *Eric*: 1–18. Accessed June 2025, https://eric.ed.gov/?id=ED144007

Gonzalez-DeHass AR, Willems P & Holbein D M (2005) Examining the relationship between parent involvement and student motivation. *Educational Psychology Review* 17(2): 99–123

Goodall J & Montgomery C (2014) Parental involvement to parental engagement: A continuum. *Educational Review* 66(4): 399–410

Harrison N & Waller R (2018) Challenging discourses of aspiration: The role of expectations and attainment in access to higher education. *British Educational Research Journal* 44: 914–938

Hoberg SM (Ed.) (1999) *Education Research Methodology*. UNISA Study Guide 2 for MEDEM2-R. Pretoria: University of South Africa

Jaiswal SK (2017) A review of the relationship between parental involvement and students' academic performance. *International Journal of Indian Psychology* 4(3): 110–123

Lareau A (1987) Social class differences in family–school relationships: The importance of cultural capital. *Sociology of Education* 60(2): 73–85

Maluleke M (2014) Perceptions of secondary school managers and teachers regarding out-of-field teaching in the Johannesburg North District. MEd thesis, University of Johannesburg

Matshe PFA (2014) Challenges of parental involvement in rural public schools in Ngaka Modiri Molema District of North West Province. *International Journal of Humanities, Social Sciences and Education* 1(6): 93–103

Mbokodi SM & Singh P (2011) Parental partnerships in the governance of schools in the Black townships of Port Elizabeth. *Perspectives in Education* 29(4): 38–48

Mestry R (2014) A critical analysis of the National Norms and Standards for School Funding policy: Implications for social justice and equity in South Africa. *Educational Management, Administration & Leadership* 42(6): 851–867

Mestry R & Grobler B (2007) Collaboration and communication as effective strategies for parent involvement in public schools. *Educational Research and Review* 2(7): 176–185

Mncube VS (2007) Social justice, policy and parents' understanding of their voice in School Governing Bodies in South Africa. *Journal of Educational Administration and History* 39(2): 129–143

Mosoge MJ & Van der Westhuizen PC (1997) Teacher access to decision making in schools. *South African Journal of Education* 17(4): 196–202

National School Public Relations Association (2006) *How strong communication contributes to student and school success: Parent and family involvement.* Virginia: National School Public Relations Association

Nichols TM, Kotchick BA, McNamara BC & Haskins DG (2010) Understanding the educational aspirations of African American adolescents: Child, family, and community factors. *Journal of Black Psychology* 36(1): 25–48

Onikama DL, Hammond OW & Koki S (1998) *Family involvement in education: A synthesis of research for Pacific educators.* Honolulu: Pacific Resources for Education and Learning. Accessed April 2025, https://files.eric.ed.gov/fulltext/ED420446.pdf

Oyserman D, Brickman D & Rhodes M (2007) School success, possible selves, and parent school involvement. *Family Relations* 56: 479–489

Republic of South Africa (1996) South African Schools Act, No. 84. *Government Gazette* 377(17579): 1–50, 15 November

Reutzel R & Cooter R (1996) *Teaching children to read: From basals to books.* Englewood Cliffs, NJ: Prentice-Hall

Rivera M (2010) Parents are key to closing the achievement gap. *The Hispanic Outlook in Higher Education* 20(22): 40

Rumberger RW, Ghatak G, Poulos G, Ritter PL & Dornbusch SM (1990) Family influences on dropout behaviour in one California high school. *Sociology of Education* 63(4): 283–299

Salami IA & Okeke CIO (2018) Absent fathers' socio-economic status and perceptions of fatherhood as related to developmental challenges faced by children in South Africa. *South African Journal of Childhood Education* 8(1): a522. Accessed June 2025, https://doi.org/10.4102/sajce.V8i1.522

Sayed Y & Ahmed A (2009) Promoting access and enhancing education opportunities? The case of 'no-fees schools' in South Africa. *Compare: A Journal of Comparative and International Education* 39(2): 203–218

Sayed Y & Ahmed A (2015) Education quality, and teaching and learning in the post-2015 education agenda. *International Journal of Educational Development* 40: 330–338

Sayed Y, Badroodien A, Omar Y, Balie L, McDonald Z et al. (2017) Social Cohesion Report 2017. Engaging Teachers in Peacebuilding in Post-conflict contexts: Evaluating Education Interventions in South Africa. ESRC/DFID Research Report, University of Sussex, UK & Centre for International Teacher Education (CITE), South Africa

Sayed Y, Kanjee A & Nkomo M (2013) *The search for quality education in post-apartheid South Africa.* Cape Town: HSRC Press.

Sayed Y & Motala S (2012) Equity and 'no fee' schools in South Africa: Challenges and prospects. *Social Policy & Administration* 46(6): 672–687

Sayed Y, Motala S, Carel D & Ahmed R (2020) School governance and funding policy in South Africa: Towards social justice and equity in education policy. *South African Journal of Education* 40(4): 1–12

Sayed Y & Soudien C (2005) Decentralisation and the construction of inclusion education policy in South Africa. *Compare: A Journal of Comparative and International Education* 35(2): 115–125

Shriberg D (2008) Social justice through a school psychology lens: Definition and applications. *School Psychology Review* 37(4): 453–468

Singh P, Mbokodi SM & Msila VT (2004) Black parental involvement in education. *South African Journal of Education* 24(4): 301–307

Smith JG (2006) Parental involvement in education among low-income families: A case study. *School Community Journal* 16(1): 43–56

Spaull N (2013) Poverty & privilege: Primary school inequality in South Africa. *International Journal of Educational Development* 33(5): 436–447

Tan CY, Lyu M & Peng B (2020) Academic benefits from parental involvement are stratified by parental socioeconomic status: A meta-analysis. *Parenting* 20(4): 241–287

Tikly L & Barrett AM (2011) Social justice, capabilities and the quality of education in low-income countries. *International Journal of Educational Development* 31(1): 3–14

Topor DR, Keane SP, Shelton TL & Calkins SD (2010) Parent involvement and student academic performance: A multiple mediational analysis. *Journal of Prevention & Intervention in the Community* 38(3): 183–197

Trusty J (1999) Effects of eighth-grade parental involvement on late adolescents' educational expectations. *Journal of Research & Development in Education* 32(4): 224–233

US Department of Education (2000) The Condition of Education 2000. Washington: National Center for Education Statistics. Accessed May 2025, https://nces.ed.gov/pubs2000/2000062.pdf

Van Wyk N (2010) The South African education system. In E Lemmer & N van Wyk (Eds) *Themes in South African education: For the comparative educationist.* Cape Town: Pearson Education

Van Wyk N & Lemmer E (2009) *Organising parent involvement in SA schools.* Cape Town: Juta

Wherry JH (2009) Shattering barriers to parent involvement. *Principal* 88(5): 7

Wilder S (2014) Effects of parental involvement on academic achievement: A meta-synthesis. *Educational Review* 66(3): 377–397. Accessed April 2025, https://psycnet.apa.org/record/2014-16557-008

Woolman S & Fleisch B (2006) South Africa's unintended experiment in school choice: How the National Education Policy Act, the South Africa Schools Act and the Employment of Educators Act create the enabling conditions for quasi-markets in schools. *Education and the Law* 18(1): 31 75

Yang D, Chen P, Wang K, Li Z, Zhang C, & Huang R (2023) Parental involvement and student engagement: A review of the literature. *Sustainability* 15(7): 5859. Accessed April 2025, https://www.mdpi.com/2071-1050/15/7/5859

2 *Linking Politics, Policy, and Practice in Understanding Parent Involvement*

Bakang Mputle

Introduction

This chapter examines how contextual factors, ideological constraints, policy production/implementation, and local practices intersect to create understandings of parental and caregiver involvement. Practices like parent/caregiver involvement operate within broader sociopolitical contexts and it is against these contexts that participation is interpreted. The chapter explores historical and contemporary perceptions of parental and caregiver involvement, using these to offer an analysis of how the concept of parent involvement is understood and how it has evolved over time.

Reference is made to parent and caregiver involvement in South Africa and, briefly, in the United Kingdom, but some general observations illuminate how perceptions of parent and caregiver involvement are mediated across contexts by class, race, language, and other aspects of identity.

Parental and caregiver involvement is multidimensional, encompassing various practices from study habits to communication with the school aimed at promoting a child's success in education (Dias 2023). However, barriers exist that hinder active parental/caregiver participation in their children's education, despite its potential benefits (DBE & NECT 2016). It is essential to acknowledge that parents' and caregivers' involvement orientations are shaped by their backgrounds, including social class, race, and prior educational experiences, as well as their perceptions of schools and educational outcomes.

Work in the sociology of education highlights the ways in which local knowledges, practices, policies, and ideologies intersect to shape discourses associated with key educational concepts, including parent and caregiver involvement. Stephen Ball's research explores the complex relationship between contextual factors, text production, policy formulation, and local practices in shaping understandings within the educational policy landscape (Iftimescu et al. 2020). This approach provides a detailed analysis of how these elements impact concepts such as parental/caregiver involvement in education. Contextual factors, including class, race, language, and identity, are crucial in influencing the level and nature of parental/caregiver engagement in education (Seikkula-Leino et al. 2019). These factors affect how parents/caregivers perceive their roles in their children's education as well as shaping their interactions with schools and teachers. Policy development can either support or hinder parental/caregiver involvement in education (Michael, Wolhuter & Van Wyk 2012). Policies set at various levels of governance establish expectations for parental/caregiver engagement in educational settings. The implementation of these policies further determines their actual impact on parental and caregiver behaviours and responses in practice (Kushnir & Yazgan 2023). The outcomes of policy implementation significantly influence the dynamics of parent–school interactions and the overall success of parental/caregiver involvement initiatives. Avelar, Nikita and Ball's work emphasises the significance of comprehending the broader educational policy landscape and its intersection with local practices in influencing parental involvement (2018). By examining the intricate connections between policy decisions, text production, and contextual factors, we can gain insights into the mechanisms that drive parental/caregiver engagement in education. This holistic approach enables a more thorough understanding of the challenges and opportunities in fostering effective parent–school partnerships.

Contextual and policy-related factors play out in a wider ideological context: currently, the effects of neoliberalism on education shed light on the ways in which market-driven reforms also impact parental/caregiver involvement. Neoliberal policies emphasise individual choice and competition, influencing parents'/caregivers' decision-making processes and their level of engagement with schools (Van Zanten & Kosunen 2013). Schools' interactions with parents/caregivers are therefore framed by broader socio-cultural contexts that influence specific notions of what it means to be a good or bad parent or teacher.

Contexts influence relationships, and political and legal frameworks inhibit and constrain interactions with parents (Chavkin 1998). There are several pragmatic implications for the way parents and caregivers are constructed by educational policy, governing the ways they access information, decision-making processes, and the spaces and times by which they are entitled or expected to be part of their children's school life. These pragmatic factors have a broader significance, with implications for how both power and accountability are distributed between parents and schools. By extension, notions of good and bad parents/caregivers are constructed in relation to the degree to which they and the school conforms to these expectations.

In terms of current understandings in liberal democratic settings, the concept of parental/caregiver involvement implies that parents or caregivers dedicate resources for their child's benefit and participate in activities, contributing either directly or indirectly towards the education of their children (Đurišić & Bunijevac 2017). Their motivation for participation assumes that involvement generally impacts positively on the education of their children. A normative assumption is that parental/caregiver involvement is likely to improve the quality of education through taking parental viewpoints into consideration (see Kaplan Toren 2013). In South Africa, participation ensures that education realises the democratic principles and processes stipulated in documents such as the South African Schools Act.

These observations illustrate how the concept of parent/caregiver involvement and the practices conventionally associated with it are shaped by culturally mediated forms of knowledge, the production of policies, and the ideological underpinnings of modern nation states. Some of these ideas are now applied to the history of parent/caregiver involvement in the United Kingdom in a case study that illustrates the changing nature of this construct and how ideology intersects with local practices.

A brief history of understandings of parent/caregiver involvement in the United Kingdom

As the bureaucratisation of education and the professionalisation of teaching evolved in the United Kingdom in the early 1900s, understandings of appropriate parental/caregiver involvement emerged in educational settings. This occurred without parents' or caregivers' input in terms of what was acceptable and appropriate support for schools and their children (Barge & Loges 2003).

The introduction of state secondary education in the 1950s led to what Chavkin (1998) has identified as an initial discursive error, characterised by a clear demarcation of responsibilities between teachers and parents/caregivers. Teachers were regarded as the authoritative educational experts that assumed control over the school. Parents/caregivers were expected to have limited involvement to the extent that they were frequently forbidden from physically entering school premises to engage in any meaningful participation. Understandings of parents'/caregivers' appropriate roles in education were heavily shaped by teachers' perspectives, leaving caregivers with the expectation of adhering to the educational framework prescribed by educators. Alternatively, they could assert control over their children's learning process by opting out of state-provided education. An authoritative dichotomy emerged, whereby parents and caregivers were presented with the choice of either conforming to the teacher's authority or withdrawing from the system.

This again changed in the 1960s, when an emerging interest in differential educational achievement led to the notion that the home was a crucial variable in educational achievement. The Plowden report of 1967 stated that parental involvement was an essential and necessary element in the educational equation, changing educational discourse on the subject. However, involvement was conceptualised very much within the terms of the school, with parents/caregivers considered extensions to this authority. Parents/caregivers were expected to support the activities of teachers at home, producing a relationship between themselves and schools. A further effect of this discursive turn was the emergence and articulation of "the bad parent", one who did not act in ways that educational authority expected. The "bad parent" highlighted the dangers of a pathological home, toxic to the educational potential of children.

On the other hand, Chavkin (1998) refers to educators expressing their concerns about parents or caregivers who are excessively involved, persistently seeking additional reading materials or more challenging homework for their children. Another emerging discourse centred on the challenges of engaging parents and caregivers, be it at formal events such as parent evenings or casual conversations at school gates. An intriguing aspect within both conversations lies in the portrayal of the "bad parent" at opposite ends of the same spectrum, either too engaged or deficient.

The interest in differential achievement continued through the 1960s and 1970s, first focusing on class but later shifting to gender and ethnicity, and the influence of the home remained important.

The 1980s saw a new discursive turn towards the marketisation of education, with parents and caregivers having a choice in their child's school, essentially becoming consumers of education and thereby redrawing lines of power and authority. In fundamental ways, parents began to exert new kinds of influence on education, punishing undesirable schools and rewarding preferred ones with their children's presence.

What actually happened outside of school was still limited to the emerging emphasis on the governing body, of which parents/caregivers were a part (Bowe, Gewirtz & Ball 2006). Parents became expected to make choices and to keep themselves informed about schools and education, something which had varying effects on different groups. Those with social contacts and who are familiar with the workings of schools could better exercise this informed choice, with the result that in practice this favoured the middle-classes. Parents/caregivers from disadvantaged and working-class backgrounds, as well as those with less social and cultural capital, were left disconnected, expected to exercise their rights without a firm foundation or understanding of the many ways in which education operates.

At this point a new discursive turn was introduced into the parent–school relationship: the notion of partnership, with parents and caregivers expected to assume part of a more cooperative relationship, one in which lines of authority were blurred, and where both the school and the parents/caregivers are intended to exercise collaborative expertise over the child (Ball 2010). In practice, power dynamics shape these partnerships, which are regularly skewed either to parents or educators (Bowe, Gewirtz & Ball 2006). Partnerships are further problematised by the authority conferred on teachers by schools, with contracts establishing these partnerships in legalistic terms, rather than through mutual respect and interest.

This brief history from the UK demonstrates how ideology and policy shape prevailing societal expectations regarding the extent and nature of parental/caregiver involvement in schools. Expectations are contingent upon a legal and cultural construction of what constitutes appropriate involvement, a concept that has evolved over time.

Policy and parent/caregiver involvement in South Africa

Expectations of parents/caregivers and understandings of what constitutes healthy involvement have also changed considerably over time in South Africa, with post-apartheid legislation exerting a significant effect on these issues. The South African Schools Act of 1996 promotes the role of parents/caregivers in education by providing them with a democratic right to serve on the school governing body (SGB). Parents and caregivers are supported by the regulation that states that there must be one more parent than the total of other members on the SGB who have voting rights. Thus, parents/caregivers constitute 60% of the SGB, in which the chairperson is also a parent (Mbokodi & Singh 2011).

Even though the South African Schools Act places parents/caregivers on an equal footing with school-based decision makers and managers, as Manilal (2014) suggests, parental involvement in South Africa remains a challenge and its form is not stipulated in the Act. Above all, while having SGB and voting rights is important, it is arguably of equal importance to have each parent and/or guardian involved in the teaching and learning of their children.

In South Africa, the legacy of apartheid and historical policies have contributed to inequalities that persist in society, affecting various aspects of life, including family dynamics and parental/caregiver involvement (Booi et al. 2019). The disparities created by past government actions have had lasting effects on communities, leading to challenges in economic empowerment, access to resources, and opportunities for families to thrive. These inequalities can exacerbate the difficulties faced by parents/caregivers in being actively involved in their children's upbringing, especially in disadvantaged communities where access to support systems may be limited.

Challenges like work demands, single motherhood, and differences between rural and urban settings further complicate the landscape of parental/caregiver involvement in the country. These challenges can hinder parents/caregivers, especially single parents, from actively participating in their children's lives, impacting the overall well-being of families and children. This can be seen in parents' and caregivers' poor attendance at meetings, children's poor matric results, and parents' lack of interest in learners' schoolwork and homework. Parents/caregivers do not deliberately distance themselves from their children's education: their involvement can instead be attributed to a complex interplay of factors including historical legacies, socio-economic challenges, educational disparities, and the evolving work landscape. Addressing these multifaceted issues requires a holistic approach that considers the broader societal context in which families operate.

Class, race, culture, and language shaping notions of desirable parent/caregiver involvement

Parents and caregivers from less affluent backgrounds in South Africa and elsewhere may not fit the widely accepted definition and dominant culture of involvement in schools. Working-class and unemployed parents/caregivers emphasise school readiness skills and attributes, but these may not be observable to teachers or fit with middle-class parental/caregiver involvement practices.

Jeynes (2023) contends that the race and class of parents can affect parental involvement when that involvement is conceived of as home-based and school-based.

Educators regularly create and adopt assumptions, perceptions, and notions of parental/caregiver involvement based on the '"observed" level' of parental/school involvement (Foster, Young & Young 2017). From the observed level, educators build the assumption that affluent families are involved, which leads to their forming a positive perception about those parents/caregivers and learners. However, this view is biased. The assumptions have become the yardstick for measuring and defining parental/caregiver involvement in education, leading to educators having a negative perception of those whose involvement does not meet their perceived standard (Trainor 2010). Parents and caregivers from less affluent backgrounds may be involved in their children's education, but this may not present itself in the same fashion as that of affluent parents/caregivers operating in the observed level and perception of educators.

These differences relate to the forms of capital or resources that working-class parents/caregivers bestow on their children, which are often not recognised by the school as they are not the forms of involvement the school values. Cultural capital misalignment occurs when teachers fail to recognise other forms of parental/caregiver contributions, largely due to an educational system that maintains a pre-existing social order; a gap exists between learners endowed with unequal amounts of cultural capital (Bourdieu 1986). Hattam et al. note that one aspect of teachers' perceptions of parental/caregiver involvement is that 'the dispositions of children's life contexts favour those with alignment to the cultural arbitrary of the … middle-class schools' (Hattam et al. 2009: 20).

Learners from low-income groups are effectively misaligned with middle-class cultural capital. Fataar (2012) characterises this misalignment as a pedagogical injustice, where learners from low-income groups do not fit into the school code. Statistically these learners make up a substantial portion of school enrolment figures (Fataar 2012). Eighty per cent of children in South Africa's school system come from working-class backgrounds, are impoverished, and are structurally destined for educational disengagement. The resources that working-class parents/caregivers bestow on their children, including a range of linguistic repertoires, often remain unacknowledged in the schooling system.

It is therefore problematic for educators to have expectations that parents/caregivers of every child must participate in traditional middle-class ways. In South Africa, this assumption is widely held by educators in lower quintile schools in rural areas and townships. Literature suggests that educators in these schools have a singular definition and standard of parental/caregiver involvement, mirroring that of middle-class ways.

Language plays a significant role in validating certain ways of discussing parents/caregivers and marginalising alternative perspectives. Language is shaped by educational policy at the school, national, and global levels, but it also perpetuates specific notions about parental roles and involvement.

Teachers' perceptions of parental/caregiver involvement are influenced by their racial backgrounds, pre-service training, the geographical location of schools, and teacher self-efficacy (Foster, Young & Young 2017). These perceptions can be detrimental to teaching and learning efficacy and can become teachers' reality if they are left uninterrogated (Foster, Young & Young 2017).

Conclusion

Norms and expectations around parent/caregiver involvement are embedded in ideologies, power relations, and the practices of dominant groups. This is pertinent to education in South Africa, where teachers and learners from different ethnic groups, geographical and socio-economic backgrounds interact in schools, with a range of expectations of parental/caregiver involvement that are culturally, racially, and socio-economically diverse.

An understanding of how socio-economic class, race, and culture shape different perceptions of parental/caregiver involvement provides insightful tools to understand that involvement and to develop co-created practices that serve the interests of all groups concerned. When working towards productive and inclusive forms of parental/caregiver involvement, it is important to establish a common understanding of what is expected from both sides, which can also help facilitate partnerships between schools and local communities. Unequal power relations, and social and economic status will always be present, but the negative effects of these can partly be dealt with by making assumptions explicit. Parents/caregivers are their children's first and most important teachers and they have an immense impact on the development, values, and identity of the child. Children need guidance, support, and encouragement from parents/caregivers, who are often intimidated by schools where they may themselves have had negative experiences as learners.

Reflecting on these insights can contribute to school reform, enable parental/caregiver involvement, and cultivate success for those typically marginalised and failed by schools, all of which are necessary tasks for educational researchers and activists concerned with injustice.

References

Avelar M, Nikita DP & Ball SJ (2018) Education policy networks and spaces of 'meetingness': A network ethnography of a Brazilian seminar. In A Verger, M Novelli & HK Altinyelken (Eds) *Global education policy and international development: New agendas, issues and policies* 2nd edition). London: Bloomsbury

Ball SJ (2010) New class inequalities in education: Why education policy may be looking in the wrong place! Education policy, civil society, and social class. *International Journal of Sociology and Social Policy* 30(3/4): 155–166

Barge JK & Loges WE (2003) Parent, student, and teacher perceptions of parental involvement. *Journal of Applied Communication Research* 31(2): 140–163. Accessed May 2025, https://doi.org/10.1080/0090988032000064597

Booi S, Chigona W, Maliwichi P & Kunene K (2019) The influence of telecentres on the economic empowerment of the youth in disadvantaged communities of South Africa. Paper presented at the International Conference on Social Implications of Computers in Developing Countries (ICT4D), Dar es Salaam, Tanzania (1–3 May). Accessed May 2025, https://doi.org/10.1007/978-3-030-18400-1_13

Bourdieu P (1986) The forms of capital. In J Richardson (Ed.), *Handbook of theory and research for the sociology of education*. New York: Greenwood

Bowe R, Gewirtz S & Ball SJ (2006) Captured by the discourse? Issues and concerns in researching 'parental choice'. In L Barton (Ed.) *Education and society*. Abingdon: Routledge

Chavkin NF (1998) Making the case for school, family, and community partnerships: Recommendations for research. *The School Community Journal* (8): 9–21

Croll P (2004) Families, social capital, and educational outcomes. *British Journal of Educational Studies* 52(4): 390–416. Accessed May 2025, http://www.jstor.org/stable/1555829

DBE & NECT (Department of Basic Education & National Education Collaboration Trust) (2016) *School–parent–community engagement framework*. Centurion: NECT

Dias D (2023) Parental involvement in school: Parents' and students' perceptions. *Psicologia Escolar e Educacional* (27). Accessed May 2025, https://www.scielo.br/j/pee/a/tt4rYPfRvFCNpsnTtFdTBpC/?lang=pt

Đurišić M & Bunijevac M (2017) Parental involvement as an important factor for successful education. *Center for Educational Policy Studies Journal* (7): 137–153

Fataar A (2012) Pedagogical justice and student engagement in South African schooling: Working with the cultural capital of disadvantaged students. *Perspectives in Education* 30(4): 52–75

Foster MD, Young J & Young JL (2017) Teacher perceptions of parental involvement and the achievement of diverse learners: A meta-analysis. *Journal of Ethical Educational Leadership* 4(5): 1–18

Hattam R, Brennan M, Zipin L & Comber B (2009) Researching for social justice: Contextual, conceptual and methodological challenges. *Discourse: Studies in the Cultural Politics of Education* 30(3): 303–316. Accessed May 2025, https://doi.org/10.1080/01596300903037010

Iftimescu S, Ion G, Proteasa C, Iucu R, Marin E & Stîngu M (2020) Closing the circle: Research and policymaking in education. In A Curaj, L Deca, R Pricopie (Eds) *European higher education area: Challenges for a new decade*. Cham: Springer. Accessed May 2025, https://doi.org/10.1007/978-3-030-56316-5_21

Jeynes W (2023) A theory of parental involvement based on the results of meta-analyses. In W Jeynes (Ed) *Relational aspects of parental involvement to support educational outcomes*. New York: Routledge

Kaplan Toren N (2013) Multiple dimensions of parental involvement and its links to young adolescent self-evaluation and academic achievement. *Psychology in the Schools* 50(6): 634–649

Kushnir I & Yazgan N (2023) The politics of higher education: The European Higher Education Area through the eyes of its stakeholders in France and Italy. *Humanities and Social Sciences Communications* (10): 774. Accessed May 2025, https://doi.org/10.1057/s41599-023-02300-x

Manilal R (2014) Parental involvement in education: A comparison between a privileged and an underprivileged school. MEd dissertation, University of KwaZulu-Natal

Mbokodi SM & Singh P (2011) Parental partnerships in the governance of schools in the Black townships of Port Elizabeth. *Perspectives in Education* 29(4): 38–48

Michael S,, Wolhuter CC & Van Wyk N (2012) The management of parental involvement in multicultural schools in South Africa: A case study. Centre for *Educational Policy Studies Journal* 2 (1): 57–82

Seikkula-Leino J, Ruskovaara E, Pihkala T, Rodríguez ID & Delfino J (2019) Developing entrepreneurship education in Europe: Teachers' commitment to entrepreneurship education in the UK, Finland, and Spain. In A Fayolle, D Kariv & H Matlay (Eds) *The role and impact of entrepreneurship education*. Cheltenham: Edward Elgar Publishing

Trainor A (2010) Educators' expectations of parent participation: The role of cultural and social capital. *Multiple Voices for Ethnically Diverse Exceptional Learners* 12(2): 33–50

Van Zanten A & Kosunen S (2013) School choice research in five European countries: The circulation of Stephen Ball's concepts and interpretations. *London Review of Education* 11(3): 239–255

3 Silencing Marginalised Voices in Early Childhood Development Policy

Lydia-Anne Plaatjies

Introduction

This chapter investigates the representation and participation of "weak publics", namely parents and caregivers, in South Africa's Early Childhood Development (ECD) policy. Nancy Fraser's concept of marginalised or "weak publics" is used to illuminate how vulnerable parents and caregivers of young children in ECD are often excluded from policy-making and implementation processes, with the result that they are unable to advocate for the interests of their children. Parental/caregiver exclusion from these processes also likely contributes to the lack of provision for parent/caregiver support programmes in ECD policy.

Weak publics produce "voice gaps", a term that refers to missing voices or people who are unable to challenge gaps in policy provision and implementation, despite their being integral to implementation, and directly affected by provision – in this case, of care for young children. The National Policy Development Framework (NPDF) (The Presidency 2020) emphasises the importance of public participation rather than perpetuating "voice gaps", but challenges persist in effectively incorporating diverse perspectives into policy-making and implementation. In 2020, the South African government adopted the NPDF, which sets out guidelines for future policy implementation through monitoring and evaluation processes. The NPDF acknowledges that the government's most significant challenge is bridging the gaps between policy development, enacting public policies, and implementation. Despite these noble intentions, equal participation regularly fails to occur within the public sphere and the "voice" of citizens is differently "heard" within public policy-making, debate, and implementation. Weak publics therefore produce voice gaps, where power relations between various stakeholders are unequal.

In this chapter, gatekeeping theory is used to understand how weak publics and their resulting voice gaps are produced, excluding parents and caregivers from the policy-making process. South Africa has developed a robust ECD policy framework, making provision for this crucial period of development, but the voices of parents and caregivers are completely excluded from the production and implementation of policy due to gatekeeping processes. Some instances of gatekeeping are unintentional while others are more explicit uses of exclusionary power; both, however, function to concentrate power with gatekeepers, limiting the representation of weak publics and contributing to the exclusion of certain voices in policy-making. Structural forces entrench these gatekeeping dynamics, as social, economic, and cultural inequalities hinder marginalised people from influencing policy outcomes.

The chapter therefore highlights the need for coherence, inclusivity, and active public participation in shaping ECD provision, opening the gate for a variety of voices to be heard. To bridge the voice gap, the South African government must prioritise the needs of vulnerable parents and caregivers, ensuring equitable access to participate in policy and programmes. Collaboration among government departments, non-governmental organisations, community-based organisations, and parents/caregivers should be enhanced to address the complexities of ECD provision and parenting support. The South African government has admirably made legal and political commitments to provide quality ECD services to young children, parents/caregivers, and families. However, by adopting a more inclusive approach to policy implementation in particular, South Africa could make significant strides towards achieving the Sustainable Development Goals of inclusive and equitable education, and lifelong learning for all. Analysing parent/caregiver participation therefore requires an understanding of the dynamics of weak publics, gatekeeping mechanisms, and cultural contexts, in order to identify inequalities and challenges.

Weak publics and voice gaps in ECD policy-making and implementation in South Africa

Think about a community meeting discussing a new ECD policy or how an existing policy is implemented. In attendance are government officials, educators, and parents/caregivers. Amidst the discussions, the group of parents/caregivers has limited resources, less access to education, and little influence. These parents and caregivers may not be as confident in expressing their views and might not have the time or means to attend every meeting. Their voices are regularly drowned out by those who are more privileged and accustomed to participating in such discussions.

In this context, parents and caregivers can be understood through Fraser's notion of weak publics (1990), a concept that emphasises how marginalised voices are regularly not given the same weight or consideration as those of more powerful or influential groups. It is not that these weaker publics do not have concerns or ideas; rather it is that social dynamics and structural inequalities often prevent their perspectives from being fully recognised and integrated into policy decisions and how policy is implemented. Weak publics are not able to obtain parity of participation in institutional settings, nor able to ensure that valuable resources that have been obtained unfairly or through coercion are redistributed (Fraser 2000). Fraser's (1990, 2000) focus was on the socio-institutional factors that enable or inhibit parity of participation. For Fraser, full participation in social processes is restricted through institutionalised rules for engagement. Fraser claims that at least two conditions need to be satisfied for parity of participation to occur. First, resources must be adequately distributed such that people can participate independently and with 'voice' (Fraser 1990: 69). Second, the institutionalised norms and values that underpin and shape evaluations of participation should treat people equally and enable opportunities for all of those involved. Fraser was therefore interested in how social structures make it possible for some people to participate more easily in social practices. In essence, weak publics represent those who have difficulty making their voices heard due to their socio-economic status, cultural background, or historical disadvantage. Fraser's work (1990) urges us to reflect on the inclusivity of policy-making and implementation processes and to recognise that the true democratic ideal is achieved only when all voices, especially the weak ones, are given a fair chance to contribute to shaping the policies that affect their lives.

South African parents/caregivers as a weak public in the National Integrated Policy for Early Childhood Development

Figure 3.1 illustrates the roles of various government departments in implementing an integrated response to ECD in South Africa, and asks the question: *Where are the voices of the parents and caregivers of young children?* The National Integrated Policy for Early Childhood Development (Department of Social Development 2015) has clear guidelines on which South African government sphere is responsible for ECD provisions – national, provincial, or local. However, the place for parents/caregivers to actively participate in, and give feedback to, the system is completely missing.

Figure 3.1 *The roles of government departments in achieving an integrated response to ECD in South Africa*

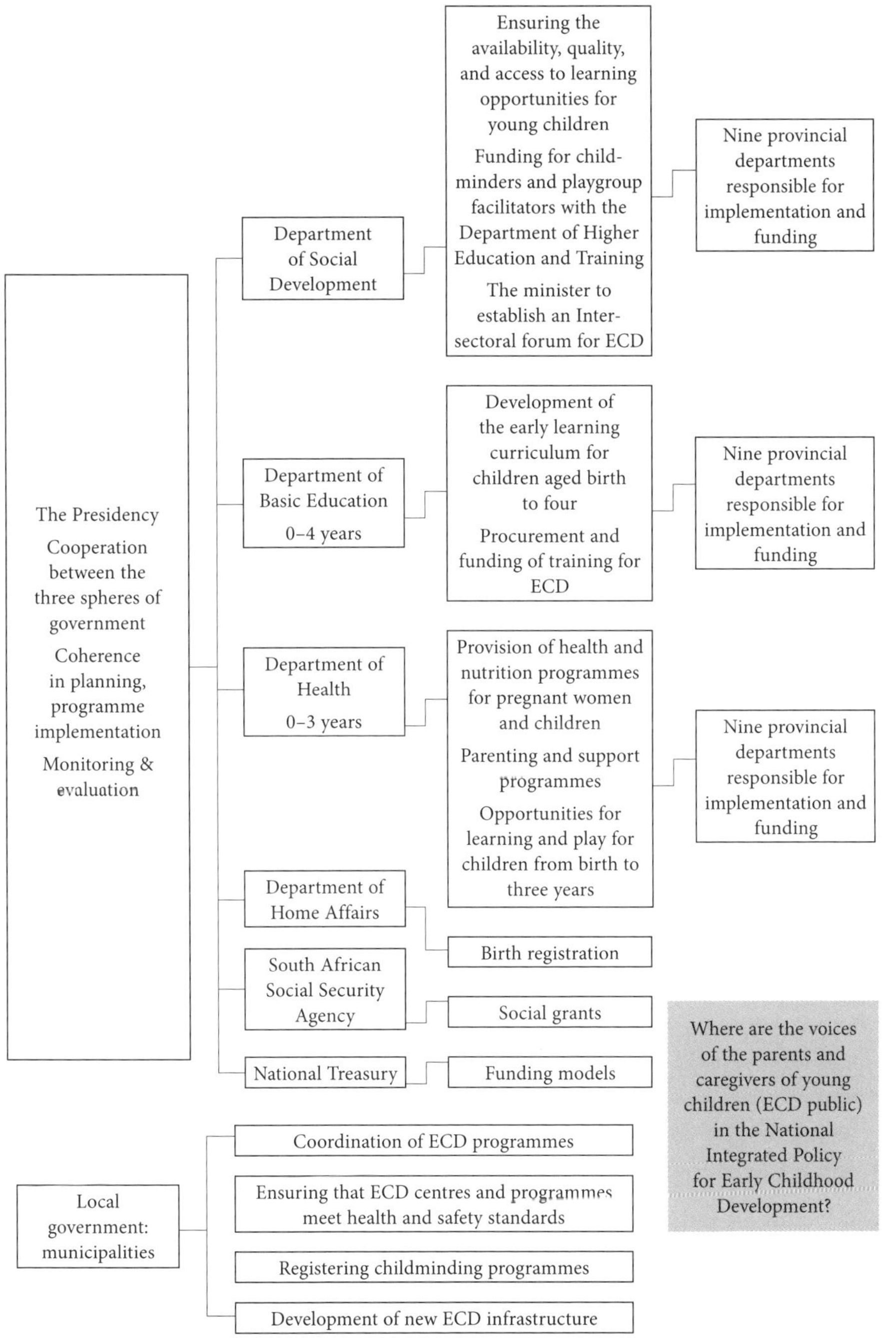

Figure 3.1 shows that South Africa has a comprehensive policy framework for ECD, anchored in the National Integrated Policy for Early Childhood Development released in 2015. This policy aims to provide quality ECD services for all young children, regardless of their socio-economic background. However, the place for parents/caregivers to actively give feedback on this policy and the system in general is nowhere to be found.

Unlike many other countries, Figure 3.1 confirms that the South African government has made admirable legal, political, and financial commitments to ECD, as shown in various documents including the National Development Plan 2030 and the Constitution. These commitments emphasise the importance of ECD in ensuring children's rights and their holistic development. The policy is implemented through South Africa's three-tiered system of government comprising national, provincial, and local spheres. Each of these levels has specific ECD responsibilities, including the provision of subsidies, training, curriculum development, funding for ECD practitioners, and ensuring safety standards. The system is not without its challenges, which stem from the differing roles of the three government spheres, variations in implementation by government departments, and the involvement of non-governmental organisations. The involvement of these multiple groups has sometimes led to confusion in policy statements, budgeting, and ECD provision implementation. The political will to make provision for ECD is apparent, but no space is created for involving parents/caregivers in the implementation of the policy, or in receiving feedback from them about how their needs and their children's are met.

In terms of financial commitments, provision is made for ECD funding in South Africa, since government supports children in formal ECD facilities. Children under the age of four benefit from government grants when enrolled in ECD facilities, highlighting the support available for such programmes through different government spending frameworks and subsidies. Challenges certainly exist — ECD facilities have reported that funding applications are complex, leading to irregular and delayed subsidies — but the policy provision for funding is at least in place.

The South African government has therefore demonstrated strong political and financial commitments to the provision of ECD, but the involvement of parents/caregivers in the production and implementation of these policies is totally ignored, something which is not in the spirit of the Constitution and its democratic principles.

It could be argued that non-governmental organisations (NGOs) and community-based organisations (CBOs) play a significant role in addressing the challenges faced by communities, and advocating for and amplifying the voices of the marginalised. The South African government collaborates with various NGOs, CBOs, and community development workers, implementing home- and community-visiting intervention programmes. However, this process has its pitfalls: in February 2022, the Department of Social Development revealed that only 50% of the non-profit organisation (NPO) sector is compliant with the NPO Act, raising governance concerns about those that are non-compliant. These shortcomings highlight the importance of parents and caregivers advocating directly for their own interests and holding those, including NGOs, to account when failures in the system emerge.

Besides silencing the voices of parents and caregivers in giving feedback on policy implementation, provision has not been made in the policy for parent support programmes. Analysis of the policy text highlights the challenges parents and caregivers face, particularly those who cannot afford to send their children to an ECD programme, but it does not explicitly mention provisions for parent support programmes. There is a need for the provision of parenting support programmes that include preparing for parenthood; promoting children's early growth, development, learning, language, and education; enabling appropriate and positive child behaviour management; promoting parental well-being, child protection, and safety; and providing information about identification documents and social grants. These programmes could equip parents and caregivers with the necessary skills and knowledge to care for their children better. The complex and difficult process of obtaining subsidies for ECD facilities, irregular funding, and delayed subsidies could impact the availability and accessibility of quality parenting programmes.

While public participation is considered vital for democratic policy-making and implementation processes, as enshrined in the Constitution, the voices of parents and primary caregivers are omitted from ECD policy development and implementation, and parent support programmes are not prioritised. The National Integrated Policy for Early Childhood Development therefore clearly demonstrates the concept of the "voice gap" (Fraser 1990). South Africa has a comprehensive ECD policy framework alongside legal commitments to support early childhood development, yet there are persistent challenges related to the inclusion of marginalised voices in policy processes, which hinders eradicating poverty and economic disparities. Key to addressing these challenges and ensuring that all children in South Africa have equal access to quality early childhood development opportunities is including in the policy implementation process those people most affected by it.

Often seen as part of what Fraser terms "weak publics", parents and caregivers find themselves on the outskirts of policy implementation processes. South Africa's performance against global expectations for investing in quality ECD, lifelong learning, and access to information and communication technologies has been mixed, but it can be enhanced by more robust forms of public participation.

Reasons for the silence of parents' voices: Gatekeeping

Gatekeeping refers to the interaction between power and information, a kind of selection process involving the 'decision whether to allow information to pass through a gate' (Barzilai-Nahon 2008). The gatekeeper is seen as the 'actor with power', who 'gatekeeps' people or groups who are held outside the gate (Barzilai-Nahon 2008: 5). The voices of marginalised parents/caregivers are regularly kept outside the gate, excluded from the implementation of ECD policy.

This may not be a conscious and intentional process, nor may the fault lie with a single entity or policy implementation mechanism. When citizens' voices are not adequately heard it may be due to bureaucratic inefficiencies, lack of transparency, or the biases and priorities of decision-makers. Silencing and gatekeeping may be due to inadequate or limited mechanisms for public participation, which can hinder citizens' access to policy-making and implementation processes. If channels for engagement are not well established or widely publicised, certain voices may be left out.

In some instances, gatekeeping may be due to time and resource constraints, since engaging with all citizens' voices can be costly and time-consuming. Policy-makers may prioritise efficiency over thorough engagement. Practical challenges can also lead to groups being excluded, as policy-making and implementation is fraught with governmental fragmentation and groups working in silos. Different departments and agencies may be segregated in large government systems, leading to fragmented policy-making, and holistic perspectives being overlooked.

While some forms of gatekeeping are unintentional, gatekeepers can also wield their influence subtly, by framing issues in particular ways, controlling the flow of information, and even setting the agenda in ways that disadvantage marginalised parents/caregivers on the outskirts of the policy making and implementation ecosystem (Barzilai-Nahon 2008). This process can lead to specific ECD issues being prioritised while others are pushed to the sidelines. Gatekeepers decide which elements are emphasised and which are downplayed, on the basis of personal biases, political agendas, and social pressures. Barzilai-Nahon's work (2008) highlights the influence gatekeepers wield, often subtly but profoundly, in shaping policies that affect societies and individuals. Gatekeepers' choices are more than just administrative; they are instrumental in guiding the narratives, priorities, and outcomes of policies.

Gatekeeping may be unintentional or subtle, but it is regularly built into the architecture of societal power dynamics, functioning to exclude marginalised and disadvantaged groups, including parents/caregivers with low incomes, minorities, or those without access to resources: groups who face significant barriers to participating in policy-making. Gatekeeping can be due to political forces and pressures from powerful groups. Political leaders play a significant role in shaping policies and setting agendas, and they regularly prioritise the interests of powerful groups, which has the effect of excluding certain citizens' voices. Pressure from powerful interest groups, corporations, or lobbyists can sway policy decisions, with the possibility of overshadowing the interests and needs of the broader public.

Gatekeeping is therefore often integral to how power functions. It may not be intentional and pernicious, but it certainly acts to set agendas and inhibit change in society (Barzilai-Nahon 2008). Gatekeepers are rarely attentive to marginalised voices, positioned at the peripheries of policy-making and implementation, as the ECD policy framework in Figure 3.1 demonstrated. Though significant and relevant, the voices of parents and caregivers may not be heard. Even when parents/caregivers are able to participate, they may not hold power equal to that of government officials, for example. This contaminates public debate due to inequalities in economic resources and subtle social and cultural distinction processes, such as dress codes, speech patterns, and body language (politics of recognition). If policy-making bodies do not intentionally include diverse representation from various demographic and social backgrounds, particular perspectives may be ignored or under-represented.

Addressing gatekeeping requires openness, inclusivity, and transparent policy-making and implementation processes to ensure that diverse voices are heard and considered. Mechanisms for public participation in policy-making, implementation, and feedback should be strengthened and made accessible to all citizens. Information control occurs through issue selection and omission, and in the way information is displayed, channelled, shaped, manipulated, repeated, localised, integrated, and disregarded (Barzilai-Nahon 2008; Pearson & Kosicki 2017; Singhal & Wassenaar 2016). It is also about vocabulary and the kinds of language that are used, whether they are accessible and encouraging of participation or, on the other hand, inhibitory. Gatekeeping is not just about letting information pass or not, it is about how those controlling the gates encourage participation through the way information and processes enter and circulate in the public domain.

While being aware of silences and gatekeeping tendencies that have negative effects on marginalised parents/caregivers, an effort should be made to work with policy-makers and implementers productively. The concept of "gatekeeping" frames the subject within a critical approach. This critique is frequently directed at the policy-makers themselves and may have divisive tendencies that further alienate marginalised groups. Healthy critique should be adopted without threatening those who hold power in ways that are counter-productive.

Conclusion

The concepts of weak publics and voice gaps, with gatekeeping theory, have provided valuable insights into the complexities of involving parents and caregivers in producing and implementing South Africa's ECD policy. Poverty and historical injustices play a significant role in excluding parents/caregivers and shaping access to ECD services. The South African government must address these challenges and actively involve all stakeholders, especially parents and caregivers, in policy development and implementation. By doing so, the legacy of poor education and economic disparities can be challenged, leading to a more inclusive and equitable society.

"Voice gaps" have repercussions that ripple through policies affecting early childhood development, education, and family support. As decisions are made and policies drafted, the perspectives of parents and caregivers may be under-represented, leading to solutions that miss the mark for those they are meant to serve. Economic, cultural, and social barriers compound this gap, leaving the gatekeepers' doors even more difficult to breach.

Scholars like Fraser (1990, 2000) and insights from gatekeeping theory remind us that understanding and addressing these voice gaps is essential for creating policies that genuinely reflect the needs of all. This calls for a more inclusive approach to policy-making and implementation, where gatekeepers actively seek out and amplify the voices of parents, caregivers, and those dedicated to the well-being of young children. It is a journey toward policy development that embraces the richness of perspectives, bridging the divide between gatekeepers and "weak publics", ensuring that no voice goes unheard. The South African national government — especially those who care for future generations — ought to realise that communicating with all their citizens contributes to delivering essential services.

References

Barzilai-Nahon K (2008) Toward a theory of network gatekeeping: A framework for exploring information control. *Journal of the American Society for Information Science and Technology* 59(9): 1493–1512. Accessed May 2025, https://doi.org/10.1002/asi.20857

Department of Social Development (2015) National Integrated Policy for Early Childhood Development. Accessed May 2025, https://www.gov.za/sites/default/files/gcis_document/201610/national-integrated-ecd-policy-web-version-final-01-08-2016a.pdf

Fraser N (1990) Rethinking the public sphere: A contribution to the critique of actually existing democracy. *Social Text* (25/26): 56–80. Accessed May 2025, https://doi.org/10.2307/466240

Fraser N (2000) Rethinking recognition. *New Left Review* 3: 107–120

Pearson GDH & Kosicki GM (2017) How way-finding is challenging gatekeeping in the digital age. *Journalism Studies* 18(9): 1087–1105. Accessed May 2025, https://doi.org/10.1080/1461670X.2015.1123112

The Presidency (2020) National Policy Development Framework. Accessed May 2025, https://www.presidency.gov.za/sites/default/files/2022-05/National%20Policy%20Development%20Framework%202020.pdf

Singhal M & Wassenaar DR (2016) Contextualising the role of the gatekeeper in social science research. *South African Journal of Bioethics and Law* 9(1): 42–46

Section

B

Contexts

The second section of the book looks at the multiple, intersecting contexts that shape social justice issues when South African parents/caregivers and schools interact. While the first section looked at macro-level issues of socio-economic inequality, policy and ideology, this section delves deeper into the more immediate conditions that shape parity of participation and how social justice plays out between parents/caregivers and schools. Chapter 4 acts as a bridge between these macro and more local issues, describing the landscape of South African parents and caregivers, who they are, and how they perceive schools. The study showed that parents/caregivers in a range of contexts perceive schools extremely positively, appreciating the pastoral role these institutions play in helping to raise and support their children. Admittedly, most said they knew relatively little about the everyday workings of teaching and learning in their children's classrooms.

Chapter 4 lays the foundation for a deeper dive into South African communities, with Chapter 5 showing how knowledge of educational processes may be possible for parents and caregivers, if authentic partnerships are built. The chapter focuses on early childhood care and education in community centre contexts, showing that knowledge may become reciprocal if educators acquire a deeper understanding of families' cultures, which can enhance children's educational experiences as educators have greater insights into children's home environments.

The following chapter, Chapter 6, goes to the heart of complex intersecting contexts in which social justice plays out between parents/caregivers and educators, looking at the work of school principals in the community of Phoenix, KwaZulu-Natal and their struggles amidst tense race relations during and beyond the July 2021 uprisings. School leadership that achieved positive parental and caregiver participation described communication as dialogical, operating from school to home and vice-versa. Positive participation also involved carefully inducting parents and caregivers into the SGB, while demonstrating the ability to adjust practices and be flexible, in the light of local conditions.

Reciprocal interactions between parents/caregivers and educators may also be negative, as Chapter 7 shows, with blame and blaming operating through feedback loops, contributing to a cycle of distrust and limited accountability in some school communities. Blame can be expressed explicitly or through inference and it usually has a corrosive effect on collaborative parent – teacher and school relationships that promote learner achievement.

In the final chapter of the section (Chapter 8), Myende and Myende reflect autobiographically on their child's education. Despite both being highly educated, they felt frustrated that their child's school struggled to understand their home and work lives, for example using homework as a generic way to prevent idleness, rather than primarily to support their child's intellectual development. Their chapter shows the challenges schools face when confronted with a highly diverse set of South African homes. In a frank reflection the authors grapple with their feelings of vulnerability in relation to the school, providing insights into the power relations that exist between parents/caregivers and schools, and the work that needs to be done for parity of participation. The contexts in which social justice plays out therefore traverse community settings, schools, and homes where race, class, and gender intersect, interacting in complex ways to enhance or inhibit parity of participation.

4 *Who Are South African Caregivers, How Do They Feel About Educational Quality, and What Is Their Involvement in Schools?*

Tarryn de Kock and Adam Cooper

Introduction

This chapter reports on the first nationally representative study of South African parents' and caregivers' perceptions of educational quality and their self-reported involvement in schools. A module of the South African Social Attitudes Survey (SASAS) was designed to elicit a holistic picture of parents' and caregivers' current experiences with and participation in their children's schooling. Data that was collected provides detailed information on who South African parents/caregivers are, their financial and living conditions, and how they choose schools for their children. Additionally, the research was able to develop an understanding of how parents/caregivers assess educational quality and the extent of their involvement in their child's school.

The importance of understanding parent/caregiver attitudes and perspectives towards schooling cannot be overstated. Globally, research has underscored the positive influence that parent/caregiver participation and engagement can have on learner confidence and performance (Williams & Sánchez 2012; Baquedano-López, Alexander & Hernandez 2013; Mncube 2010; Đurišić & Bunijevac 2017; Munje & Mncube 2018). However, research on parent/caregiver involvement regularly overlooks the fact that parents/caregivers are not a homogeneous group, as their personal identities and circumstances intersect with contextual differences between states and regions, the nature of education systems and societies, and the interactions between these dimensions at school level. The variation in how researchers and scholars conceptualise parent/caregiver participation needs to be informed by historical and contextual conditions, as the South African example so vividly demonstrates.

Taking differences into account by framing our data around an exploration of "who parents are", we show that South African parents/caregivers believe that schools, including leadership and educators, are generally performing effectively, and providing essential pastoral care and social support, despite most parents/caregivers admitting to knowing little about the daily workings of their child's school. The findings raise interesting questions about how parents can support their children better, and help schools to improve the educational ecosystem, keeping in mind that parent/caregiver involvement may differ across culture, class, and racial divisions. Diversity should inform understandings of, and possibilities for, parental/caregiver involvement, mediated by the power various role players may access through resources and social or political capital, in ways that are uneven and historically embedded. The survey provides a point of departure to engage with these issues, and it also highlights the absence of a culturally and sociologically informed understanding of the factors influencing parent/caregiver participation and engagement with schools in South Africa. Finally, we offer some initial analysis towards interpreting this wellspring of data in order to further support meaningful parental/caregiver engagement in the education ecosystem.

Contextualising parent/caregiver participation

A global trend in school governance described as "decentralisation" has played a key role in reframing parental/caregiver participation at schools as a necessary component of stable school management, governance, and educational success. This in turn is defining a stream of research concerned with the role of parents and caregivers in the educational attainment and success of learners (Crozier 2001; Henderson 1981; Tinkler 2002). Decentralisation involved central governments ceding power to local governments and, in the case of education, schools themselves. This trend is observed locally in the South African Schools Act (No. 84 of 1996) and the power it gives to school governing bodies (SGBs), of which parents/caregivers are the majority constituent group. The global turn towards educational decentralisation and new forms of public management began in the late 1970s, with a wave of political and economic reforms geared towards infusing public bureaucracies with the managerial efficiency of private companies, making them more responsive to "consumers" (citizens), and finding ways to reduce public spending on traditional public services such as health and education (De Kock et al. 2018). This "trend" needs to be understood in conjunction with the deeply contextual ways in which reforms took root in different societies, with their own historic, political, and cultural contexts.

With this contextual framing in mind, the focus in this chapter is on the South African experience of parent/caregiver participation in "decentralised conditions", while drawing key lessons from elsewhere. The contemporary South African case is not an exceptional one, as the discussion will show, but consists of an overwhelming assortment of contextual "layers" that contribute to what happens in schools and how parents/caregivers engage with these schools, including the implicit and explicit effects of the country's apartheid past (Mncube 2010). It is also important to consider how parents and caregivers, as an interest group, are socially and historically located role players whose engagement with schools is enabled (or constrained) by their own experiences, circumstances, and capacities. Parent/caregiver involvement and participation in schools differs significantly from context to context, in South Africa and elsewhere, and policy provisions for this involvement may further reduce or expand the opportunities parents/caregivers have to engage meaningfully and collaboratively with schools (Baquedano-López, Alexander & Hernandez 2013).

Decentralisation has led to different types of schools in post-apartheid South Africa because of the distinction made between fee-paying and no-fee public schools, which is determined on the basis of a wealth quintile system. Fee-paying schools are considerably stratified in cost and infrastructure, and fee payment itself has a significant effect on how parents/caregivers relate to educators on either side of the economic divide. Parents/caregivers at no-fee schools, which make up three of the five quintiles, may feel disempowered by their lack of "contribution", for example, while also responding positively to the additional welfare interventions offered to their children. These dynamics lead to a variety of parent/caregiver attitudes and types of involvement. Support for parent/caregiver involvement in schools uniformly draws on the argument that their involvement positively impacts learning achievement, boosts learners' confidence and socioemotional skills, and supports effective whole school management, without necessarily understanding differences between parents/caregivers at a range of schools (Munje & Mncube 2018). Research tends to frame parent involvement within quite restricted "roles" or formal functions, without necessarily giving credence to the alternative and informal ways that marginalised parents/caregivers may participate and positively contribute to schools (Baquedano-López, Alexander & Hernandez 2013). It also takes for granted that parent/caregiver involvement influences learner achievement in observable ways and, conversely, that uninvolved parents/caregivers are to blame for low-performing learners.

Research, therefore, often fails to ask "who parents are" and how this may influence the nature of their relationships to schooling and education more broadly, leading to a series of "tropes" (or stereotypes) that underlie perceptions of parent involvement (Baquedano-López, Alexander & Hernandez 2013). This aligns with our argument in this chapter that "who parents are" influences how they conceptualise the role of the public sector, and how they are located in relation to it. Schools are important sites through which parents/caregivers and learners engage with other state interventions, such as welfare provision and immigration services, or disengage from them by opting into private education institutions (Baquedano-López, Alexander & Hernandez 2013). The COVID-19 pandemic in South Africa underlined the crucial role schools play in offering pastoral care, information, and food security for families, thus extending narrow understandings of schools as teaching and learning institutions.

Even if parental/caregiver involvement influences learning attainment, it is certainly category- and context-specific (LaRocque, Kleiman & Darling 2011). Research has shown that low-income minority parents in the USA were more likely to impact their children's learning attainment positively through school-based involvement. Possible reasons for this included strengthening parent confidence in school services, facilitating understanding of institutional processes, and supporting parents through unlearning negative experiences or impressions of educational institutions (LaRocque, Kleiman & Darling 2011; Makgopa & Mokhele 2013). This is important to bear in mind, considering that the mainstream field of research on parent/caregiver involvement takes the view that involvement positively impacts learning attainment, without much clarity on how this takes place or what the contributing environmental or social factors may be. Researchers, including Makgopa and Mokhele (2013) and Bouguen, Gumede, and Gurgand (2015) argue that a limited connection exists between increased parent involvement and learner outcomes in poor schooling contexts, suggesting that the impact of this involvement is couched within a number of other enabling conditions that, together, form a supportive architecture for learner success.

In Makgopa and Mokhele's work, for example, the greater predictor of improved learner performance was the presence of SGB teachers (in other words, teachers hired in addition to the state's allocation of teachers at a given school), which points to a range of other factors playing a role, such as the race and class make-up of schools (2013). Research in impoverished settings therefore needs to engage with the social, cultural, and historical influences on educational participation, and how these may differ from the dominant class-based and culturally mediated notions of parent/caregiver involvement. Education also intersects with, for example, religious undertakings and long histories of socio-cultural survival strategies, as is the case for many Black South Africans; these factors need to be considered when thinking about parental involvement in schools (Bähre 2020).

The mechanisms through which parents/caregivers impact learning outcomes may be related to the normative ideals underpinning how parents and families are framed within education policy. Baquedano-Lopez, Alexander and Hernandez (2013) caution that middle-class parent–school relations are taken for granted in these framings, with particular assumptions about parent/caregiver education and work status, access to resources and learning materials, the home environment, and shared cultural norms. For example, Makgopa and Mokhele (2013) present an idealistic picture of what parents/caregivers *should* be doing, while offering little acknowledgement that this is far from a reality or even a possibility in the majority of South African schools. Time, poverty, lack of financial resources, lack of access, and lack of awareness all limit parent/caregiver involvement for poor and minority parents (Williams & Sánchez 2012).

A common notion is of parents/caregivers as "partners" or "consumers", working with schools and teachers to support improvement in learning outcomes, in effect serving as enforcers of school academic policy. As consumers, the choices of parents/caregivers are influenced by the resources available to them, and they therefore feel more entitled to demand accountability for schooling as a service rendered (Baquedano-Lopez, Alexander & Hernandez 2013; Williams & Sánchez 2012). The converse of these framings highlights how inequality is diffused through education systems based on de-contextualised notions of individual choice and the market value of an education. Race- and class-based divisions mean that some parents/caregivers may be treated as perpetual learners or children, while others take on the role of partner or consumer with ease. Choices made by powerful parents/caregivers shape education systems by stratifying them according to resources, identity differences, geography, or gender, harming poorer families and school communities as a result. The decision to opt into testing regimes, for example, may impact disciplinary processes of low-performing learners with behavioural problems, while parent mobilisation for changes in language policy might serve as a subtle way of excluding particular families from the school community (Mncube 2007; Williams & Sánchez 2012).

Homogenising parents and caregivers in research means that, despite decentralisation policies like the South African Schools Act claiming to empower local communities by including parents in school governance, many parents/caregivers remain excluded from decision-making processes. In contexts where race, class, and geography function in such a way that parents/caregivers cede decision-making responsibilities to principals or more vocal parent governors, the gap between policy and reality remains stark (Mncube 2007; Mohapi & Netshitangani 2018). Part of this relates to role confusion in the implementation of decentralised governance, especially in the formation of school governing authorities populated by principals, teachers, parents/caregivers, and other key stakeholders (Echaune, Ndiku & Sang 2015; Mncube 2007; Mohapi & Netshitangani 2018). But it also points to how power relations problematise parent/caregiver involvement and educational success.

The above highlights that parent/caregiver involvement in schools is conditioned by "who parents are" and to what extent they are able to negotiate the structures of school governance in order to benefit their children most effectively. Despite a significant dimension of research on parent/caregiver involvement focusing on securing the buy-in of poor and minority parents/caregivers in order to remedy low learning outcomes, there is a lack of critical reflection on who parents/caregivers are, the factors that shape their involvement, how these emerge through school–parent relations, and the ways in which marginalised parents/caregivers understand interactions. It is critical to identify those dynamics that act against parent-empowering forms of involvement, as well as to note the lack of a clear link between parent/caregiver involvement and concrete learning outcomes. These are two ongoing gaps in the research that this survey makes an incisive contribution towards. A further gap, particularly in South Africa, is the lack of engagement with how poverty shapes people's engagement with public institutions, and how these engagements further shape their overall sense of moral worth (Ross 2009). Poverty complicates these relationships with public institutions, such as when learners and their families access welfare and other services through schools. While the research cannot address all of these issues, findings from the data underscore the complexity of fostering durable parent/caregiver connections with teachers and schools, as well as the factors influencing parent/caregiver perceptions of education quality. As the discussion will demonstrate, these are both historically located and contextually conditioned.

Parent involvement in schools: Research from the South African Social Attitudes Survey

A module on parent/caregiver involvement in, and attitudes towards, schools was included as part of the 2021 round of the Human Sciences Research Council's longitudinal and nationally representative public opinion survey (the SASAS). Each round has accommodated rotating modules on specific themes to provide detailed attitudinal evidence to inform policy and academic debate concerning topical issues. Alongside these rotating modules, the survey includes background variables to allow a representative picture of key demographic variables such as:

- sex;
- race;
- level of education; and
- employment status.

The module aimed to understand the attitudes of parents and caregivers towards school: (a) climate; (b) leadership; and (c) quality. In addition, there was an interest in parental agency and the role that parents/caregivers play in their children's education, as well as their children's experiences of the South African educational system. Many respondents had children enrolled in multiple schools, with quite divergent experiences with each child and its school. One child of these respondents was randomly selected, and fieldworkers were directed to ask questions about the selected child's school experience. This child was labelled the "focal child". "Parent" in this research is defined as any adult acting as one of the primary caregivers to a child currently attending primary or secondary school. Although this can be a somewhat limited definition of a "parent" in the general sense, it is the most useful one for the research purposes of this study.

The sampling frame used for the survey was based on Statistics South Africa's 2011 population census (Statistics South Africa 2012). Estimates were obtained of the population numbers for various categories of census variables, forming the basis for drawing a nationally representative sample for the current study. Five hundred primary sampling units were selected, made up of individual dwelling units and constituting a nationally representative sample of parents living in South Africa. Four parents from each primary sampling unit were randomly selected to be interviewed. This ensured that the sample size target of 1 600 was reached. The inclusion of geographic type and majority population group as additional stratification variables guaranteed that the sample reflects the demographic and population distribution in each province. Table 4.1 provides a breakdown of the sample size at both a national and provincial level.

Table 4.1 *SASAS sample for 2021*

	Dwelling Unit	Primary Sampling Unit
Eastern Cape	176	50
Free State	134	38
Gauteng	319	81
KwaZulu-Natal	383	93
Limpopo	146	42
Northern Cape	125	32
North West	137	36
Mpumalanga	151	38
Western Cape	134	53
Total	1 705	463

This is the first large-scale public opinion study of parents/caregivers in South Africa, a major contribution to our collective understanding of parent/caregiver perceptions and behaviour in the country.

Findings

Demographics and family composition

South African families are complex and often do not conform to the model of a nuclear family, with previous studies of parenting in the country struggling to classify "who" a "parent" is. To deal with this, we conducted a detailed investigation into the composition of families of school-enrolled children, allowing the primary caregivers of children to define themselves through their answers in the survey. Understanding how parents/caregivers view the quality of education and their participation in schools requires an initial analysis of "who parents are". The representative sample used in the survey gives a coherent picture of South African parents/caregivers and the kinds of households they live in. There is a small but significant proportion of parents who are either very young (in the 16–25 years old category) or well past middle age (from 56 years old and upwards). Women make up the majority (78%) of primary caregivers in the study, evidence of the ongoing phenomenon of absentee fatherhood in South Africa. Only a fifth of parents/caregivers in South Africa identified themselves as male. The history of colonial and apartheid-era labour policies and practices may explain this finding (for a detailed discussion of this phenomenon, see Van den Berg, Ratele and Makusha [2021]). It was interesting, therefore, to note that absentee fatherhood was especially a problem in the rural areas where only 12% of parents are male. This urban–rural disparity in fatherhood helps explain the substantial provincial variations that were observed in the data. The majority of male participants in the study were racially classified as white (34%) or coloured (31%) and over the age of 46. The province with the highest number of male respondents was the Western Cape (40%), followed by North West (26%), Northern Cape (25%) and Limpopo (22%). Table 4.2 provides similar demographic data on "focal children" in the study.

Figure 4.1 further disaggregates data on focal children's school enrolment. The majority of focal children were enrolled in public schools, with 47% in fee-paying schools and 38% attending no-fee schools.

Table 4.2 *Characteristics of focal children of respondents*

	Unweighted N	Per cent
Gender		
Male	778	50%
Female	790	50%
Population Group		
Black African	989	63%
Coloured	250	16%
Indian/Asian	176	11%
White	152	10%
Age Group		
6 years and under	104	7%
7–9 years	337	21%
10–13 years	523	33%
14–16 years	373	24%
17 years and above	231	15%
Relationship to Parent		
Grand/great grandchild	217	14%
Son/daughter	1124	72%
Brother/sister	84	5%
Other relation	143	9%
School Grade		
Grade 0–3	439	26%
Grade 4–7	571	34%
Grade 8–12	661	40%

Figure 4.1 *Enrolment by school type*

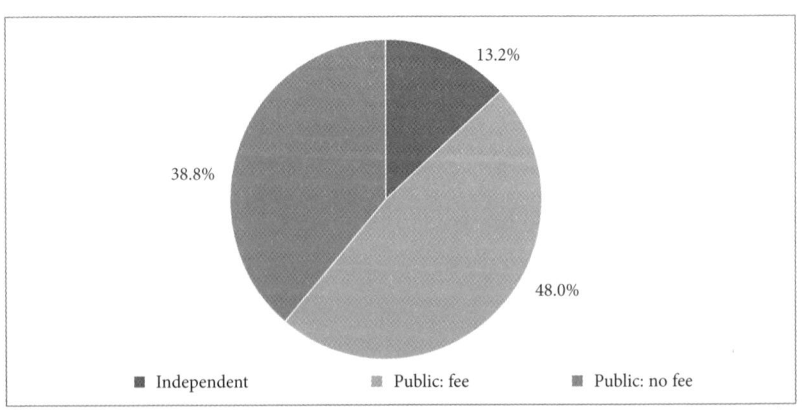

It is also interesting to note the variance in the nature of the relationship between the focal child and the parent/caregiver, as shown in Table 4.2. While two-thirds (66%) of focal children were the biological children of the parent or caregiver respondent, 13% of children were grandchildren or great-grandchildren of their caregiver. This speaks to further evidence on the varied household composition of respondents in the study.

Figure 4.2 *Distribution of inter-generational households by province*

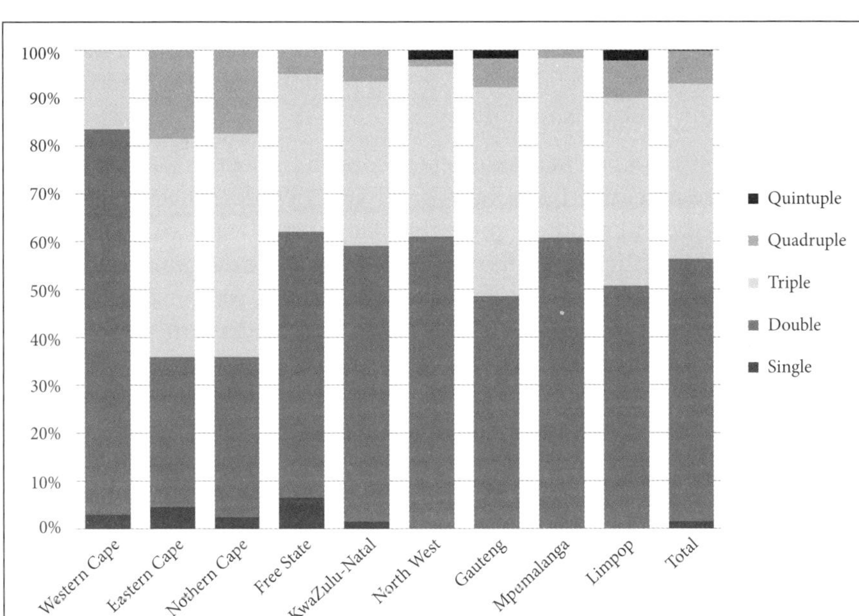

Figure 4.2 describes the average household composition, disaggregated by province. It is informative to examine the generational composition of the parent/caregiver population, keeping in mind that generational cut-offs points aren't an exact science and there is no agreed-upon formula for how long the span of a generation should be. For the purposes of our research, a generation is designated as 20 years. We selected generations based on five age cohorts: (a) Generation Z (0–19 years); (b) Generation Y (20–39 years); (c) Generation X (40–59 years); (d) Post-War (60–79 years); and (e) Pre-War (80–100 years). About half (51%) of the populace was part of Generation Y while 34% belonged to Generation X and 12% were from the Post-War Generation. The research team found that there was substantial variation in household composition based on an inter-generational configuration by province, as shown in Figure 4.2.

Nationally, 55% of parents/caregivers live in households that were classified as double generation while 37% of households were categorised as triple generation households. Approximately one twentieth (6%) of households contained four generations and 1% contain five. Only a small minority (2%) of parents lived in single generation households, indicating the low number of teenage households within the populace. The research team found that 6% of parents lived in skipped generation households: households without middle generations (that is, those in the 20–39 and 40–59 age cohorts).

The prevalence of multigenerational households speaks to the fact that the nuclear family is not the South African blueprint; households and families also comprise extended and fictive kinship relations that are important to the rearing and education of children.

Just a third (30%) of parents/caregivers lived with a romantic partner of any kind; of these parents, 81% were married and 15% described themselves as living together. In addition to the third of parents living with a partner, 19% of respondents indicated having a partner that they were not currently living with. Urban (especially metropolitan) parents were more likely to report having a live-in partner than their rural counterparts. More male than female respondents lived with a partner (43% compared to 27%), further affirming the realities of single motherhood in South Africa. It is also interesting to note clear racial differences in household composition, for example, a higher proportion of white (74%) and Indian/Asian (61%) respondents reported living with a partner. Furthermore, living with parents or siblings was especially common for younger parents (35 years old and under), while living with a partner was more prevalent among parents over 36 years old. On average, roughly 40% of parents lived with a sibling, parent, or other relative. The small proportion of predominantly female parents living with romantic partners, and the fact that 40% live with extended family, provide invaluable insights into "who parents are" and the social resources at their disposal to assist with parenting and education.

Income and socio-economic status

The bulk of household income for South African parents/caregivers comes from two primary sources: (a) wages and salaries; and (b) social grants. Other main sources (such as remittances) were mentioned by only a small segment of the parent/caregiver population. When parents/caregivers were asked what the main source of income in their household was, a somewhat larger percentage mentioned wages and salaries (45%) than social grants (40%). The majority of parents/caregivers in the country (78%) lived in a household that received at least one social grant.

The labour market dynamics of the parents/caregivers in South Africa are, perhaps unsurprisingly, similar to the adult population as a whole. Just about a third of all parents/caregivers described themselves as permanently employed. Of these working parents/caregivers, the vast majority (88%) are wage labourers or salaried employees of some kind. More than a quarter (or 10% of the entire parental population) of working parents/caregivers were in skilled employment, working in managerial or other white-collar forms of employment. Roughly, a third of all parents/caregivers were looking for work, and the remainder (33%) were outside the labour market.

To provide a comprehensive analysis of the socio-economic character of parents and their households, the research team designed an index to measure an adult's socio-economic status – the asset living measurement (ALM). This index comprises more than 20 questions on a respondent's asset ownership and access to services. The ALM divides the population into 10 groups, ranging from the least affluent (with a ranking of 1) to the most affluent (with a ranking of 10). It is considered superior to income as a measure of economic status as income does not capture access to basic services or household assets and is therefore a flawed indicator of socio-economic position. The mean ALM score for parents in South Africa was 5.2 (SE=0.090).

Table 4.3 *Mean ALM by school type*

School Type	Mean		[95% Conf. Interval]		Scheffe test	
Independent	7.9	(0.293)	7.3	8.4	ref.	
Public: fee	5.3	(0.135)	5.1	5.6	–2.54	***
Public: non-fee	4.4	(0.106)	4.2	4.7	–3.42	***

Notes: 1 Standard error in parenthesis. 2 The signs *, **, *** indicate that mean score differences are significantly different (based on ANOVA testing) at the 5%, 1% and 0.5% levels respectively.

Interestingly, a more pronounced difference in ALM exists between independent schools and public schools, rather than between fee and no-fee public schools. Only a relatively small difference existed in the average ALM between parents/caregivers whose focal child attended a fee-paying public school compared to those whose child attended a no-fee public school.

Parents were also asked about the nature of their financial contribution, if any, to the child's schooling. Most parents, regardless of school type, made some form of contribution towards their child's education, although more affluent and educated parents were likely to spend more. More than 69% of parents were making some form of financial contribution to their child's schooling. Just over half (54%) of all parents/caregivers were the only ones financially responsible for school expenses, with 46% of parents/caregivers receiving support from someone else. Younger parents/caregivers were more likely to receive additional financial support from parents and extended family networks.

Data on transportation expenses indicated that these were highest among parents in metropolitan areas, those in the upper range of ALM (>7.5), employed parents/caregivers, and those with children at independent schools and fee-paying public schools. This confirms that a significant proportion of South African learners are commuting across neighbourhoods to get to school on a daily basis, shifting the foundation of who forms part of a school's immediate "community". Fataar (2015) refers to the complex changes that these learners usher into historically exclusive school environments, as well as the factors that form part of their decision to move outside the confines of racially segregated neighbourhoods, as forms of educational and socio-spatial access.

Social mobility

A component of the survey looked at inter-generational mobility through the lens of educational attainment in respondents' families of origin. Nearly a quarter (24%) indicated that they attained a higher level of education than their parents, and 16% had accomplished a much higher level. The remainder had either reached a level of education equivalent to their parents (36%) or lower (12%). A combined 12% did not know or did not answer. Those in rural areas (48%) were more likely to report having a better educational level than their parents. A substantial percentage of the parent populace did not know what their mother (40%) or father (50%) did for work. The majority (66%) of the parent population considered themselves to be better off than their parents while only a minority of 13% considered themselves worse off. The fact that people perceive themselves to be better educated than their parents and feel that their lives have improved in comparison to their own parents may influence their perceptions of education in general, remembering that South African parents generally have extremely positive views of their child's schooling.

The research team evaluated what respondents think their children should do after secondary school. The bulk of the parent population told fieldworkers that they considered further education would be best. Half (54%) of those who had achieved a lower level of education than their parents favoured a university education for their children. This figure can be compared to 69% of those who had achieved a better level of education, and 72% of parents who had achieved a much better level of schooling. One of the largest drivers for parents' post-secondary preference was socio-economic status. More affluent individuals were much more likely than their counterparts to believe that their child should continue their studies at a university or further education and training college. More educated and economically advantaged parents/caregivers reported a greater likelihood of having a mother or father with a post-secondary qualification. This speaks to the reproductive nature of inequality in South Africa and how this continues to hinder the country's poor from unlocking the opportunities promised by democracy. It follows that if education and economic status are positively related, and this accords with past and present racial imbalances, then South African parents/caregivers are likely justified in their belief that quality education is an essential driver of economic mobility. This influences their attitudes to their children's schooling and towards education in general.

The demographic data highlight the reality that South African parents/caregivers are a heterogeneous group. Many of their lives do not fit the norm of a middle-class nuclear family, an issue which impacts how they engage with the focal child's school and the level of confidence that they have in negotiating these spaces. Moreover, the data demonstrate significant breadth in the relationships, resources, and networks that are mobilised in support of children's education, even where this is unrecognised or under-valued in school contexts. In considering the findings presented, it is worth considering how specific beliefs and norms about parent/caregiver participation may undermine the realities faced in most South African schools and communities.

Parent/caregiver perceptions of school and personnel quality

"Quality education" is a multidimensional concept (Tikly & Barrett 2011). Literacy skills, for example, form the foundation of a child's future development and are widely seen as essential to most learning activities (Gustafsson et al. 2010). But what about other educational dimensions like interpersonal skills or critical thinking? A quality education incorporates a diversity of meanings, and there is no dominant list of what it comprises. To obtain a greater understanding of how parents/caregivers in South Africa think about quality education, we will examine this theme in detail, paying special attention to what parents/caregivers think constitutes a quality school; how they assess interactions with teachers, principals and SGBs; and their evaluation of the safety of the school environment.

Parents/caregivers were asked to select the three factors they considered most important for a school to offer high quality education (see Figure 4.3).

Figure 4.3 *Important factors for high-quality education*

I want you to think about how important the following things are for high quality education in general. Which, in the following list, are the most important for a high-quality education?

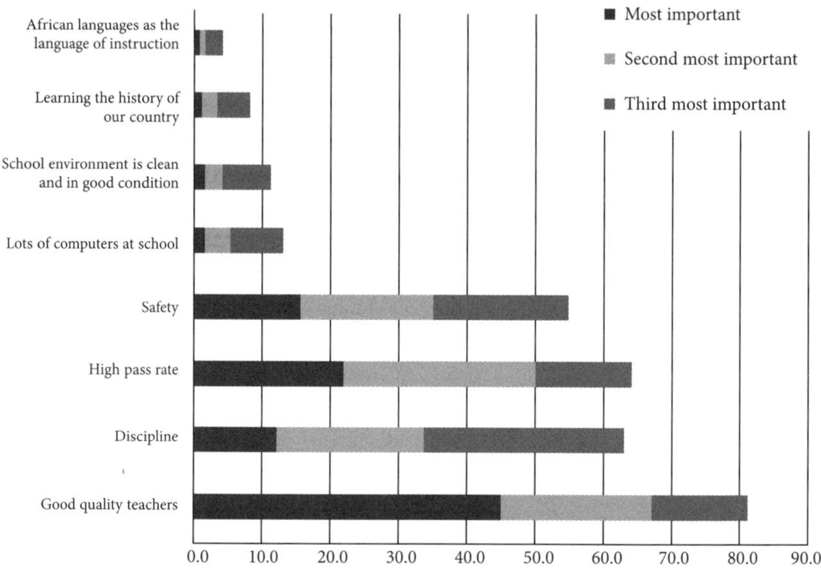

By far the most important feature listed by parents/caregivers was good quality teachers (listed by 45% of the parental population). A cumulative total of nearly 80% of parents included quality teachers in their articulation of what constituted high-quality education. Other features that were highly rated included discipline, a high pass rate, and safety. We noted some interesting disparities between how male and female parents/caregivers thought about school quality. When compared to their male counterparts, female parents/caregivers were more likely to list good teachers and safety as important. Discipline and pass rates were more likely to be selected by male parents/caregivers than their female peers.

When compared to their counterparts with children at primary schools, parents/caregivers with children at secondary schools were more likely to identify a high pass rate as an important feature of a high-quality school. The feature identified least often by parents/caregivers was African languages as the medium of instruction. Of respondents' ethnolinguistic backgrounds, Xitsonga speakers were much more likely to think that this was a top priority. It was interesting to note that features related to environment or infrastructure were only considered important by a small subset of parents/caregivers. However, parents/caregivers with children at public fee-paying schools were twice as likely as their peers to think that school environment was important.

The research found that perceptions of teachers influenced parents'/caregiver's perceptions of the school principal. Good principals were seen to be strong leaders, cultivating a culture of safety and order in schools, receptive and responsive to parents/caregivers, and promoting high achievement and learner success. It is notable that while parents/caregivers generally advocate for collaboration and horizontal lines of communication, there is still an expectation that principals will be strict, commanding heads of school, and that this reflects a high quality of teaching and learning. This underscores the historically embedded nature of parents'/caregivers' own school experiences: many parents/caregivers were old enough to have been educated under the authoritarian, deeply conservative system of Christian National Education under apartheid, where strictness, rote learning, and highly regimented lines of authority in schools were the norm across racial groups. This system was not designed to cultivate critical thought or positive, emancipatory attitudes towards society. Rather, it was intended to deliver different race groups into their designated social and economic roles under the apartheid system, deliberately limiting the social and economic mobility of countless Black, coloured and Indian people. The effect of this history on parent/caregiver participation and navigation of school contexts should not be underestimated.

It is also noteworthy that parents/caregivers with children in independent schools were more likely to admit to being intimidated by the school principal. A clear pattern emerging in the data is that while high-ALM parents/caregivers spend more on school fees, transport, and other educational resources, they are not necessarily as hands-on in other ways, nor do they inherently have better relationships with their children's schools. One factor influencing this is the desegregation of South African schools, which has had both localised and systemic effects. It should not be assumed that all parents/caregivers with children in independent schools or high-fee public schools are wealthy or able to provide the necessary educational and economic support. Indeed, it may be that in these cases parents step back from participation in school activities precisely because they do not feel confident engaging with these institutions. In fact, these institutions may feel alien to them although they may perceive them to be necessary to provide an educational foundation as well as social capital for their children. On the other hand, the research also found that white and high ALM parents/caregivers have low knowledge of teacher expectations of learners, suggesting that wealthier parents/caregivers have higher levels of trust in their children's schools and are more likely to be hands off, knowing the financial and social benefits that will accrue from their child's enrolment at a particular school.

It was surprising to note that good education quality was a deciding factor in school choice in only a third (34%) of parents/caregivers. Three-fifths of parents/caregivers said that the proximity of the school to their residence was a major factor when deciding on a school. Learners may not attend schools in their immediate location, especially those learners in fee-paying and independent schools.

Other important criteria listed by parents/caregivers include affordability and safety. More affluent parents were less likely to list geographic proximity as a factor in school choice. If parents/caregivers had selected a fee-paying school, then they were less likely to report using geographic proximity as a major decisional factor and more likely to list good quality education.

A clear majority of the parent/caregiver population gave SGBs at their child's school a positive assessment, suggesting that most people think their SGB performs well. If parents/caregivers rated the teachers and principal at their child's school positively, they were more likely also to rate the SGB as effective. SGB elections were less well appraised. Just about a fifth of participants said that the elections were fair and democratic. While SGBs form part of the vision of cooperative governance under the new democracy, they are also sites of significant power struggles in South African schools. It is therefore not surprising that parent perceptions of the fairness of SGB elections are varied.

Parent/caregiver responses to questions about school and staff quality illustrate an emphasis on school safety, academic performance, and communicative, supportive relationships with educators and other staff members. Despite low participation in school governance overall, parents/caregivers were positive about the relationship with SGBs. It is notable that high-scoring aspects of school quality (such as academic success, discipline, and safety) are about visible and tangible indicators of how the school functions. A similar pattern can be observed in parent responses on SGB quality, with a focus on financial management, positive relations, and having the capacity for school management. Parent assessments of quality are also conditioned by the semi-privatised nature of the schooling system: parents at independent and fee-paying public schools spend a significant proportion of their resources on transport, school fees, and other educational expenses but do not necessarily report knowing more about, or feeling more confident about, engaging with their child's school. It may be that in such cases parents spend more in the hope that this guarantees higher quality education and that they are more readily able to leverage their financial contribution as a form of power than they are able to draw on knowledge of school operations that can support their child's success. The next section focuses on the issue of parent knowledge in further depth.

Parent/caregiver knowledge and participation

The research probed parent perceptions of their own participation in the focal child's school, delivering valuable insights that allow us to stitch together what we know about "who parents are" with the decisions they make and the perceptions they have.

The survey asked parents/caregivers to self-report on their knowledge of – and participation at – the focal child's school. Twenty-seven per cent of parents/caregivers agreed with the statement, 'I do not know what is happening at my child's school'. Parents/caregivers with children at independent and no-fee public schools were most likely to agree with this statement. On the whole, parents/caregivers indicated having low general knowledge of what happened at school. The survey identified four issues that schools are likely to share information about with parents/caregivers:

1. the performance of other learners in the child's class or grade;
2. learner absenteeism at school;
3. teacher absenteeism at school; and
4. school finances.

If parents/caregivers are deficient in understanding one of these areas, then they may be unable to evaluate the quality of education provided to their child. The bulk of the parental/caregiver population was not aware of basic information about the school. Parents/caregivers were most likely to report knowing about school finances and learner performance, and knowing very little about learner absenteeism. The research also asked parents/caregivers about their level of interest in six types of information that could be shared by schools (see Figure 4.4).

Figure 4.4 *Parent/caregiver interest in information about the school*

Please indicate the extent to which you would be interested in receiving information on the following topics.

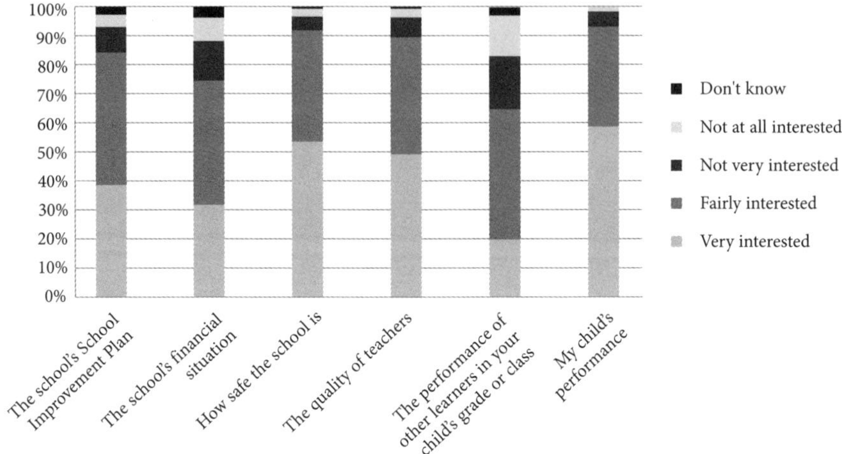

The vast majority of parents/caregivers were either very interested (60%) or fairly interested (30%) in learning about their child's performance. Outside of this indicator, it was apparent that a clear majority of the parental/caregiver population wanted other general information about their child's school. Of the other five indicators, the area that received the most interest was the safety of the school, and the area receiving the least interest was the performance of other learners. It is possible, though, that knowledge of general performance trends can enable parents/caregivers to advocate for additional support for learners where necessary or pick up whether a teacher is performing poorly.

The research showed that parents/caregivers regularly make assessments about a school's teachers based on their child's experience at school, rather than their own knowledge of personnel or school conditions. The more a parent/caregiver thought their child enjoyed school, the more prone that adult was to give their child's teachers a positive evaluation. Parent/caregiver perceptions of teachers form an important part of their overall perception of quality, and their level of satisfaction with the school in general, with this information generally being obtained from conversations with their children.

When investigating their participation in school governance, it was found that parents were more likely to have met the school principal if the focal child was their direct relation (son/daughter), and if the focal child was in primary school. This echoes several other findings that indicate that parent/

caregiver figures who are related to the focal child in a different way (such as a grandparent or aunt) were less likely to take an active role in the child's education, including voting in SGB elections. Parent/caregiver participation declined overall at secondary school level. The research did not probe this in further detail, but it would be interesting to understand the reasons for this phenomenon. Two clear potential factors emerging from the data are the influence of language and educational level on parents'/caregivers' ability to support learners with homework. Parents/caregivers were more likely to struggle with understanding learners' homework if their own educational foundation was weak. Additionally, parents/caregivers who spoke any of South Africa's indigenous languages were more likely to struggle with homework assistance than those who spoke English or Afrikaans. The fact that homework increases in complexity as children progress in the education system would also likely contribute to a decrease in parental/caregiver participation in, and knowledge of, their children's schooling.

While most parents/caregivers viewed principals and SGBs positively, their actual knowledge of school governance was weak. One anomaly could be found among Indian parents/caregivers, who scored highly in participation in school activities, having positive relationships with teachers, and keeping in regular contact with the school. This created a mutually reinforcing connection between home and school that benefited learner performance and parent attitudes towards their child's school. When probed about participation in SGB elections, less than 50% of all parents/caregivers indicated having voted in SGB elections in the past three years. Abstention from voting may signify unwillingness to express tacit support for school governance. Some parents/caregivers also said that they were not interested in these processes or did not have the time to attend meetings.

It is also possible that a lack of knowledge, inaccurate perceptions, or uncertainty about their potential contribution may hold parents/caregivers back from engaging with SGBs, which may be compounded by poverty, being unemployed, or not having much education – particularly if parents/caregivers feel unwelcome in the school generally. While 60% of all parents/caregivers indicated that they at least felt welcomed at their child's school, only 16% said that they felt a sense of community at the school.

If parent/caregiver participation at schools were graded on a scale, participation in school governance would arguably be at the upper range of the activities that engaged parents/caregivers would opt into, given the space this offers for them to influence the management of their child's school.

However, a number of foregoing conditions would need to be met, including feeling empowered and confident to act in their child's interests, having a positive relationship with the school and its staff, and being able to access school events and information. When some or all of these conditions are not met, it is unlikely that parents/caregivers will progress towards greater involvement in their child's school. Schools in South Africa are complicated sites, and parents'/caregivers' experiences of their own schooling may also shape their attitudes and choices in participating in their children's schools as well as their perceptions of school staff. Parents/caregivers were critical, for example, of schools and teachers assuming that they could easily provide homework help or extra resources for projects. Underlying this was an awareness of the constraints of their economic circumstances and how this negatively impacted the focal child's school experience, as well as the relationship between parent and school. This is not to suggest that all parents/caregivers were equally invested, but rather that parent/caregiver investment in general was rarely understood within its historic and social context.

Discussion

The research on parent/caregiver participation in South African schools delivered vital insights into an under-investigated constituency of the educational ecosystem. In presenting the findings from the survey, a number of important threads have emerged. These include "who South African parents are"; the effect of financial power on parents'/caregivers' choices and perceptions of quality; the broad range of roles that schools play in the lives of learners and parents; and the cumulative effect of historically laden inequalities on parents' sense of ownership and engagement with their children's schools.

In terms of who parents/caregivers in South Africa are, they are overwhelmingly female, often supported by kin, with nearly a quarter living with a sibling and 40% living with extended family. Large numbers experience economic hardship and rely on government grants. Familial experiences of schooling shape attitudes to education in an inter-generational way, reproducing inequalities over time. That said, the most poor, marginalised, and rural parents/caregivers still hold very positive views of education generally, something that requires further exploration.

Interestingly, parents/caregivers at more affluent schools were often less impressed by the quality of education received by their children.

It may be that parents/caregivers with different backgrounds and socio-economic status assess school quality in a variety of ways. This was illustrated during the COVID-19 pandemic: not for the first time, schools fulfilled a welfare and social protection function for learners and their families, affirming the critical role that schools continue to play in ensuring that some of the most grinding aspects of poverty can be ameliorated on a day-to-day basis. Parents/caregivers across the economic spectrum reported ongoing interaction with schools during the pandemic: the difference was that wealthier parents were more likely to report the continuation of teaching and learning, and having to support the school's educational programme at home. Poorer parents/caregivers noted the additional welfare support that schools offered, while acknowledging that teaching was significantly disrupted by the pandemic or came to a complete stop. When poor parents/caregivers describe schools, educators, and principals as co-parents or similar, it is because of an established awareness that schools "share the load" of providing for their children, offering a safe learning environment; access to books, uniforms and meals; and sometimes additional support to learners' families. This also places these schools – mostly no-fee schools – in positions of relative power over learners and their families, as access to the school combines access to education with further access to welfare support. In this way, schools become instruments of state welfare and surveillance, organising those requiring food aid, stationery, or uniforms. This requires striking a careful balance between ensuring that learners and families are able to access what they need to survive, while managing attitudes of distrust or fear towards public institutions (Mohapi & Netshitangani 2018). There are real consequences underlying this fear – for example, the risk of an undocumented parent's status being revealed and the overall security of a learner's family being compromised.

Parents/caregivers at fee-paying public and independent schools may arguably wield financial power that their no-fee counterparts do not, but this does not automatically result in higher parent participation or even knowledge of what happens at schools. Parents/caregivers are clearly historically and socially located actors, but the degree of parent/caregiver engagement cannot be attributed to any racial designation, or economic or geographic subgroup. Rather, parents/caregivers enter their children's schools conditioned by their own educational experiences, including their perceptions of schools as state institutions. South African schools have historically mirrored the authoritarian nature of the apartheid state, which is one of the key reasons for post-apartheid reforms focused on developing cooperative and collaborative forms of school governance. However, it is likely that the cultural effects of this educational history continue to influence some parents'/caregivers' attitudes towards their appropriate role within school environments, as well as their confidence in navigating the space being offered to parents/caregivers through national policy.

In terms of factors influencing parents' perceptions of school quality, the most important factor in the survey was the quality of educators (both teachers and principals). Parents/caregivers perceived educators and themselves as collectively responsible for child-rearing, favouring styles of communication that are interactive and dialogic. Most parents'/caregivers' perceptions of the quality of educators were formed through discussions with their children, rather than first-hand experience, indicating how they glean knowledge about their children's schools. The barriers to marginalised parents/caregivers interacting with schools and educators directly have been consistently pinpointed in this chapter, including material challenges like time and money, as well as confidence and past experiences of schooling. The divide between fee and no-fee schools in South Africa might have adverse effects on how parents/caregivers engage, as fee payment and financial contribution could shape parents'/caregivers' sense of ownership and "having a right" to interact directly with schools. In cases where learners attend no-fee schools or where parents/caregivers cannot afford school fees, parents'/caregivers' sense of autonomy or ownership over their child's schooling may be undercut by their lack of financial contribution, whether this is an empirical reality or an insecurity shaping parent/caregiver behaviour.

But the research also hinted that socio-cultural factors may serve as a positive driver of parent participation, finding that Indian parents scored highly in their overall knowledge and engagement with schools, based on regular interactions with teachers and engagement in the school community. This suggests that positive and sustained parental/caregiver involvement in schools can offset some of the limitations created by historical disadvantage or lower socio-economic status, as well as that continued involvement is necessary even where parents/caregivers trust the school and associate the high cost of education with high quality.

Some parents/caregivers mentioned that they were not interested in school affairs. It would be interesting to consider how much of this lack of interest was conditioned by past experiences of their own schooling or of negative experiences with a child's school. When discussing conflict resolution at the focal child's school, the majority of parents responded positively when asked how they felt the conflict had been resolved. However, parents/caregivers indicated that they would prefer to resolve these issues via email in future, perhaps due to the time demanded by a school visit, or as a way of maintaining some form of authority and distance from school authorities. Parent/caregiver involvement declines overall at high school level: parents/caregivers are more likely to attend events, participate in fundraising, and engage regularly with schools up until the end of primary school. However, this has class and race contours since middle-class, white and Indian parents/caregivers are more likely to continue to participate in school activities and support fundraising.

The nature of school fee policy, a direct effect of decentralised school governance in South Africa, therefore shapes the space available for parental/caregiver involvement in a variety of ways. It is not surprising, then, that fundraising is a major activity – particularly at fee-paying schools – that supplements the government contribution with fee income and funds raised through donations, alumni contribution, and school events. In comparison, no-fee schools have limited authority to fundraise because their expenses are intended to be fully covered by government, closing off one of the key spaces through which parents form social and collegial linkages with schools. These data from the survey on South African parents/caregivers highlight the heterogeneous ways in which they interact with schools, something which cannot be ignored in studies of parent/caregiver involvement.

In conclusion, we set out to establish who South African parents/caregivers are and how their identity shapes their involvement in their children's schools. We have presented a complex picture of parents/caregivers located at the intersection of multiple experiences, historic conditions, economic constraints, and educational choices. These parents/caregivers and their children are further embedded in an education system struggling to emerge from the material and symbolic inequalities of our recent past. The result is that positive policy provisions for collaborative school governance may fall short of addressing the lingering inequities that hold parents back from taking ownership of the space being offered to them. Additionally, lack of quality, comprehensive information – about school governance, national education policies, and even curricula – may deter parents/caregivers from engaging with schools, given that they do not know how they may contribute to school improvement, or even what happens at their child's school on a daily basis. Parents/caregivers who had one or two initially positive experiences were more likely to take an interest in a school, be open to participating in school events, or demonstrate greater knowledge of school operations, whereas parents/caregivers with little to no contact with the school were more hesitant to participate or consider how they might contribute. Therefore, it is necessary to consider how South African parents/caregivers are constructing a sense of agency (or lack of agency) in relation to their children's schooling, and what the factors may be that act against forms of involvement that they experience as empowering.

References

Bähre E (2020) Wealth-in-people and practical rationality: Aspirations and decisions about money in South Africa. *Economic Anthropology* 7(2): 267–278

Baquedano-López P, Alexander RA & Hernandez SJ (2013) Equity issues in parental and community involvement in schools: What teacher educators need to know. *Review of Research in Education* 37(1): 149–182

Bouguen A, Gumede K & Gurgand M (2015) *Parent's participation, involvement, and impact on student achievement: Evidence from a randomised evaluation in South Africa.* Paris School of Economics (PSE) Working Paper. Accessed June 2025, https://ideas.repec.org/p/hal/psewpa/halshs-01241957.html

Crozier G (2001) Excluded parents: The deracialisation of parental involvement. *Race, Ethnicity and Education* 4(4): 329–341

De Kock T, Hoffmann N, Sayed Y & Van Niekerk, R (2018) *Public–private partnerships in education and health in the Global South focusing on South Africa*. Equalities in Public Private Partnerships (EQUIPPPs) Working Paper. Accessed May 2025, https://sussex.figshare.com/articles/report/Public-private_ partnerships_in_South_African_healthcare_provision_scholarship_from_the_ South/23471285?file=41179862

Đurišić M & Bunijevac M (2017) Parental involvement as an important factor for successful education. *Center for Educational Policy Studies Journal* 7(3): 137–153

Echaune M, Ndiku JM & Sang A (2015) Parental involvement in homework and primary school academic performance in Kenya. *Journal of Education and Practice* 6(9): 46–53

Fataar A (2015) *Engaging schooling subjectivities across post-apartheid urban spaces*. Stellenbosch: African SUN Media

Gustafsson M, Van der Berg S, Shepherd DL & Burger C (2010) *The costs of illiteracy in South Africa*. University of Stellenbosch Economic Working Paper No. 14/10. Accessed May 2025, http://dx.doi.org/10.2139/ssrn.1727649

Henderson A (1981) *Parent participation–student achievement: The evidence grows*. NCCE Occasional Papers. Accessed May 2025, https://eric.ed.gov/?id=ED209754

LaRocque M, Kleiman I & Darling SM (2011) Parental involvement: The missing link in school achievement. *Preventing School Failure* 55(3): 115–122

Makgopa M & Mokhele M (2013) Teachers' perceptions on parental involvement: A case study of two South African schools. *Journal of Educational and Social Research* 3(3): 219–225

Mncube V (2007) Social justice, policy, and parents' understanding of their voice in school governing bodies in South Africa, *Journal of Educational Administration and History* (39)2: 129–143. Accessed May 2025, https://eric.ed.gov/?id=EJ814607

Mncube V (2010) Parental involvement in school activities in South Africa to the mutual benefit of the school and the community. *Education as Change* 14(2): 233–246

Mohapi SJ & Netshitangani T (2018) Views of parent governors' roles and responsibilities of rural schools in South Africa. *Cogent Social Sciences* 4(1): 1–14

Munje PN & Mncube V (2018) The lack of parent involvement as hindrance in selected public primary schools in South Africa: The voices of educators. *Perspectives in Education* 36(1): 80–93. Accessed May 2025, https://journals.ufs.ac.za/index.php/ pie/article/view/3585

Ross F (2009) *Raw life, new hope: Decency, housing, and everyday life in a post-apartheid community*. Cape Town: UCT Press

Statistics South Africa (2012) *Census 2011 Statistical release - P0301.4*. Pretoria: Statistics South Africa

Tikly L & Barrett AM (2011) Social justice, capabilities, and the quality of education in low income countries. *International Journal of Educational Development* 31(1): 3–14

Tinkler B (2002) *A review of literature on Hispanic/Latino parent involvement in K–12 Education*. University of Denver, 25 March. Accessed May 2025, https://eric.ed.gov/?id=ED469134

Van den Berg W, Ratele K, & Makusha T (eds.) (2021) *State of South Africa's fathers 2021*. Cape Town/Stellenbosch: Sonke Gender Justice, Human Sciences Research Council, & Stellenbosch University. Accessed May 2025, https://genderjustice.org.za/publication/state-of-south-africas-fathers-2021/

Williams TT & Sánchez B (2012) Parental involvement (and uninvolvement) at an inner-city high school. *Urban Education* 47(3): 625–652

5 An Inclusive Learning Environment in Early Childhood Care and Education: Enhancing Parent and Family Partnerships

Ashnie Mahadew

Introduction

There is no question that the involvement of parents and families in the early years is beneficial to educators, children, and their families; however, the practice of building authentic partnerships with the families of children is seldom taken seriously. For early childhood care and education (ECCE) centres to become inclusive, families need to be collaboratively involved in various ways, with the voices of all families being heard, valued, and embraced (Meresman 2014). This would foster a climate where families increase their knowledge of children's needs, educators acquire a deeper understanding of the family's culture and diversity, and children's learning is extended outside the school, resulting in a more positive experience. Building partnerships with families goes deeper than just signing a communication book, attending meetings four times a year, or completing reply slips. For centres to be inclusive, they need to function as a microcosm of society, since social and cultural factors influence the relationship between schools and the wider community (Ewulley et al. 2023). Families and communities are, therefore, a rich resource that can strengthen inclusion in an early years programme. The purpose of this chapter is two-fold: to ascertain the situation of family partnerships in an ECCE centre; and to explore how this centre could enhance partnerships with families.

The context of the study

The study is located in the informal early childhood care and education (ECCE) sector, which caters for the care, education, and holistic development of children from birth to four years (Zulu, Aina & Bipath 2022). ECCE falls under the umbrella of early childhood development (ECD), which encompasses the child from birth to nine years. In South Africa, children from their fifth year are mainly accommodated in formal schools while ECCE centres cater for those aged from birth to four years. An ECCE centre could be a crèche, a home-based facility, a mobile centre, a day-care centre for young children, a playgroup or a pre-school. ECCE has been recognised in the United Nations sustainable development goals, where it is acknowledged that early intervention predicts positive outcomes across the human lifespan.

In South Africa, this sector has also been identified as a means to level inequalities and contribute to social and economic transformation.[1] As part of the current national interest in the professionalisation of ECCE as a university degree and the migration of the responsibility for ECD from the Department of Social Development to the Department of Basic Education, this study hopes to make a valuable contribution to knowledge in the sector. There is no doubt that fostering partnerships with parents/caregivers and the community is a vital aspect of creating inclusive and quality ECCE programmes. Drawing from a wider study on diversity in ECCE, five research participants consisting of two teachers, one supervisor, one master's student, and a field monitor were purposively selected based on their experience in ECCE. The field monitor was employed by a non-profit organisation and her main duties were to monitor and train the ECCE teachers in that area.

Inclusion

Inclusion refers to equal opportunities and access to educational institutions for all groups of learners. This understanding of inclusion portrays an all-embracing broad view that includes all children vulnerable to marginalisation, not just those experiencing barriers to learning (Cologon 2019; Walton 2018). Studies on inclusion, however, generally focus on children with disabilities or special needs, and there is thus a need for research on how to create inclusive environments involving all vulnerable children, not just those with special needs or disabilities (Paulsrud & Nilholm 2020). Children could be excluded due to various marginalised identity markers including race, skin colour, gender, sexual orientation, trauma, learning style, or disability (UNESCO 1994: 6). According to my previous research, an inclusive learning environment is context-driven and may be created using multiple approaches, including: positive attitudes and the conscientisation of teachers; inclusive, play-based, culturally responsive, participatory pedagogies; challenging stereotyping and bias; and the building of partnerships with parents and families in the early learning environment (Mahadew 2022). Educational institutions are the centre of the community, and when educators work together with families and community members, an important facilitator of inclusion comes into effect (Meresman 2014). This is because the involvement of parents and families enables teachers to understand the diversity of learners and their unique cultural backgrounds. This chapter, therefore, focuses on building partnerships with and involving parents and families in ECCE, as this is a vital factor for creating an inclusive learning environment.

Parental/caregiver involvement in education

Quality early childhood education has been identified as a means for social and economic transformation in South Africa, but a quality educational programme is difficult to achieve without adequate parental involvement (Epstein 2018). Numerous studies have highlighted the benefits of parental involvement in a child's development (Kwatubana & Makhalemele 2015; Lemmer 2007; Nevski & Siibak 2016; Pineda et al. 2018). For instance, it has been demonstrated that parental involvement in early childhood education has the ability to enhance children's cognitive development and future literacy and numeracy skills (Desforges & Abouchaar 2003; Dickins 2014). A quantitative study in Zimbabwe by Chansa-Kabali (2016) confirmed that the involvement of even low-income parents in children's schooling has a positive impact on the children's academic skills. The study, which was conducted using nine purposively sampled schools in order to capture data from a range of schools representing the population of the area, highlighted that children can benefit from parental/caregiver involvement, and teachers need to be equipped with knowledge on how to guide parents to become more involved.

Parent involvement and family involvement

Due to a myriad socio-economic factors in the South African context, a rich diversity of family structures is apparent in our country, including those where extended family members or older siblings have taken on the responsibility of the biological parents. While both fathers and mothers have equal responsibility for the upbringing of children, a cycle of absent fathers is common in South African society (Moodly et al. 2019). According to Mavungu, Thomson-de Boor and Mphaka (2013), absent fathers include those who do not live with their children, who do not communicate with them or who do not pay maintenance for them. In addition to absent fathers, which result in increased responsibilities for mothers and extended family members, some children's parents may both be absent. The number of South African children who have lost both parents is 471 000, as revealed in a report by Hall and Sambu (2019). A result of this situation is the phenomenon of child-headed households, where older siblings take on the role of a parent (Thwala 2018). Hall & Sambu (2019) also reveal that 55 000 children in South Africa were found to be living in a total of 33 000 child-headed households. Of further significance is a study by Damian, Mashau, and Tugli (2019) that found that, for various reasons, grandmothers may be responsible for raising their grandchildren, and although they may experience enormous difficulties in doing so, they provide a positive influence in significant ways.

As parental figures, grandmothers serve as role models and as custodians and transmitters of culture, also offering nurturing, love, and support (Schultz & Shirindi 2019). Thus, in the South African context of diverse family structures, this study uses the term "family" to encompass families headed by parents, and families headed by other family members who take on the responsibilities of parents.

Family involvement versus family partnerships

Family involvement in an education programme may occur to varying degrees and could be important to the programme or not. The concept of family partnerships, however, is more likely to result in a meaningful contribution to the education programme (Driessen 2019).

The word "partnership" emphasises the complementary role played by parents and families in the education and development of children in schools or centres (Beveridge 2013). Epstein (2018) agrees that establishing partnerships is a superior approach as it encourages families and schools to work together, and recognise their shared responsibilities in the education and development of children. However, as pointed out by Blue-Banning et al. (2004), parents may not feel recognised as equal partners in this process. The authors assert that one reason for the lack of collaborative partnerships could be a failure to define the constructs of family partnerships in educational programmes. This study, therefore, attempts to determine how teachers, by enhancing family partnerships, can create inclusive early learning environments.

Family partnerships and inclusion

The concept of promoting family partnerships aligns with the philosophy of inclusion in which democratic participation in educational settings is emphasised, and the exclusion of children and their families is rejected (Beveridge 2013). Thus, to foster inclusivity, teachers need to demonstrate an ability to value the voices of children and families in educational settings. This means that teachers should not engage in teaching without understanding the diverse backgrounds of the children they teach as well as their family situations. Early studies highlighted that while there are cultural differences between home and school, teachers were found to lack interest in familiarising themselves with the cultural beliefs and practices of the children they were teaching (Vincent 1996). Moreover, Crozier

(2001) points out that teachers may incorrectly assume that all children and families have the same needs, while parental partnership policies may ignore the diversity among children and their families. As Allen et al. (2021) assert, in order to ensure that all children and their families feel a sense of belonging, teachers need to make an effort to connect school and home by acknowledging this diversity.

Theoretical perspectives

The study is underpinned by the ecosystemic perspective, which attempts to understand the child as a product of a multilayered environment, and by Epstein's theory, which presents a framework and a comprehensive typology for different levels of parental participation. Although Epstein offers a comprehensive framework to address the interaction between families, schools, and communities, there are limitations when it comes to inclusion of diversity, hence the need to include the ecosystemic perspective as a complement to the theory.

Ecosystemic perspective

The ecosystemic perspective places the young child at the centre of concentric circles representing layers of the factors that influence the child (Moodly et al. 2019). To create inclusive learning environments, teachers need to consider the complexity of these and other interrelated factors that impact the child. Urie Bronfenbrenner, a Russian-born American psychologist, developed the Ecological Systems Theory, which resembles Russian nesting dolls, with each aspect of the system fitting neatly inside the other systems (Bronfenbrenner 1979). Bronfenbrenner argued that the family requires the support and involvement of the entire society to raise children successfully. This "it takes a village" philosophy was based in part on the weaknesses of many families in modern American society. According to Bronfenbrenner, American children were more often raised by television and peers than by parents, who were busy working to survive.

Thus, according to Bronfenbrenner's Ecological Systems Theory, a child is influenced by the interrelationships among a number of superimposed ecosystems, namely, the microsystem, mesosystem, exosystem, macrosystem, and the chronosystem. Just as the family requires the collaboration of schools in raising children, schools require partnerships with parents and caregivers to function successfully. Bronfenbrenner's model is useful for understanding the interactions between the child, the home, the school, and the community in creating an inclusive learning environment in ECCE. The various spheres that comprise this model are described in the section that follows.

The microsystem is the layer that represents the child's direct interactions in the home and school, mainly with the family and the teacher. The mesosystem signifies the relationships between the significant role players in the microsystem. For instance, positive relationships between the ECCE teacher and the child's family may result in a more inclusive schooling experience. This could be due to the family volunteering or having a say in the ECCE programme's decision-making processes. The third layer, the exosystem, represents factors not directly linked to the child, for example, the career demands of a parent/caregiver. According to Moodly et al. (2019), when a parent needs to work away from home for a few weeks, this may impact the emotional state of the child in a negative way. However, it is important to note that the effects of parental absence may also have positive results such as fostering greater independence, self-confidence, and resilience in children. The fourth layer is the macrosystem, which highlights the impact of socio-economic status, race, culture, and ethnicity on the child's development. For example, a study conducted by Steenkamp (2021) on the presence of cultural diversity at a full-service school indicates that interactions with people from diverse, multicultural backgrounds led to greater overall wellness for school role players, deeper learning, and the development of a greater sense of belonging for all. This greater sense of belonging could have a positive impact on family partnerships and inclusion in educational programmes. Bronfenbrenner's theory thus offers a framework to support our understanding of contextual factors that have a bearing on inclusion in the ECCE centre, as well as on the fostering of family partnerships in schools. This framework can be complemented by Epstein's typology that offers a structured framework describing how family involvement may be enhanced.

Epstein's typology

Joyce Epstein (1996) outlined a typology that can be used to guide ECCE teachers in fostering partnerships with the family. Epstein highlights that when partnerships are fostered, families and schools acknowledge their joint responsibilities and work together to enhance the early learning programme (Epstein 2018). The typology outlines six types of parental/caregiver involvement in children's education, including parenting, communicating, volunteering, learning at home, decision-making, and advocacy and collaborating with the community (Sibanda 2021).

Research on exploring diversity in early childhood care and education

The remainder of the chapter discusses a segment of a larger study on exploring diversity in ECCE carried out by the author in a township in KwaZulu-Natal in 2022. The research objectives of the study were:

1. to establish the current situation regarding family partnerships in the ECCE learning environment; and

2. to enhance family partnerships in the ECCE learning environment.

The first research objective was underpinned by the ecosystemic theoretical perspective, while the second research objective used Epstein's typology to establish guidelines for educators to enhance family partnerships in the ECCE learning programme.

Findings and discussion

The findings section begins with an exploration of the current experiences of the research participants in relation to the ecological layers that influence the child. The data generated from semi-structured interviews reveals that families experienced both physical and social barriers to their successful partnerships with the ECCE centre. Underpinned by Epstein's typology, the findings also reveal suggestions made by the participants to enhance family partnerships at the centre.

Physical barriers to family partnerships: 'Parents are hardly ever there'

Research participants indicated that certain physical or practical barriers impacted negatively on the involvement of parents in the early learning programme. Research Participant 2, who works as a field monitor and is responsible for the training of ECCE educators in the eThekwini region, mentioned:

> Some parents are hardly ever there. They don't even ask their children about school. There were books that were given to the children. The parents were supposed to read to them and then [the children would] come back the next day to tell the teacher about the story. In 15 children, maybe only three parents read those stories to the children. They have a communication book but some don't even check that. If teachers write in the communication book, they need to follow up by phoning them. They need to phone and say there is a message in someone's bag, you need to check that. (Research Participant 2: field monitor)

Research Participant 2 mentioned that apart from the centre in this study, other schools that were monitored experienced similar problems with parents/caregivers. Some of the parents, even though physically present, did not show an interest in the child's schoolwork. Research Participant 2 also mentioned that it was mainly grandparents who were responsible for the primary care of the child:

> Some children are living with grandma and the actual parents, the biological parents, are maybe in town while the child is living in the township with grandma. So the grandma first of all can't read. There will be a gap on that. Also, the grandma can be old or sick. (Research Participant 2: field monitor)

When asked for possible reasons for this kind of situation, Research Participant 1, a master's student researching ECCE, mentioned that in some cases:

> The mother has a child when she is very young in my culture. Then she gets married after 20 years to another man who does not take care of the child. She has to leave that child with the grandmother, and she goes to get married. (Research Participant 1: student researcher)

Other likely causes mentioned by the research participants included parents or caregivers working away from the area due to increasing unemployment there, grandmothers often being illiterate or in ill health and unable to provide adequate support with reading or any type of schoolwork, and the absence of fathers in the daily lives of their children.

> It is more like the father is the provider. That's his role. He will pay for things, but he won't be a part of checking on the child's education and all of that, and it's more of a cultural thing. It is a common thing for the father to not even be present in our African culture. Because of unemployment, the father has to go and work far away for a couple of months. So he only comes when the schools are closed. I think it's a common thing for the role of the father to be to provide and pay for the school fees. (Research Participant 1: student researcher)

In line with research by Moodly et al. (2019), in the South African context, the above findings reflect a breakdown of the nuclear family system, with children living apart from one or both biological parents. To thrive, children require the presence of both parents and a stable environment (Ogodogu-Chima 2024). The phenomenon of teenage pregnancy also seems to be a contributing factor to the findings above, as very young mothers, having become parents while unmarried, sometimes leave their children with grandmothers when they get married to a person other than the firstborn's father. Aligning with Mavungu, Thomson-de Boor and Mphaka (2013), absent fathers also seem to contribute to poor family partnerships, as single mothers find it difficult to be providers while also supplying the child with adequate emotional care and support. This assertion is supported in the literature, which states that a majority of South African children live in households where their fathers are absent (Mavungu, Thomson-de Boof & Mphaka 2013; Moodly et al. 2019).

Various reasons for absent fathers have been cited, and these include unemployment, poor socio-economic conditions, divorce, the labour migration system, cultural beliefs, and so forth (Mavungu, Thomson-de Boor & Mphaka 2013). The findings also reveal that grandmothers play an important role in the upbringing of children. A number of factors have given rise to this situation. For instance, grandmothers may take over the care of their grandchildren when HIV and/or Aids infection results in the death of their own children (Ardington & Leibbrandt 2010). Another possible contributor to the grandmothers' changed role is parental neglect. This situation arises when a parent fails to meet the basic needs of their child or children (Dubowitz & Poole 2012). According to Amin et al. (2024), neglect usually has negative effects on a child's development. Drawing on the ecosystemic theory, as the primary microsystem, parents are a child's first and most important teachers and play a crucial role in the child's holistic development. The absence of parents results in a break in the mesosystem, leading to poor family connections with schools.

Despite these seemingly negative impacts of the physical barriers to family partnerships mentioned above, the spirit of ubuntu reigns in instances when extended family members adhere to the principle of "it takes a village to raise a child". Ubuntu is an African concept that refers to the philosophy of humaneness in the interactions of community members. Aligned with the ecological systems theory, the ubuntu philosophy encourages mutual inter-dependence and cooperation among community members, so, in the case of absent parents, extended family members step up to exercise collective responsibility for the benefit of the children in the community.

Socio-cultural barriers to inclusion: 'They call them these names, that is why they don't come'

ECCE centres are places where children from diverse cultures, linguistic groups, religions, and nationalities may come together for the first time. According to Banks (2006), the teacher needs to plan strategies to enable all groups of children and their families to be included, irrespective of differences. Engaging in activities with children in the early years provides an opportunity for teachers to address social injustices caused by bias against minority groups (Kissinger 2017). Research Participant 2, the field monitor, verbalised how difficult it is to correct discriminatory behaviour taught by parents/caregivers:

> Learning starts at home. So, if children are learning wrong things at home there is a problem. It is very hard to change a child who is speaking hate speech. It is so difficult for teachers to correct the child and tell the child it is wrong … when the child is hearing it from home. Everything comes from home and we need to have meetings for parents to avoid this. (Research Participant 2: field monitor)

Research Participant 3, the supervisor of the centre, reported that a diversity of children from families of different nationalities who speak different languages attended the centre. Children from the minority groups had to learn to master isiZulu quickly and were called names due to being different.

> In my centre, the children are coming from different countries. Some are coming from Zimbabwe, Lesotho, Malawi, and some are Zulu. They speak different languages when they are with their peers, but when they are in the classroom, we have to use Zulu. Those who don't understand – they learn so quick I tell you! People who come from out of South Africa are discriminated against, for example they are called names. When they come in our country, they feel like they do not belong – but we need to make them feel like they belong. (Research Participant 3: centre supervisor)

Similarly, Research Participant 4, an educator at the centre, noted that there were differences among the children at the centre and that the four-year-olds were able to identify these differences. They sometimes refused to play with children they perceived as being different.

They also called these children names, a behaviour they picked up from their homes and families. Research participant 4, who had a long history teaching at the school, discourages this behaviour, also spending much of her personal time supporting the foreign nationals in her community.

> The children look the same, but the language and culture is different. They also eat differently, they do not like maas [sour milk] and milk, so we try to accommodate different foods. They do eat pap like us …. The children were not playing with them normally. They were fighting with them. They say kwere don't come to this side. They are always saying no don't play with me … They are learning from their parents who are using these words at home – so in school it comes out of their mouths. I was talking to them and now it is better. (Research Participant 4: ECCE teacher (four-year-old group))

Research Participant 1 explained how children who were culturally different were expected to fit into the dominant school culture; for example, those with dreadlocks were expected to cut their dreadlocks off, just as they were expected to speak only isiZulu in class. Daniels (2018) defines this as assimilation, where the child is required to adapt to the existing learning environment by losing their own culture and language. Assimilation promotes standardisation and conformity, with minority groups becoming part of the dominant group and differences being side-lined. Reygan, Walton and Osman (2018) maintain that assimilation creates a situation where there are no separate social structures for diverse identities, and exclusion is perpetuated.

Research Participant 1, a post-graduate student stated that:

> If a child has dreadlocks, according to the family belief the child is not allowed to cut the dreadlocks as it has a spiritual meaning. The school policy will not allow the dreadlocks, and the parents would fight the policy or remove the child to go to another centre. (Research Participant 1: student researcher)

The ECCE centre supervisor described a similar incident that she had personally experienced as a parent:

> My daughter is schooling in one of the schools – from not around here, and then she has long hair. They told her to make her hair in a certain way. We have Afro hair and they don't understand that. Indian hair, white hair is different from Afro hair. It is almost as if our type of hair needs to change to fit with the school rules. (Research Participant 3: centre supervisor)

These efforts to make children conform to the language and appearance of the dominant group are examples of assimilation. While an ECCE centre may be perceived as inclusive, children may only be included on condition that they lose their personal identity so that they fit into the dominant school culture. Parents are aware of this but seldom have much say in the policies of the centre or school. The use of school governing bodies (SGBs) to facilitate parent partnerships in the ECCE centre's policy making was identified as an area of need.

Research Participant 1 noted that teachers need to make a special effort to make parents and caregivers feel welcomed and needed at the centres. This could be achieved if children from different cultures were welcomed, and their unique identities were appreciated. The ECCE student reflected:

> Parents are not happy to come in. They don't feel welcome. They don't feel like they want to participate in the school activities. They feel like they don't actually belong here. It is some kind of a block that is preventing them. Also, they feel that the teachers do not need them. They do not want them within the school. (Research Participant 1: student researcher)

To prevent this situation, teachers need to make a concerted effort to seek knowledge about the characteristics of children and their families from different cultures (Gordon & Browne 2017). The supervisor stated:

Sometimes, when we say the names of children, we may say it wrong and this may hurt them without us meaning to hurt them. Therefore, it is important for teachers to learn about their names, and the different cultures and languages in the classroom. To handle differences and to work with differences, teachers need to work together with the parents. (Research Participant 3: centre supervisor)

Socio-cultural factors align with the fourth layer or the macrosystem, which highlights the impact of socio-economic status, race, culture, linguistic group, and ethnicity on the child's development. A study by Hanson et al. (1998) found that language differences between homes and schools affected the amount and type of communication that occurred between teachers and parents/caregivers, as well as the relationships between them and centres. Similarly, socio-cultural differences appear to be a barrier to the development of family partnerships. When children in minority groups are expected to remove their dreadlocks or eat the same food and speak the same language as the dominant group, they are being asked to lose their individuality to fit in. Socio-cultural barriers hinder the authentic participation of minority cultures and result in the exclusion of certain children and their families.

A way forward: Teachers need to know that families are partners

For sound family and ECCE centre partnerships, much effort is required on the part of teachers and ECCE staff. Teachers need to acknowledge that they can create an inclusive learning environment by understanding the child in the context of the family and community (Bronfenbrenner 1979). Both families and teachers have a common goal and an equal responsibility for the child's optimal development. The field monitor emphasised that teachers need to believe that family partnerships enhance an inclusive learning programme, with families feeling valued and welcomed:

> Parents know that they need to be involved but they are not getting involved. We need to implement some kind of training to get teachers to get parents more involved in the centre. We feel that parents are partners, but teachers need to know that parents are partners because they need to be a part of the policy-making of the school. (Research Participant 4: ECCE teacher (four-year-old group))

The ECCE student mentioned that in addition to making families feel welcomed as partners in the child's education, teachers may also design experiences where children see themselves represented in the displays, books, and resources in the early learning environment. She stated that:

> If the child has amadreads [dreadlocks], we must try to include the child in a subtle way. For example, they could have stories about heroes or characters with dreads. The story needs to represent the people that they are teaching. The charts also need to show different races, cultures, languages, families to make children and their families feel welcome. (Research Participant 1: student researcher)

Research participants also felt that teachers need to ensure that families are not just called to meetings for negative reasons, for example, to discuss a problem or to collect money. For instance, the baby and toddler group educator indicated that:

> When we call the parents in for meetings, we are mainly discussing money. That is the problem. Teachers call the parents in to discuss school fees and fundraising. So, the parents feel that whenever they are called in, it has to do with money. We need to be careful about doing this. (Research Participant 5: ECCE teacher (baby and toddler group))

The findings also indicate a need for positive interactions between ECCE centres and families. These interactions could include informal activities where families interact with the educators in a relaxed manner.

> Fun events like a pyjama party are held with the children, but they hardly ever involve parents. Except at the end of the year when the Grade R children graduate, then they involve the parents. But some parents do not even come for that. Maybe we should invite them often for fun events at the centres. (Research Participant 2: field monitor)

For teachers and families to build relationships, opportunities need to be created for them to interact and build trust. According to the first level of Epstein's typology, teachers may organise workshops or conferences to allow diverse families the opportunity to share beliefs regarding parenting skills, child development, and ideal home conditions to facilitate the optimal development of children. It is, however, important for teachers to note differences in cultural beliefs on parenting and to be open to learning from parents and caregivers.

Aligned with the second level of Epstein's typology, teachers also need to establish clear channels of communication with families regarding the child's progress. Two-way communication enables teachers to understand the child's home situation and make accommodations according to the child's needs. Communication needs to be regular and in a language that families understand. A communication book was generally used by the educators at this centre for this purpose. However, Research Participant 5 stated that parents/caregivers did not always understand the language used in the communication book. She said:

> When teachers write in English or isiZulu in the communication book, it
> is another problem because some parents do not understand. There is a
> language barrier. Even the parent meetings, if I am calling a meeting, if I have
> 16 parents who are Black and two of you are speaking English, we will speak
> isiZulu but you will not feel like you attended that meeting because you did
> not understand what I was saying. So, I will suggest that teachers need to
> make sure that the parents understand them. (Research Participant 5: ECCE
> teacher (baby and toddler group))

Taking such language barriers into account is also important for parent meetings, newsletters, and school reports.

The third level of Epstein's typology emphasises the importance of parents or caregivers volunteering at the school. When parents share their expertise, they are able to make meaningful contributions and, at the same time, gain an understanding of how the school operates.

Parents and caregivers from minority groups should be encouraged to volunteer as they may offer unique insights and serve as a valuable resource to facilitate inclusion. Research participants mentioned that parents could volunteer in the school garden, set up displays, and assist with reading and story time. The ECCE student noted:

> Teachers need to realise how important it is to get the parents in, not just for
> signing the reply slips and communication books. We need to get them into
> our schools as partners. Whereas I have 50% responsibility as a teacher and
> you have 50% responsibility as a parent, we need to come together. I don't
> think teachers understand their role in bringing in parents to school. The
> only time teachers invite parents to school is when there are issues with the
> child's work or behaviour. Instead, parents need to be a part of the school in
> other ways like volunteering, telling stories, and doing reading. (Research
> Participant 1: student researcher)

The fourth level of Epstein's typology encourages teachers to extend children's learning into the home by providing opportunities for parents and caregivers to be a part of the curriculum. In the early years, these learning activities generally comprise practising songs, poems or reading stories to children. Research Participant 4, in charge of the four-year-olds, noted that teachers received poor support in this regard, as parents were uninterested in carrying school through to the home. She indicated that parents often felt that it was the teacher's responsibility, which they were paid to do.

> When we send some work home for the children to practice, maybe they will
> need to practice something like a poem or song. One child asked, 'Why am
> I taking work home to do? Mum says she is paying you to teach me. Why

am I taking work home now?' (Research Participant 4: ECCE teacher (four-year-old group))

To foster partnerships with family, Epstein's fifth level suggests that parents and caregivers need to be an integral part of the school's policy-making. Aligned with this idea, the South African Schools Act of 1996 calls for SGBs consisting of parents, guardians, educators, school management, and even community leaders to assist the school in policy development. It is mandatory that parents of learners in a school constitute the majority of the SGB members (Kekana & Makura 2020) and that diverse groups are represented. The field monitor mentioned:

> These centres have a governing body, but most do not use the school governing body as they should. It is just a name. They need to have a governing body that is why they have a governing body – but they do not know how to use them. They need to include different parents (from diverse groups). But they do not do that. They choose the same race. If it is a Zulu school, they will choose the isiZulu parents, if it is Indian or white it is the same story. I remember at my school there never was a Black person on the governing body. The Black person was the security guy. We used to call him uncle. Even the cleaners, you never found a white lady cleaning. This sends a message that certain races are good at only the minor jobs. Certain groups are only good for cleaning. (Research Participant 2: field monitor)

ECCE centres are generally a first point of contact for families within the wider community. Cultural factors have an influence on the relationship between schools and the community (Meresman 2014), and ECCE centres can encourage inclusion of, and social interaction between, diverse groups of people. Epstein's sixth level suggests that communities are a rich resource that can strengthen inclusion in the early years programme. For instance, the ECCE student mentioned that the community can be roped in to foster inclusion or simply be regarded as a valuable source of knowledge.

> The parents have skills and strengths that can be useful. A clinic nurse can speak about HIV and AIDS, and dispel discrimination against these people. Young children have false beliefs that if you touch a person with HIV or AIDS you can get it too. Other parents may work at the dentist and speak to the children about how to care for their teeth. (Research Participant 1: student researcher)

Families generally possess the greatest knowledge about their children, and they are invaluable resources in the creation of an inclusive learning environment. Aligned with Epstein's typology, families need to be recognised as equal stakeholders in an inclusive ECCE centre. Undoubtedly, for families, this would mean not just being involved in the education programme but making a positive contribution to the everyday running of the school. Fostering family partnerships definitely entails more than just requiring parents or caregivers to sign reply slips and communication books; rather it is encouraging them to play a part in advocacy and in the policies of the centre.

Conclusion

As families play a pivotal role in the creation of an inclusive learning environment in ECCE, this study sought to establish the current situation regarding family partnerships and ways in which they can be enhanced in the ECCE learning environment. Underpinned by the ecosystemic perspective, physical and socio-cultural factors were identified as barriers to parental/caregiver involvement. In the microsystem, parents or caregivers and ECCE teachers are the key role players. A home environment that lacks the presence of one or both parents, or the care of a capable adult, presents a barrier to the child's development. Physical barriers to family partnerships in this study included absent fathers, single mothers, and grandparents and extended family members adopting the role of primary caregivers in the microsystem. According to Bronfenbrenner (1979), these disruptions in the microsystem have an impact on the mesosystem, which comprises the interconnections between the home and the school. Despite the presence of these physical barriers, extended family members such as grandparents, aunts or uncles did step up in the spirit of ubuntu to ensure children were cared for. Nonetheless, the study found that these changes or breakdowns in the home microsystem impacted on the extent of family and ECCE centre partnerships.

In terms of the ecosystemic theory, we found that the exosystem, consisting of factors not directly relating to the child, also has an impact on family partnerships with educational institutions. Here, we found that parents and caregivers were sometimes forced to leave their children and work away from home due to high unemployment in the local area. Research participants felt that this was one of the reasons for the absence of parents, either one or both, for most of the school term. The macrosystem comprising social, cultural, and linguistic differences also was felt to influence family partnerships. Cultural and linguistic differences between the ECCE centre and the families led to poor family partnerships. The participants in the study felt that parents/caregivers from minority groups needed to be welcomed and included in the activities of the centre. This goes deeper than just inviting all parents/caregivers to meetings and including them in communications: rather, it requires teachers to learn about the different cultures present in the learning environment. To be inclusive of all cultural and linguistic groups, teachers need to be aware of assimilation, where minority groups are expected to fit into the dominant culture of the ECCE centre, and adopt the hairstyles, food habits, and the language of the dominant group. For children from minority groups, this results in a loss of identity. Teachers and centre managers need to be aware that assimilation is indeed a form of exclusion as it negates differences.

Bearing in mind the concerns raised, research participants were asked to consider ways to enhance partnerships between home and school in the early learning programme. The findings supported the use of Epstein's model, which calls for deep-rooted partnerships between the school and families, rather than family involvement. In this model, families and ECCE centres are seen as equally important in the development of young children. The findings align with the first level of Epstein's typology, suggesting that schools should create workshops or conferences at which diverse families can exchange perspectives on parenting approaches, children's developmental milestones, and supportive home environments that promote children's optimal growth.

The participants also suggested ways to enhance two-way communication that would allow ECCE centres to learn more regarding the child's home situation and individual culture. Some of the comments from the research participants indicated negative attitudes from families regarding the extension of curriculum-related activities to the home environment. Participants also noted that parents/caregivers did not participate in decision-making or in developing the policies of the school because the SGB was not democratically elected, nor was it effective. Opportunities and ideas for the parents to volunteer were also suggested as a means for families to become fully engaged in the daily running of the school. Finally, aligned with Epstein's sixth level, participants suggested introducing community members and their unique skills to enhance the ECCE centre's programme. This would ensure that centres are inclusive and represent the cultural beliefs of the society that they serve.

The study highlights a need for awareness to be created amongst families and teachers regarding their joint accountability in the education and optimal development of young children. Stumbling blocks to the fostering of family partnerships in the form of physical and socio-cultural barriers were unique to the ECCE centre in question. However, similar barriers could be present in other ECCE centres in South Africa. The findings of this study may also offer valuable insights into how family partnerships may be enhanced by ECCE centres. The study used only a small selection of research participants. Therefore a wider study could build on this one by selecting ECCE centres from a range of cultural and economic backgrounds. This may lead to comprehensive suggestions to enhance family partnerships in ECCEs. As a way forward, I suggest that teachers should be given pre- and in-service training to recognise parents and caregivers as equal stakeholders in the education of young children. With the diversity of the community in mind, these training programmes could use Epstein's typology as a framework to enhance partnerships with families. In the journey to create quality inclusive ECCE centres, teachers need to ensure that families are authentically welcomed to ECCE centres. The narratives of the research participants represent stories of trauma in which physical and social barriers impede authentic partnerships with families. Despite these stories of trauma, stories of hope were also captured when participants suggested ways to enhance family partnerships at ECCE centres.

Notes

1   Bipath K & Joubert I, The birth of a new curriculum for Early Childhood Development. *Mail and Guardian*, 27 May 2016. Accessed May 2024, https://mg.co.za/article/2016-05-27-00-the-birth-of-a-new-qualification-for-ecd

References

Allen KA, Slaten CD, Arslan G, Roffey S, Craig H & Vella-Brodrick DA (2021) School belonging: The importance of student and teacher relationships. In ML Kern & ML Wehmeyer (Eds) *The Palgrave handbook of positive education.* Cham: Springer

Amin U, Rashid B, Jan R, Jan R & Malla AM (2024) Child abuse and neglect. *Indian Journal of Continuing Nursing Education* 24(2): 104–109

Ardington C & Leibbrandt M (2010) Orphanhood and schooling in South Africa: Trends in the vulnerability of orphans between 1993 and 2005. *Economic Development and Cultural Change* 58(3): 507–536

Banks JA (2006) Improving race relations in schools: From theory and research to practice. *Journal of Social Issues* 62(3): 607–614

Beveridge S (2013) *Children, families and schools: Developing partnerships for inclusive education.* Oxford and New York: RoutledgeFalmer

Blue-Banning M, Summers JA, Frankland HC, Nelson LL & Beegle G (2004) Dimensions of family and professional partnerships: Constructive guidelines for collaboration. *Exceptional children* 70(2): 167–184

Bronfenbrenner U (1979) *The ecology of human development: Experiments by nature and design.* Cambridge, MA: Harvard University Press

Chansa-Kabali T (2016) Parental involvement in early schooling: Exploring parent and teacher views in a low income African context. *Journal of Education, Society and Behavioural Science* 14(4): 1–9

Cologon K (2019) *Towards inclusive education: A necessary process of transformation.* Clifton Hill, VIC: Children and Young People with Disability Australia (CYDA)

Crozier G (2001) Excluded parents: The deracialisation of parental involvement. *Race, Ethnicity and Education* 4(4): 329–341

Damian JU, Mashau NS & Tugli AK (2019) Experiences of grandmothers raising their grandchildren in Vhembe District, South Africa. *Journal of Gender, Information and Development in Africa* S1(1): 137–151

Daniels D (2018) Educating in diverse worlds: The immigrant Somali parent as a strategic partner of South African education. In E Walton & R Osman (Eds) *Teacher education for diversity: Conversations from the Global South*. London: Routledge

Desforges C & Abouchaar A (2003) *The impact of parental involvement, parental support and family education on pupil achievements and adjustment: A literature review*. London: Department for Education and Skills

Dickins M (2014) *A-Z of inclusion in early childhood*. Berkshire: Open University Press

Driessen G (2019) Parental involvement, parental participation, parent-school-community partnerships. *Encyclopedia*. Accessed June 2025, https://www. researchgate.net/publication/335397199_Parental_Involvement_parental_ participation_parent-school-community_partnerships

Dubowitz H & Poole G (2012) Child neglect: An overview. *Encyclopedia on Early Childhood Development*: 1–6

Ewulley F, Anlimachie MA, Abreh MK & Mills EE (2023) Understanding the nexus of school types, school cultures and educational outcomes and its implication for policy and practice. *International Journal of Educational Research* 121: 102237

Epstein J (1996) Advances in family, community, and school partnerships. *Community Education Journal* 23(3): 10–15

Epstein JL (2018) *School, family and community partnerships: Preparing educators and improving schools*. New York: Routledge

Gordon AM & Browne KW (2017) *Beginnings and beyond: Foundations in early childhood education*. Boston: Cengage Learning

Hall K & Sambu W (2019) *Demography of South Africa's children*. Cape Town: Children's Institute, University of Cape Town

Hanson MJ, Wolfberg P, Zercher C, Morgan M, Gutierrez S, Barnwell D & Beckman P (1998) The culture of inclusion: Recognising diversity at multiple levels. *Early Childhood Research Quarterly* 13(1): 185–209

Kekana LM & Makura AH (2020) The importance of school governing bodies in the effective governance of the public schools: Do women have a role? Paper presented at ADVED 2020, 6th International Conference on Advances in Education, Virtual Conference (5–6 October)

Kissinger K (2017) *Anti-bias education in the early childhood classroom: Hand in hand, step by step*. New York and Oxford: Routledge

Kwatubana S & Makhalemele T (2015) Parental involvement in the process of implementation of the National School Nutrition Programme in public schools. *International Journal of Educational Sciences* 9(3): 315–323

Lemmer EM (2007) Parent involvement in teacher education in South Africa. *International Journal about Parents in Education* 1(1): 218–229

Mahadew A (2022) An inclusive learning environment in early childhood care and education: A participatory action learning and action research study. Doctoral Thesis, University of KwaZulu-Natal

Mavungu EM, Thomson-de Boor H & Mphaka K (2013) *So we are ATM fathers. A study of absent fathers in Johannesburg, South Africa.* Johannesburg: Centre for Social Development in Africa, University of Johannesburg and Sonke Gender Justice

Meresman S (2014) *Parents, family and community participation in inclusive education.* Webinar 13 Companion Technical Booklet. Paris: United Nations Children's Emergency Fund (UNICEF)

Moodly A, Sotuku N, Schmidt K & Phatudi N (2019) *Early childhood care and education (0– 4): A transdisciplinary approach.* Cape Town: Oxford University Press Southern Africa

Nevski E & Siibak A (2016) The role of parents and parental mediation on 0–3-year olds' digital play with smart devices: Estonian parents' attitudes and practices. *Early Years* 36(3): 227–241

Ogodogu-Chima A (2024) *Parenting styles and forms (single parent vs two parents) and their impact on children's wellbeing.* Preprint. Accessed June 2025, http://dx.doi.org/10.13140/RG.2.2.36382.96324

Paulsrud D & Nilholm C (2020) Teaching for inclusion: A review of research on the cooperation between regular teachers and special educators in the work with students in need of special support. *International Journal of Inclusive Education* 27(4): 541–555

Pineda R, Bender J, Hall B, Shabosky L, Annecca A & Smith J (2018) Parent participation in the neonatal intensive care unit: Predictors and relationships to neurobehavior and developmental outcomes. *Early Human Development* 117: 32–38

Reygan F, Walton E & Osman R (2018) Assimilation and celebration? Discourses of difference and the application of critical diversity literacy in education. In E Walton & R Osman (Eds) *Teacher education for diversity: Conversations from the Global South.* London: Routledge

Schultz P & Shirindi L (2019) Reflections on the experiences and needs of grandparents caring for their grandchildren with a substance use disorder. *Social Work* 55(4): 359–378

Sibanda R (2021) 'I'm not a teacher': A case of (dys)functional parent–teacher partnerships in a South African township. *South African Journal of Education* 41(3): 1–13

Steenkamp U (2021) Cultural diversity and its influence on role players in a full-service school in Soshanguve. A wellness perspective. *European Journal of Education* 4(1): 23–39

Thwala S (2018) Experiences and coping strategies of children from child-headed households in Swaziland. *Journal of Education and Training Studies* 6(7): 150–158

UNESCO (United Nations Educational, Scientific and Cultural Organisation) (1994) *The Salamanca Statement and Framework for Action on Special Needs Education.* Paris: UNESCO Special Education, Division of Basic Education

Vincent C (1996) *Parents and teachers: Power and participation.* London: Falmer Press

Walton E (2018) Decolonising (through) inclusive education? *Educational Research for Social Change* 7(SPE): 31–44

Zulu PP, Aina AY & Bipath K (2022) Education and training experiences of early childhood care and education practitioners in rural and urban settings of Durban, South Africa. *South African Journal of Childhood Education* 12(1): 1–11

6 Learning From School Principals' Experiences of Parental and Caregiver Involvement at Primary Schools in Low-Income Communities

Bongani Nhlanhla Mkhize and Kerishka Govender

Introduction

In this chapter, we present and discuss some of the learnings gleaned from conversations we had with principals at three primary schools that serve low-income communities in Phoenix township, an impoverished area largely populated by Indians who share common cultural and socio-economic backgrounds. The schools selected for this study have large Indian populations. Indian culture depicts parenting as a communal task, shared by family members, relatives, and neighbours. Therefore, parental/caregiver involvement in the Indian community includes everyone who shares responsibility for children's education. From our conversations, we sought to understand the principals' experiences of parental/caregiver involvement in the selected schools. Furthermore, we sought to understand what the principals perceived as factors that inhibited involvement, and the strategies they used to promote and sustain parental/caregiver involvement in their schools. Such insights could be useful for school principals and policy-makers alike in understanding what works in promoting and sustaining parental involvement in schools situated in low-income communities. We begin the chapter by briefly discussing the concept of parental/caregiver involvement and the context of low-income communities. We then move on to discuss Epstein's model for parental/caregiver involvement as the chapter's conceptual framework. Thereafter, a discussion of the study's methodology follows. We present and discuss our findings through two broad themes and three sub-themes. The two themes are: (a) principals' experiences of parental/caregiver involvement in the schools in the low-income communities; and (b) strategies implemented by the principals to promote parental/caregiver involvement in the schools in low-income communities. The three sub-themes are: frequent communication with parents/caregivers; creating a welcoming and inviting environment for parents and caregivers; and building the leadership capacities of school governing body (SGB) members. We then conclude the chapter by drawing pathways for implementing an effective programme of parental/caregiver involvement in low-income communities in South Africa.

Parental/caregiver involvement in education

Parental/caregiver involvement in education can be conceptualised in a multitude of ways: it involves the active participation of parents/caregivers in all facets of their children's social, emotional, and academic development (Castro et al. 2015; Eden, Chisom & Adeniyi 2024; Ndwandwe 2023). Research by Vandergrift and Greene (1992) and Sheldon (2002) found that there are two segments that work conjointly to build the concept of parental/caregiver involvement. The first segment is the level of commitment that parents show to support their children's learning. This includes encouraging their children to perform to the best of their ability, and being sympathetic and understanding towards them. The other segment of parental/caregiver involvement refers to the levels of parental/caregiver activity and active participation displayed by the parents/caregivers. These activities are usually observable and include assisting children with their homework and reading to them (Hornby & Blackwell 2018; Vandergrift & Greene 1992). School-based parental involvement activities are things done by parents/caregivers to support the school and their children's learning in school. These types of activities include attending parents' meetings or volunteering time and services to the school. However, several researchers show that parental/caregiver involvement in South Africa is largely limited to attending parents' meetings and paying school fees (Ndwandwe 2023; Sibanda 2021). Research by Sibanda (2021) shows that while the majority of parents/caregivers in South Africa are committed to driving learning amongst their children, socio-economic complexities in their communities act as barriers to parental/caregiver involvement. This affects parental/caregiver involvement in many schools in South Africa.

In South Africa, the South African Schools Act (SA Schools Act) of 1996 is a national policy that recognises the importance of parental involvement in education. The SA Schools Act acknowledges parents as equal partners in their children's achievement of success, and seeks to empower and capacitate parents to participate in school governance (Manilal 2014; Ntuli & Mncube 2020). Additionally, the SA Schools Act seeks to forge a bond between the school and the parents, allowing the latter to feel a sense of ownership of, and accountability for, decision-making processes and giving them a sense of responsibility for their children's education (Chetty 2017).

The significance of parental/caregiver involvement in a child's education

The significance of parental/caregiver involvement in a child's education and in the school is acknowledged in the literature (see for example, Amponsah et al. 2018; Đurišić & Bunijevac 2017; Eden, Chisom & Adeniyi 2024; Ikechukwu 2017; Myende & Nhlumayo 2020; Ndwandwe 2023; Segoe & Bisschoff 2019). We note and support the notion highlighted by the literature that there is a positive correlation between a high level of parental/ caregiver involvement and improved academic achievement. Parents/ caregivers are one of the most significant influences on a child's education and development due to the critical role they play in the child's life (Đurišić & Bunijevac 2017; Magwa & Mugari 2017). Parental involvement supports and leads to educational growth and the social and emotional development of the child (Roy & Giraldo-Garcia 2018). Furthermore, research by Đurišić and Bunijevac (2017) and Segoe and Bisschoff (2019) shows that children whose parents/caregivers are actively involved in their education and perform home-based parental involvement activities such as assisting children with their homework, reading to them or hiring private tutors to assist them, often perform better academically and have better attitudes towards learning than children without parental support. Segoe and Bisschoff (2019) elaborate that children who receive high levels of support and encouragement from their parents are likely to manage stressful situations more efficiently and perform better academically. Drawing from the literature cited above, we argue that the opposite is true for children who receive low levels of support and encouragement from their parents/ caregivers.

In most cases, poor parental involvement is prevalent in schools situated in low-income communities despite the policies and guidelines that are in place to increase parental/caregiver involvement, particularly in South Africa (Msila 2009; Myende & Nhlumayo 2020; Ndwandwe 2023). The level of parental involvement experienced is often linked to a parent's socio-economic background. Research by Sibanda (2021) reveals that socio-economic complexities such as time and financial constraints, and low literacy levels experienced by parents in low-income communities, negatively impact the ways in which they can be involved in their children's learning. In addition, Poole (2017) notes that the parents often have a strained relationship with the education system, attributing this to negative experiences they retain from their schooling years and other contextual factors such as low literacy levels, language barriers, and time constraints. Principals have to deal with such factors that inhibit parental/caregiver involvement, and devise strategies to promote and sustain involvement in their schools.

Low-income communities in the context of the study

A low-income community is an area characterised by low-income households, poor infrastructure, a high unemployment rate, overpopulation, and inadequate availability of health facilities, transport, and educational resources (Cant 2017; Matshabane 2016). Parents/caregivers in these communities are generally less educated compared to those in high-income areas, and they usually do labouring work (Du Plessis & Mestry 2019). This type of time- and energy-consuming work finds parents/caregivers working for longer hours and more days, thereby depriving them of ample time to assist their children with homework activities (Du Plessis & Mestry 2019; Munje & Mncube 2018; Ndwandwe 2023). Their work schedules also sometimes prevent them from attending parent meetings and other school events. In addition, parents/caregivers from these communities often experiences low levels of literacy and language barriers (Ndwandwe 2023; Poole 2017).

The study took place in Phoenix township, which is characterised as a low-income community. Phoenix is one of many impoverished townships in KwaZulu-Natal that has a large Indian population; hence it is commonly referred to as an Indian township (Jagganath 2020). While Phoenix is rapidly developing, Reddy (2013) highlights the destitute state of those living there, stating that many families receive little to no weekly and/or monthly income due to the high unemployment rate. Like many low-income communities in South Africa, crime and violence are common occurrences in this community, with drug and alcohol abuse the main contributing factors to this behaviour (Machethe, Obioha & Mofokeng 2022).

The role of school principals in promoting parental/caregiver involvement

Principals play a critical role in promoting parental/caregiver involvement in schools as their leadership practices can work to either encourage involvement or impede it (Yulianti et al. 2020). While this is the case, evidence from the literature suggests that principals in low-income communities experience parental involvement differently from those in high- or middle-income communities (Batista 2009; Msila 2009; Myende & Nhlumayo 2020). This is because parents/caregivers in low-income communities often experience barriers to involvement that are unique to their communities, and this shapes principals' experiences of parental/caregiver involvement in these communities (Anastasiou & Papagianni 2020). This suggests that how the principals experience and promote parental involvement in their schools are unique to these contexts

(Cruse 2021; Yulianti et al. 2020). We therefore argue that the principals' experiences and attitudes have a crucial influence on the extent to which they improve parental/caregiver involvement.

Epstein's model of parental involvement

This study is underpinned by Epstein's model of parental involvement. Epstein (1995) proposed six types of parental involvement in education. These are parenting, communicating, volunteering, learning at home, decision-making, and community collaboration. Epstein's model draws attention to what schools can do to promote and enhance parental/caregiver involvement in education, ultimately leading to school improvement and improved learner outcomes (Epstein 1995).

For successful parenting and improved learner achievement to take place, parents/caregivers need to encourage learning and provide learners with a peaceful environment that is conducive to learning (Caño et al. 2016).

Communication is a crucial component in building trusting and lasting relationships (Gu 2017), and schools can increase parental/caregiver involvement by establishing a channel of two-way communication between the school and parents. This is an effective way to involve parents in their children's education within the school sphere (Epstein et al. 2018).

Volunteering is another route that gives parents/caregivers an opportunity to be involved in their children's schools (Matthews et al. 2017). With regards to volunteering, schools could create opportunities to encourage parents to volunteer at the schools, through which they could share their time, talents, and resources to support the school and/or its members (Epstein et al. 2018).

The fourth type of parental involvement identified in Epstein's (1995) model is learning at home. This type of parental/caregiver involvement is not a new phenomenon as parents are regarded as their child's first teachers. However, when it comes to supporting children's learning at home, the literature shows that parents and caregivers need guidance on how to do this (Caño et al. 2016; Đurišić & Bunijevac 2017; Epstein 1995; Epstein et al. 2018; Ramanlingam & Maniam 2020). Schools and teachers play a pivotal role in helping parents build the knowledge to guide learning at home. Therefore, teachers should take responsibility for providing this guidance to parents to ensure learner improvement and success (Đurišić & Bunijevac 2017; Epstein 1995; Epstein et al. 2018; Ramanlingam & Maniam 2020).

Decision-making is the fifth type of parental involvement according to Epstein's (1995) model. This type of parental/caregiver involvement is achieved by allowing parents to have a say in decision-making processes at the school (Epstein et al. 2018). Đurišić and Bunijevac (2017) assert that a shared decision-making process is an essential part of a successful home–school partnership. Goshin and Mertsalova (2018) note that decentralising decision-making powers, and providing parents and caregivers with the opportunity to be part of decision-making processes empowers parents, who, in turn, develop a sense of ownership of the school, which further influences their involvement.

The sixth and last type of parental involvement identified in Epstein's (1995) model is collaborating with the community. Epstein et al. (2018) state that schools should identify and integrate resources and services from the community. By seeking resources and services from community members, the school gradually becomes part of the community, which would then support the school's initiatives (Đurišić & Bunijevac 2017). The six types of parental involvement in education proposed by Epstein (1995) frame our data analysis and discussion.

There are positive and negative aspects of Epstein's model of parental involvement, especially for parents/caregivers in low-income communities. The positive aspects of the model include recognising that parents can play a significant role in children's education. Parents have a role to play at home, including supporting educational efforts and providing an environment where educational activities are supported and encouraged (Epstein 1995). The model also acknowledges communication as a bi-directional endeavour, and encourages schools to create a place for parental/caregiver ownership within the school through shared decision-making. Studies have found connections between the use of this model and increased learner achievement (Msila 2012; Munje & Mncube 2018). However, limitations do exist with this model. One limitation is that the model fails to consider differences in cultural norms by socio-economic status in order to use parental/caregiver involvement effectively as a strategy for learner success (Munje & Mncube 2018). The tight work schedules that some parents endure, and a lack of both transportation and childcare may prevent some parents/caregivers from attending school events or volunteering at the school (Du Plessis & Mestry 2019; Msila 2012; Munje & Mncube 2018; Page 2016; Sibanda 2021). Parents/caregivers from lower-income communities sometimes use less-structured approaches, including more informal conversations and unscheduled visits to schools (Msila 2012). However, schools and teachers often view these less-structured approaches as obtrusive (Munje & Mncube 2018; Sibanda 2021). Schools need to take into account the myriad cultural differences that can impact on how parents/caregivers demonstrate parental involvement.

Methodology

This study is located within an interpretive research paradigm and uses a qualitative research approach. We conducted an in-depth exploration of parental/caregiver involvement in a geographically bound context of the Phoenix township near Durban in KwaZulu-Natal. This small-scale study drew data from three principals at primary schools in Phoenix, with both purposive sampling and convenience sampling used in selecting the schools. We generated data primarily through the use of semi-structured interviews with the three school principals and through a document review. We used content analysis to analyse the data. We present and discuss the findings below, using two themes and three sub-themes that emerged from our data analysis. To protect the participants' identities and those of their schools, we used pseudonyms for them as follows: Mr Govender, a principal at Gandhi Primary School; Mr Singh, a principal at Caneside Primary School; and Mr Pillay, a principal at Sai Primary School.

Profiles of participants and their respective schools

Mr Govender

Mr Govender is the principal of Gandhi Primary School. He has been at the school for 25 years and has been the principal at the school for seven years. Prior to becoming the principal, he had held the position of head of department at the same school for 14 years. Gandhi Primary is a small, English-medium school in a tight-knit community. The school is classified as a quintile 4 school and has an enrolment of 323 learners. The staff consists of eight state-employed teachers, one SGB-employed teacher, two secretaries, and two school management team (SMT) members. The majority of learners at the school are from the surrounding area. 96% of the school's learner population is Indian and 4% is Black. The school reported that it had neither coloured nor white learners. The majority of the Black learners at the school do not live in the immediate community but rather in surrounding low-income areas.

Mr Pillay

Mr Pillay is the principal at Sai Primary School. He has been at the school for 33 years and has been the principal for six years. Prior to his appointment as principal, he had held the position of head of department at the school for seven years. Sai Primary School is both an English medium and a quintile 4 school. The school has an enrolment of 908 learners. The staff consists of 25 state-employed teachers, three SGB-employed teachers, two secretaries, and five SMT members. Learners at the school live in various areas in and around the Phoenix Township. The school has a large Indian population, which makes up 81% of its learner body. Only 0.5 % of the school's population are coloured learners while 18.5% are African learners. There are no white learners at the school. The school is well-furnished and well-established in the community.

Mr Singh

Mr Singh is the principal at Caneside Primary School. He has been at Caneside Primary for eight years and has been the principal for a year. Prior to his appointment as principal, he had held the position of head of department at the school for four years. Caneside Primary is a relatively small school, recognised for its successful Adult Basic Education and Training programme. It is an English-medium, quintile 5 school, with an enrolment of 319 learners. The staff consists of eight state-employed teachers, two SGB-employed teachers, two secretaries, and two SMT members. The vast majority of learners at the school reside in the Phoenix township, with just a handful of them coming from the surrounding townships. Indian learners account for 95% of the school's population, coloured learners for 0.3%, African learners for 4.7%, and there are no white learners.

Findings and discussion

We wanted to elicit information about the culture of parental/caregiver involvement in schools situated in the low-income community of Phoenix and how this culture, either positively or negatively, impacted the principals' experiences of parental involvement in their respective schools. The principals in this study were thus asked to describe the current culture of parental involvement in their schools. The participating principals shared both positive and negative experiences of parental involvement, ranging from issues of trauma and wellness to hope.

The 2021 "July riots" sparked a racial war between the Indians in the Phoenix township and its neighbouring Black townships (Desai 2022). Our findings show that the culture of parental/caregiver involvement experienced in the Phoenix township was negatively impacted by these events. Mr Govender explained that, sadly, his experience of parental involvement has been highly stressful and traumatic. He cited multiple traumatic encounters with parents ranging from angry parents to parents who seemed to be reluctant to be involved in the school despite efforts to involve them. This is what he said:

> Who are the parents? They are dead or in town working or looking for work. Some of these parents are our dropouts who are showing little interest in school matters. They drink a lot and shout at us when they pass the school

as you heard them shouting that we are wasting their children's time. Some of them are part of the people who vandalise the school. So, you ask them to support their children with homework or come to school, it's just ...

Mr Govender expressed anger when he spoke about parents and caregivers who expect the school to discipline their unruly children. He also mentioned cases of learners who bully and threaten teachers, and yet the parents side with the learners. It is apparent that Mr Govender is exasperated ('gatvol') with some of the parents, feels overwhelmed, helpless, and shocked, and has difficulty processing the experiences he has had with some parents.

Similarly, Mr Singh, the principal at Caneside Primary School, explained that the majority of parents/caregivers at his school are not cooperative and that only a few of them would go out of their way to involve themselves in the education of their children. He blamed this on the poor environmental context. He said:

> Basically, the environment here is too busy and cramped. There is noise pollution; drugs and alcohol abuse; sex abuse; violence; theft; battles for survival; illness; you name it. These children come to our schools. We mould them and the context de-moulds them. As for parental involvement, it is quite minimal in that we don't get full cooperation. There are a few parents that help and go out of their way to assist the school in every way that they can, but most of the parents are not actually involved in the school activities.

Both Mr Govender and Mr Singh are aware that the current culture of parental/caregiver involvement in their schools is poor. This situation is contrary to the assertion by Caño et al (2016) that parents need to encourage learning and provide learners with a peaceful environment that is conducive to learning. Mr Govender had previously made several attempts to improve the current culture of poor parental involvement at Gandhi Primary. However, none of his attempts seem to have been successful. When we asked him what he had done to improve this poor culture of parental involvement in his school, Mr Govender said:

> I have tried many things throughout the years to change this culture, but parents just don't seem to be interested. Whatever parental involvement we get at the school is welcomed but other than that, we just have to keep trying.

Mr Singh acknowledged the current culture of poor parental/caregiver involvement at Caneside Primary School, drawing attention to the impact of the July uprisings. He decided to focus on the parents who want to be involved in the school, rather than the parents who do not. Mr Singh said:

> There's very little parental involvement in this school. I know parents are busy, but they don't seem to be interested in their children. Before the July

> riots we had our Black parents coming in and showing willingness to be involved in their children's learning but since the riots these parents don't bother entering the Phoenix township, and when they are called to school, they treat us with disrespect as if we are the enemies of their children. I just choose to focus on the parents who care and create an open pathway for them to be involved in this school.

It emerges from the discussion above that the principals of Gandhi and Caneside Primary Schools have developed a negative attitude towards parental/caregiver involvement due to their experiences of the culture of parental involvement in their schools. However, despite their negative experiences, they are still trying to change the culture of parental involvement in their schools.

A different picture is seen at Sai Primary School, where the principal focused on positive experiences of parental/caregiver involvement. When asked about the culture of parental involvement at Sai Primary School, Mr Pillay proudly declared that there is a positive culture of parental involvement. He said:

> We have a positive culture of parental involvement at this school. The school encourages maximum participation and involvement by parents. We welcome parents being involved in the education of their children; we see that we cannot, as a school, successfully complete all educational tasks by ourselves, and acknowledge that as a school, we need to get the parents involved in the teaching and learning processes. Therefore, the school welcomes whatever involvement we can get from the parent. That's the attitude we have and share.

We note from the perspectives of the principals that their attitudes towards parental/caregiver involvement display a complex interplay between parents' responses to the principals' efforts to improve their involvement and how the principals, in turn, view the parents. The principals at Gandhi and Caneside Primary Schools display negative attitudes towards improving the culture of parental involvement, while Mr Pillay's overall positive attitude towards parental involvement seems to have played a significant role in shaping the positive culture of parental involvement at Sai Primary School. In this study, the differences in the principals' attitudes seem to account for the principals' varying experiences and strategies used to promote parental involvement. We discuss these strategies in the next section.

Strategies implemented by principals to promote parental involvement at primary schools in low-income communities

As previously highlighted, creating and managing parental/caregiver involvement in schools is part of a principal's responsibilities. We therefore asked the principals to share their views on, and experiences with, strategies they used to improve and sustain parental involvement in their schools. We discuss three main strategies used by the three principals. These are: frequent communication with parents; creating a welcoming and inviting environment for parents; and building the leadership capacities of SGB members. These are discussed as sub-themes below.

Frequent communication with parents/caregivers

All three principals emphasised the importance of frequently communicating with parents to encourage and maintain parental involvement in their schools. They all believe that frequent communication with parents lays the foundation for building and sustaining a successful home–school relationship. Mr Singh highlighted the importance of communication in building this relationship and mentioned the different communication methods that can be used to relay essential information. He said:

> Communication is the key to any successful relationship. We communicate with parents on a regular basis through our different channels of communication, whether it's the telephone, email, or WhatsApp. When certain important information comes in from the department, we try to make it available to our parents through the different modes of communication that we have.

Mr Pillay also highlighted the importance of effective communication, stating that constant communication is the main strategy used to promote and sustain parental involvement at Sai Primary. Mr Pillay explained thus:

> There must be proper communication between the school and the parents. And teachers must be fully involved in that. Parents want to know what's happening in school, what the child is up to, and what is the school doing towards the education of the child. And we need to communicate, we need to listen, and we need to welcome parents to be involved in the education of the child.

A review of staff meeting minutes supported the principals' claims as the importance of home–school communication was frequently highlighted in the minutes of staff meetings. The importance of home–school communication is also supported by Epstein (1995), who likewise asserts that frequent communication between the school and the parents/caregivers lays the foundation for successful collaboration between the home and the school. Sharing similar views to those expressed by the participants, research by Kuusimäki, Uusitalo-Malmivaara and Tirri (2019) found that communication is at the heart of any successful relationship, and further, that frequent communication leads to an enhancement of trust in the home–school relationship. This is also in line with the findings of Gu (2017), who states that strong home–school communication enhances trust within the home–school relationship, ultimately leading to enhanced collaboration between the home and school.

The findings from this study reveal that the principals recognise the value of communication in promoting parental/caregiver involvement. All three schools have recently adopted WhatsApp groups as their main platform of communication. WhatsApp group settings allow for one-way and two-way communication. In the one-way approach, only the group administrator can relay information to the group, whereas the two-way approach allows for a dialogue to be created between the administrators and the users. Gandhi and Caneside Primary Schools have adopted the one-way approach to communication to keep parents/caregivers abreast of educational issues or developments impacting the learners or the school. Sai Primary has adopted a two-way approach to communication, placing an emphasis on interactive home–school communication. Mr Pillay proudly declared:

> Recently, in our WhatsApp programme, we found that more parents are getting involved in the education of the child. Whenever parents need more clarity on their child's work or any school-related issues, parents message the teacher directly.

Although Mr Singh did not adopt the two-way approach to communication, he recognises the importance of two-way home-school communication and said:

> The WhatsApp group is a singular means of communication with parents. However, the school is looking into having an alternative method of communication between teacher and parent, so that parents will be able to engage with the educator in the future more freely.

Mr Govender justified his decision to adopt the one-way approach, stating that teaching is the main responsibility of the teacher, therefore, parents should not be able to freely communicate with teachers during the school day without making an appointment. Mr Govender explained:

> In our WhatsApp groups, only the class teacher can post on the WhatsApp groups. A staff decision was taken that even if parents message the teacher

privately, they will not respond. This is because, during teaching time, teachers should not drop their responsibilities to answer to parents. If parents want to talk to the teacher, they must follow the correct channels of communication and make an appointment to see or speak to the teacher.

Our findings reveal that each school has adopted a different approach to communication. It is noteworthy that in comparison to Gandhi and Caneside Primary Schools, Sai Primary School was found to have considerably more parental/caregiver involvement. This finding is in line with the work of Epstein (1995) and Zenda (2021), who highlight the importance of two-way communication to enhance and maintain parental involvement in education.

Welcoming environment as a strategy to promote parental/caregiver involvement

The principals participating in this study indicated that they have tried to create and sustain a warm and welcoming environment for parents and caregivers to encourage them to share their time, talents, and resources to support the school. Mr Pillay explains the approach of Sai Primary School:

> We make sure that we maintain a welcoming environment towards parents in this school. The teaching staff and the administrative staff in the school have been trained on how to approach parents, how to speak to parents, and to be helpful. The whole goal is to make sure parents feel comfortable enough to be part of the school.

Similarly, Mr Singh indicated that he has created an environment that welcomes parents'/caregivers' thoughts and complaints to make them feel that they are valued members of the school community and their children's educational journey. Mr Singh explained that they have tried their best to make parents feel welcomed at the school and create a sense of belonging.

According to Mr Singh, the school involves parents/caregivers in decision-making, welcomes any suggestions, and addresses complaints from parents.

The findings from this study indicate that the principals regard the creation and maintenance of a welcoming environment towards parents/caregivers as an essential tool to encourage and sustain involvement. This finding is consistent with Alinsunurin (2020), who states that creating an inviting environment for parents must be an essential objective for all public-school principals. Further, Đurišić and Bunijevac (2017) support and advocate for the creation of a welcoming environment to encourage and sustain parental involvement. The authors highlight that schools can overcome the barrier of poor parental involvement by creating a welcoming environment, one that is built on mutual respect. Alinsunurin (2020) adds that when parents feel welcomed to be part of a school, they begin to take ownership of the school,

Building leadership capacities of SGB members

The principals emphasised the notion of building the leadership capacities of SGB members as another strategy that assists them to keep parents/caregivers motivated and wanting to be part of the school. Mr Singh mentioned that the parent component makes up the majority of his school's SGB members, and it is therefore crucial for these members to develop leadership capacities to enable them to draw on the support of other parents. He said:

> The SA Schools Act stipulates that the majority of the SGB members should be the parents. Given our context, one has to build capacity of those parents that you get. Of course, some do have leadership capacities. I am not saying they are blank. But we take it upon us to workshop them on issues such as decision-making, communication, and working for and with the community. We need to work on the common ground. In this way, the SGB becomes the front of the school when talking with other parents.

Mr Singh took it upon himself to build the leadership capacity of the SGB members to establish and create a culture rooted in shared norms, values, and beliefs.

Similarly, Mr Pillay explained that building the leadership capacity of SGB members enabled him to build the authority to tap into the abilities of stakeholders to advance parental involvement in his school. Mr Pillay explained that the SGB was performing well to advance the interests of the school and attributed this to the leadership-building workshop held to enhance the capacities of the SGB.

Evident from this discussion is that the principals are committed to building a strong and sustainable stakeholder base that can drive organisational efforts, as noted by Pless and Maak (2011), and to create synergy between the school and the community (Myende 2018) despite their experiences of the difficulties of parental involvement and the reservations expressed. The three principals are still trying to break the shackles of their schools' low-income environments and empower SGB members to be practical agents of democratic school governance (Mfeka, Makhasane & Chikoko 2018).

Discussion about lessons learned

Our analysis of the principals' experiences of parental/caregiver involvement reveals issues of trauma, wellness, hope, and resilience. For instance, Mr Govender and Mr Singh's experiences of parental involvement left them with a bitter taste. Their negative experiences stemmed from perceived parental interference in their schools, poor parental attitudes, and the parents' lack of trust in the schools. Such negative experiences have tended to influence their attitudes towards parental involvement. While the two principals have been negatively affected by the parents' attitudes and behaviours, the third principal had a positive experience of parental involvement.

While the three principals showed different attitudes towards parental/caregiver involvement, they all showed some resilience in continuing to try to promote and sustain parental involvement in their schools. The findings of this study show that the principals' efforts to promote parental involvement were limited to communication, creating a welcoming environment, and building the leadership capacity of the SGB members. While the three communication strategies align with Epstein's model of parental involvement, the difference between them is that two principals opted for one-way communication, whereas one opted for two-way communication with parents. Two-way communication is welcoming for parents and seemed to be working well as it provides the two parties with a deeper understanding of mutual expectations and children's needs. This enables both parties to assist children effectively, and to establish a basis of cooperation (Epstein & Sanders 2006). Two-way communication builds parents' interest in investing their time and resources and, as Mr Pillay highlighted, the parents participate more in decision-making involving their children. This is a plus for parents in low-income communities who would otherwise feel disconnected from schools. Decentralising decision-making powers and providing parents with the opportunity to be part of decision-making processes empowers them, enabling them to develop a sense of ownership of the school (Goshin & Mertsalova 2018).

Further to effective communication, the three principals highlighted that they created a welcoming environment to encourage parental/caregiver involvement. A welcoming environment paves the way for volunteering, participation in decision-making and community collaboration (Epstein et al. 2018).

Finally, building the leadership capacity of SGB members empowered the SGB parent-members to be actively involved in school affairs, including becoming practical agents that create synergy between the school and the community. Capacitated SGB members played a crucial role in getting parents/caregivers involved in the affairs of the school. It is evident though that Sai Primary School was more active in this regard than Caneside and Gandhi primary schools, with Sai Primary School seeming to be more successful at encouraging parental involvement than at the other two schools.

Conclusion

While Epstein's (1995) model of parental involvement may not entirely align with the unique challenges of the South African context, adapting it serves as a valuable framework for enhancing parental/caregiver engagement in primary schools in low-income communities. The finding of this study is that the principals were able to adapt their leadership practices to involve and engage with parents according to the demands of their current realities. The use of current technology (WhatsApp) has proven to be effective and efficient in bi-directional communication with parents. Further, creating a welcoming environment and building the leadership capacity of the SGB members was helpful in promoting parental/caregiver involvement in the communities served by the schools. We note as a sign of hope that the principals were able to be creative and responsive to the current situations facing their schools, and thrive despite the apathy of many of the parents in their respective communities. This study contributes to the body of knowledge by revealing the reality of parental/caregiver involvement in low-income communities and the leadership roles of school principals in promoting parents' and caregivers' involvement.

References

Alinsunurin J (2020) School learning climate in the lens of parental involvement and school leadership: Lessons for inclusiveness among public schools. *Smart Learning Environments* 7(1): 1–23

Amponsah MO, Milledzi EY, Ampofo ET & Gyambrah M (2018) Relationship between parental involvement and academic performance of senior high school students: The case of Ashanti Mampong Municipality of Ghana. *American Journal of Educational Research* 6(1): 1–8

Anastasiou S & Papagianni A (2020) Parents', teachers', and principals' views on parental involvement in secondary education schools in Greece. *Education Sciences* 6(1): 69. Accessed July 2023, https://doi.org/10.3390/educsci10030069

Batista H (2009). Principal perspectives toward parental involvement in Pennsylvania public high schools. Doctoral dissertation, Duquesne University

Caño KJ, Cape MG, Cardosa JM, Miot C, Pitogo GR, Quinio CM & Merin J (2016) Parental involvement on pupils' performance: Epstein's framework. *The Online Journal of New Horizons in Education* 6(4): 143–150

Cant MC (2017) The availability of infrastructure in townships: Is there hope for township businesses? *International Review of Management and Marketing* 7(4): 108–115

Castro M, Expósito-Casas E, López-Martín E, Lizasoain L, Navarro-Asencio E & Gaviria JL (2015) Parental involvement on student academic achievement: A meta-analysis. *Educational Research Review* 14: 33–46

Chetty T (2017) Invaluable allies? Case study of promoting effective parent–teacher relationships in three primary schools in the Phoenix-West Circuit. MEd thesis, University of KwaZulu-Natal

Cruse AV (2021) An analysis of the relationship between school culture and teachers' professional learning. Doctoral dissertation, Youngstown State University

Desai A (2022) Geographies of racial capitalism: The 2021 July riots in South Africa. *Ethnic and Racial Studies* 46(16): 3542–3561. Accessed July 2023, https://www.tandfonline.com/doi/full/10.1080/01419870.2022.2131452

Du Plessis P & Mestry R (2019) Teachers for rural schools: A challenge for South Africa. *South African Journal of Education* 39(1): S1–S9. Accessed July 2023, https://doi.org/10.15700/saje.v39ns1a1774

Đurišić M & Bunijevac M (2017) Parental involvement as an important factor for successful education. *Center for Educational Policy Studies Journal* 7(3): 137–153

Eden CA, Chisom ON & Adeniyi IS (2024). Integrating AI in education: Opportunities, challenges, and ethical considerations. *Magna Scientia Advanced Research and Reviews* 10(2): 006–013

Epstein JL (1995) School/family/community partnerships. *Phi Delta Kappan* 76(9): 701–712

Epstein JL & Sanders MG (2006) Prospects for change: Preparing educators for school, family, and community partnerships. *Peabody Journal of Education* 81(2): 81–120

Epstein JL, Sanders MG, Sheldon SB, Simon BS, Salinas KC, Jansorn NR & Williams KJ (2018) *School, family, and community partnerships: Your handbook for action.* Thousand Oaks: Corwin Press

Goshin M & Mertsalova T (2018) Types of parental involvement in education, socio-economic status of the family, and students' academic results. *Theoretical and Applied Research* 3(1): 68–90

Gu L (2017) Using school websites for home–school communication and parental involvement? *Nordic Journal of Studies in Educational Policy* 3(2): 133–143

Hornby G & Blackwell I (2018) Barriers to parental involvement in education: An update. *Educational Review* 70(1): 109–119

Ikechukwu O (2017) Exploring teachers' perceptions of parental involvement via the capability approach: A case of a low-income school community. MEd dissertation, University of the Western Cape

Jagganath G (2020) Exploring township Youth Perceptions: Vulnerable girls and their caregivers in Chatsworth, Durban. *The Oriental Anthropologist* 20(2): 292–302

Kuusimäki AM, Uusitalo-Malmivaara L & Tirri K (2019) Parents' and teachers' views on digital communication in Finland. *Education Research International* 2019: 1–7. Accessed July 2023, https://doi.org/10.1155/2019/8236786

Machethe P, Obioha E & Mofokeng J (2022) Community-based initiatives in preventing and combatting drug abuse in a South African township. *International Journal of Research in Business and Social Science* 11(1): 209–220

Magwa S & Mugari S (2017) Factors affecting parental involvement in the schooling of children. *International Journal of Academic Research and Reflection* 5(1): 74–81

Manilal R (2014) Parental involvement in education: A comparison between a privileged and under-privileged school. MEd dissertation, University of KwaZulu-Natal

Matshabane OP (2016) Exploring the influence of role models on the career development process of school-going adolescents from a low-income community in South Africa. MA dissertation, Stellenbosch University

Matthews A, McPherson-Berg SL, Quinton A, Rotunda RS & Morote ES (2017) The school–parent relationship across different income levels. *Journal for Leadership and Instruction* 16(1): 15–21

Mfeka N, Makhasane SD & Chikoko V (2018) School governance that works in deprived primary schools. In V Chikoko (Ed.) *Leadership that works in deprived school contexts of South Africa.* New York: Nova Science Publishers

Msila V (2009) School choice and intra-township migration: Black parents scrambling for quality education in South Africa. *Journal of Education* 46(1): 81–98

Msila VT (2012) Black parental involvement in South African rural schools: Will parents ever help in enhancing effective school management? *Journal of Educational and Social Research* 2(2): 303–313

Munje PN & Mncube V (2018) The lack of parent involvement as hindrance in selected public primary schools in South Africa: The voices of educators. *Perspectives in Education* 36(1): 80–93

Myende P (2018) Leadership for school–community partnership: A school principal's experience in a deprived context. In V Chikoko (Ed.) *Leadership that works in deprived school contexts of South Africa.* New York: Nova Science Publishers

Myende PE & Nhlumayo BS (2020) Enhancing parent–teacher collaboration in rural schools: Parents' voices and implications for schools. *International Journal of Leadership in Education* 25(3): 490–514

Ndwandwe ND (2023) Parental involvement and academic achievement: Voices of role players in secondary schools in Mpumalanga, South Africa. *Research in Social Sciences and Technology* 8(4): 237–256

Ntuli BA & Mncube DW (2020) Exploratory study of stakeholders' perspectives of parental involvement in school governance. *Gender & Behaviour* 18(3): 15972–15982

Page RD (2016) The role that parents play in their children's academic progress at a previously disadvantaged primary school in Cape Town. MEd thesis, University of the Western Cape

Pless NM & Maak T (2011) Responsible leadership: Pathways to the future. *Journal of Business Ethics* 98(S1): 3–13

Poole SM (2017) Developing relationships with school customers: The role of market orientation. *International Journal of Educational Management* 31(7): 1054–1068

Ramanlingam S & Maniam M (2020) Teachers' perspective on the importance of parents' roles in students' academic achievement using school and family partnership model (Epstein): A qualitative study. *Universal Journal of Educational Research* 8(8): 3346–3354

Reddy M (2013) An exploration into the dynamics of violence in two schools in Phoenix township, KwaZulu-Natal. MEd dissertation, University of KwaZulu-Natal

Roy M & Giraldo-García R (2018) The role of parental involvement and social/emotional skills in academic achievement: Global perspectives. *School Community Journal* 28(2): 29–46

Segoe BA & Bisschoff T (2019) Parental involvement as part of curriculum reform in South African schools: Does it contribute to quality education? *Africa Education Review* 16(6): 165-182

Sheldon SB (2002) Parents' social networks and beliefs as predictors of parent involvement. *The Elementary School Journal* 102(4): 301–316

Sibanda R (2021) 'I'm not a teacher': A case of (dys) functional parent–teacher partnerships in a South African township. *South African Journal of Education* 41(3): 1–13. Accessed July 2023, https://doi.org/10.15700/saje.v41n3a1812

Vandergrift J & Greene A (1992) Rethinking parent involvement. *Educational Leadership* 50(1): 57–75

Yulianti K, Denessen E, Droop M & Veerman GJ (2020) School efforts to promote parental involvement: The contributions of school leaders and teachers. *Educational Studies* 48(1): 98–113

Zenda R (2021) Implementing a parental involvement policy to enhance Physical Sciences learner's academic achievement in rural secondary schools. *Educational Research for Policy and Practice* 20: 125–143

7 What's Blame Got to Do With It?[*] Teacher and Parent Blame Narratives in South African Primary Schools

Andrew Paterson, Melanie Ehren, and Zaahedah Vally

Introduction

This chapter explores blame and blaming between teachers and parents/caregivers, an issue that also typically involves the wider school community, including principals, governing bodies, and learners. We analyse how blame is assigned in home–school relations, exacerbating unproductive relationships in schools, and creating adversarial governance and educational interactions between various stakeholders in the surrounding community.

'[P]arents are important mediators between the school and the learners, with an undeniable impact on performance', according to Munje and Mncube (2018: 88–89). In that context, the specific aim of this chapter is to explore the role and function of blame in relationships between parents/caregivers and teachers in primary schools, based on interviews of teachers and senior staff drawn from case studies of four schools in the province of Gauteng, South Africa.

In schools where blame and blaming were present, the intention was to understand how blame works. Insights into how blame operates can then be used to replace problematic narratives with forms of collaboration and shared responsibility for learners' education.

The analysis explored blame dynamics between teachers, parents/caregivers, and other school community role players through the eyes of educators. In each scenario, the interests of the blamer and blamed were deconstructed, to illustrate how feedback relationships between parents/caregivers and teachers can contribute to poor learner achievement.

Blame can be expressed explicitly or through inference, usually with a corrosive effect on collaborative parent–teacher and school relationships that promote learner achievement. Blame and blaming contribute to a cycle

---

[*] The title of this chapter paraphrases the title of a famous song recorded by Tina Turner, 'What's love got to do with it?' from her 1984 album, Private Dancer.

of distrust and limited accountability in the school community, operating through feedback loops. We propose that more attention needs to be paid to how responsibility – for the "failure of schools", the "failure of teachers", or the "failure of parents" to meet the needs of learners – is understood.

Blame and blaming in schools

International research shows that the phenomenon of mutual blaming in school communities is quite common. Research in New Zealand investigated parent, teacher, and learner beliefs regarding responsibility for student learning and participants' attribution of responsibility for student failure. All three groups deferred blame away from themselves (Peterson et al. 2011).

In her North American study, Chisley found that blame can be exchanged quite freely: 'Teachers easily blame parents and, likewise, parents blame the teachers' (2014: 66). According to that study, a key contributing factor was limited understanding between participants: 'This finding showed how blame shifts from one stakeholder to the other due to a lack of understanding of the expected roles of all concerned with the education of the children' (Chisley 2014: 54). The research identified mutual lack of understanding as the problem, but the reasons behind the "lack of understanding" or what "understanding" might mean in these situations remained unclear.

At the intersection of blame and policy-making, Pawlewicz (2022) argues that political interests impacted on the direction of school reform in the United States through blame of teachers. This shows how blame is a powerful weapon that can influence national debates about the direction of public education.

In South Africa, the public discourse of blame is widely visible, for example, in relation to government deflecting blame[1] for low national levels of reading capacity among primary school learners based on the international comparative Progress in International Reading Literacy Study.[2]

Teachers are often blamed for these poor results. Three contrasting interpretations of teacher culpability for their role in low performance are expressed in Table 7.1. The first casts teachers as unaccountable, the second casts teachers as victims of poor education system governance, and the third sees them as blameless sufferers of learner unwillingness to study. Further groups attracting blame are identifiable from the examples. These include government, or more specifically, the department responsible for school education, teacher unions, and (again) the learners. These examples usefully reflect how positions within a blame discourse can be expressed in emotive and emotionally charged language. Through metaphor and judgmental claims, teachers are viewed as "helpless passengers" and learners are presented as "lazy" with a "hatred" for reading.

Table 7.1 *Perspectives of teacher accountability*

Unaccountable	Powerless and poorly prepared	Blame the learners
'Teachers are steering the education system dangerously off course. Not only can't they teach, they don't want to and are being used as cannon fodder by politically driven unions.'	'Teachers are merely helpless passengers – strapped in the backseat alongside their pupils, powerless to stop the car.' 'They have been poorly trained, thrown into overcrowded classrooms with under-prepared pupils.'	Teachers blame learners for poor learning outcomes: 'Our teachers struggle to get the learners to read. On the whole, they are lazy and hate reading, and they hate comprehending.'

Source: DGMT (2018: 9, 24)

While teachers are blamed for poor results, parents/caregivers are regularly blamed for learner misbehaviour at school[3] and for rising levels of teenage pregnancy.[4] In response to acts of student disruptions and violence in schools in 2018, the Federation of Governing Bodies of South African Schools directed blame for student indiscipline on the parents:

> Parents … have not taken responsibility for the upbringing of their children. (In) by far the majority of cases, … the ill behaviour of a child can be directly linked to problems at home.[5]

This example can be interpreted as an attempt by SGBs to avoid responsibility for their role. As will be discussed below, blame for the most part masquerades as an explanation for a complex set of problems in a social or organisational environment.

Particularly in a place like South Africa, the danger is that blaming can go beyond attributing responsibility to an individual and slip into attributing characteristics to the group that is blamed. In South Africa, Sibanda (2021) observes how 'educators attribute low (learner) achievement to parental despondence, whereas parents (caregivers) attribute it to teacher incapability. The parents' and teachers' "blame game" suggests a dysfunctional teacher–parent partnership' (2021: 9). Sibanda argues that when either party resorts to blame, this implies that a dysfunctional relationship exists.

In their research survey on Black parental involvement in a sample of schools, Singh, Mbokodi and Msila (2004) reported that 'seventy-five per cent of the teachers stated specifically that parents' ignorance was to be blamed for the schools' lack of success. The teachers believed that the parents were not doing their share of the work' (2004: 304). The authors observed that, come examination season, blame of teachers intensifies: 'When the learners fail, the focus is on teachers who are usually blamed for the poor results' (2004: 306). This scenario reveals how blame-shifting occurs in situations where groups share responsibility for people, such as parents and teachers sharing responsibility for children. A second feature of this example is teachers' attribution of 'ignorance' to parents as an explanation for the lack of success of the school. This totalising explanation, generalised to all parents, is presented as a single explanation for a complex problem and begs further enquiry into the interplay between blame and accountability. A teacher who is blaming others – such as parents – is at the same time distracting attention from their own contribution to the problem (Mitchell 1998).

Blame and blaming does not just feature in home–teacher relations, or in how teachers assign responsibility for low student performance: it also features in wider relationships within South Africa's education system. In the South African Council for Educators' handbook on teacher rights and responsibilities for example, a scenario describes a hypothetical crisis of low accountability and high blame across the system:

> Scenario 85: There is lack of accountability. The department blames teachers, teachers blame leadership and management, management blames the department, and, in the end, in the whole system, nobody is held accountable.

> Recommendation: Strictly follow the policies and protocol. (South African Council for Educators 2020: 80)

The handbook therefore offers generic guidance, with little practical advice for problem-solving. It suggests that following the protocol will at least make the reader blameless – even if nothing is improved and understanding is not deepened. This scenario illustrates how the mechanisms of blame operate within different levels of the system, becoming entrenched in key texts that have substantial influence on teacher practice. There is clearly a need to understand how blame at the school level is generated through a combination of individual, social, organisational, and situational factors.

This chapter aims to unpack these different levels to make sense of blame and blaming at schools, with each school forming an institutional and analytic unit within which the relationships, respective responsibilities, and patterns of interaction between teachers and parents/caregivers are enacted. Our focus is the school level, but this clearly relates to national priorities, challenges, and educational relations. At the national level, the pace and scale of participation in online blaming has increased, and we observe rising occurrences of blaming on social media platforms. The immediacy of information, coupled with the possibility of bias or incomplete information, is potentially harmful, since it can feed polarisation of blame within school communities or parent groups. Insights into participants' motives, power relationships, assumptions, and blind spots can be developed through analysis of blame exchanges (Conradie 2020; Hansson 2018a; Hansson 2018b).

However, our focus on the interactions of parents/caregivers and teachers at an individual school level holds the potential to illuminate ways in which both groups can jointly bear immediate responsibility for academic improvement and pastoral care of learners, alongside school management and the SGB.

Understanding blame at four schools in Gauteng

The analysis in this chapter is based on interviews with teachers and senior staff drawn from case studies of four schools in the province of Gauteng, South Africa. These educators were part of a research project focused on the relationship between trust, capacity, and accountability in primary schools, and the implications for improving learner achievement (Ehren, Paterson & Baxter 2020a; Ehren, Paterson & Baxter 2020b; Ehren & Baxter 2021; Baxter & Ehren 2023).

The particular aim of this chapter is to investigate and advance our understanding of the forms of blame, the intentions of blame, the impact of blame on thinking, and the outcomes of blame, using evidence drawn from interviews in schools. This focus required attention to how blame or blaming statements could be differentiated from non-blame. When a person unequivocally blames another party orally or in written communication and/or uses the word 'blame', this provides concrete evidence of their intention. In a substantial proportion of cases, blame statements were quite easily recognisable, but this was not always straightforward.

Interviewers did not explicitly focus on blame, and the interview schedules did not make any reference to blame or blaming, so respondents were not alerted through any reference to blame or blaming.

A scan of the fieldwork data in each of the four case-study schools revealed some evidence of blaming. There was evidence of "blame narratives", implying that low levels of blame existed in all four schools. Based on this framing, we identified and analysed interactions between teachers and parents/caregivers involving blame narratives. We also identified and analysed parent–teacher interactions that had blaming implications. These were scenarios where blame emerged. This accorded with our assessment that none of the schools presented with high levels of conflict between the school or teachers and parents.

The challenge in identifying the presence of blame is to be able to distinguish a blame statement from a neutral observation about a person, group or other subject. This is important because it is necessary to be alert for instances where blaming may involve gender, racial, social class or other assumptions, which highlights the identity of the blamer and of the blamed. This is because understanding the difference between blaming and a "neutral observation" depends on how language is used, the social context, communication style, and also the apparent intent of the person making the statement.

An assessment of a phrase or sentence for blame needs to be based on criteria that can provide consistency. To this end, we developed the following assertion: *If a person formulates a statement that is objective, neutral, and seeks to provide an unbiased assessment of a situation without seeking to blame or criticise, then it may be interpreted as not blaming.*

We added a question: *Has the person understood* the facts, shown insight into the dynamics of a situation, reflected with empathy (without taking sides), and displayed fairness?*

However, blame is not always expressed so directly, so blame can be implied in a variety of ways that makes interpretation of what constitutes blame an interpretive challenge. Individuals may employ different non-vocal signals or language constructions to imply blame. Some of these are identified in Table 7.2.

For this reason, we developed criteria as a guide to assist in identifying blame or blaming statements. The criteria are presented in tabular form in Table 7.2.

---

* This ancillary question uses the definition of 'understand' as provided by the *Cambridge English Dictionary*. Accessed May 2025, https://dictionary.cambridge.org/dictionary/english/understand.

Table 7.2 *Identifying statements of, or text implying, blame or non-blame*

Reference points	Non-blaming identifiers	Blaming identifiers
Purpose/intention	• solution orientation • understanding orientation	• to assign fault • to attribute responsibility
Framing of language	• explicitly • indirectly by implications/ allusion	• phrases that directly attribute fault • phrases that imply negative intentions
Point of view	• objective	• subjective
Use of evidence	• concrete evidence or verifiable	• assumptions
Tone	• withholds judgement	• accusatory use of emotion
Transparency	• clarity	• ambiguity
Assigning blame	• neutral description of claim	• observable behaviour
Way forward	• engagement	• rules out dialogue
Social context	• in moderated, facilitative or restorative settings	• views given in private, in a public gathering, in an interview
Use of rhetoric	• open communication	• indirect • innuendo • insinuation
Guilt assignation	• neutral framing, withholds judgement	• guilty by implication
Use of evidence	• verifiable events	• subjective opinions • hearsay
Balance	• comparing evidence	• selection of evidence
Representation	• multiple causality	• simplistic generalisation

From a research perspective, this rubric provided a point of reference for assessing the nuances of meaning in the interview transcripts.

Analysis of selected themes related to blame in schools

We analysed a handful of themes that we identified as related to "blame narratives" or blame-driven interactions. Our aim was to deconstruct these situations in order to bring attention to how educators openly or inadvertently revealed biases in their thinking that fed into a narrative of implied blame or explicit blame.

As indicated earlier, the vignettes below are drawn from an interview schedule that concentrated on trust and accountability, and was not conceived to explicitly address blame. Also, the study was limited to in-school professional accountability of teachers related to learner achievement. A future study might give prominence to hearing parent/caregiver voices.

Low levels of parent/caregiver education

Parents' and caregivers' levels of education were regularly identified by teachers as a problem:

> Most of our parents, they are unlearnt, so they find it difficult to assist the children at home. (Teacher 1, School 3)

> Many parents have – according to the teachers – very little education themselves, so are either not interested or are scared to come to school and talk to teachers about their child's progress. (Teacher 2, School 3)

In the first teacher statement, the fact of some parents having limited education is associated with low capacity to support their children's academic learning. The second statement, without evidence, associates limited parent education with an attitudinal characteristic of being 'not interested'. However, the pattern is similar: to generalise the characteristics of parents with low education in such a way that responsibility and blame vests in them and that the obligation of the school is overlooked.

Parents/caregivers 'scared' to attend meetings at school

The idea of parents/caregivers being "scared" was expressed in several interviews, without further elaboration by the teacher. This may be grounded in an assumption that teachers are not responsible for finding out or not expected to consider whether they themselves may have contributed to these "fears":

> Some [parents] are scared to come here … you know this thing of saying, 'I can't talk with … Teacher X?' It's quite sad. There's not too much relationship between the teachers and the parents, though we are trying. (SGB member, School 3)

Referring to parents/caregivers as scared "because that's how they are" becomes a barrier to teachers' awareness and to understanding their own role. In the presence of a teacher, a parent may fear judgement, expectations, conflict or other responses linked to unequal power relations that lead to lack of parent engagement, and perceptions of the teacher as unapproachable or uncaring. This, in turn, can lead to frustration and misunderstandings that are grounds for unproductive relationships and the emergence of mutual blame.

Uncaring parents/caregivers

Parents/caregivers were regularly described simply as "uncaring":

> What he disliked about his job was uncaring parents. (Principal, School 4)

> From time to time, we will try and assist where we can: get in touch with [the
> government department of] Social Development, phone NGOs to get social
> workers to come to school. We had that – it was working for two, three years,
> then they stopped because they were short-staffed, and I accept them being
> short-staffed. (Teacher, School 4)

The same principal quoted above gave examples of learners arriving late at
school without apparent reason; learners being late because they were made
responsible for taking younger siblings to crèche first; learners' homework
not having been done because they had tasks to complete at home. Parents
claimed to be too busy and delegated these responsibilities to their older
children. The principal interpreted these cases as indicating lack of parental
care for their children's schooling.

In the same school, teacher concerns about low parental involvement
reflected deeper problems of poverty and joblessness in the society and
economy, impacting on households. Teachers recounted difficulties with
sourcing social workers to assist, revealing the shortage of public social and
welfare services, in the absence of which teachers are pressurised in and out
of the classroom with pastoral needs. In this case, taking a broader view
outside of the school is necessary for understanding systemic challenges
that teachers encounter in their classrooms.

Even parents/caregivers living close to the school were often said not to care:

> And the situation there was quite pathetic, and even the parents who were
> living closer to the school, even if you invited them to come, they would not
> come. (Teacher who is a teacher union representative, School 1)

The quotation above reveals that parent involvement does not increase
with proximity to schools, meaning that parents/caregivers who live close
to schools may be equally disinclined to participate as those living further
from schools, for reasons other than distance to the school.

The perceived lack of care may lead to frustration when parents and
teachers do interact:

> We have what is called open days every term, where all parents are called,
> and when we give out reports, especially so that teachers are going to sit
> with parents and say: 'Now let's talk. You haven't been coming. I have been
> calling you. Your child is not doing well in this subject. What is the problem?'
> (Teacher, School 1)

The account above shows how a teacher describes interactions with parents,
characterised by legitimate frustration. However, it leads to the teacher
speaking from a position of authority, using language that is accusatory
and interrogative. It reflected assumptions that the problem or "blame"

lies with the parents/caregivers and it failed to offer open discussion on an "open day" intended to promote shared responsibility. This snippet of conversation does not indicate admission from the side of the teacher that the school may share responsibility for why the parents had struggled to attend. In a similar vein, a circuit manager who was interviewed expressed regret about occasions earlier in their career when they called parents to meetings and expressed blame, rather than trying to convince them to act differently. These examples provide insight into how hierarchies in the schooling system and power dynamics impact negatively on collaboration.

Parents/caregivers deny responsibility

Educators said that parents and caregivers did not necessarily appreciate the full extent of their responsibilities and blamed teachers for poor discipline of their children:

> Some others [parents], they will say [to their child]: 'I won't waste my time to go to school. I send you there to get educated, so why are they [the teachers] looking for me?' (SGB member, School 3)

> [Learners are] growing up without discipline at home, so they come to school, and parents think that the teachers should be able to educate and teach them discipline. (SGB member, School 1)

The statements above from SGB members in different schools represented opinions that were also shared by teachers, who reported that some parents knowingly distanced themselves from their responsibilities. The scenario generated blame-shifting, highlighting how it is necessary to make sense of each set of unique school-level circumstances and the importance for local stakeholders to be involved in addressing the challenges together.

Parent/caregiver estrangement from the SGB destabilises governance

There were indications that parents and caregivers did not trust school governing bodies:

> If they see a new car, [parents say] 'You bought a car with our money. You are SGB. We know how things they are.' You know how the parents they are. Yes, you have to say that because they say [to the SGB], 'You are eating our money, and what'. (Teacher, School 3)

This scenario indicated parental/caregiver lack of trust in the SGB, with suspicions about finances, control, or allocation of funds for which the SGB is responsible. Many schools service the needs of low-income and impoverished communities and are declared no fee-paying schools. Yet parents still contribute financially if requested by the SGB to fund academic, sporting, and cultural outings for learners. Some schools request support when the government subsidy for consumables (such as photocopying paper) runs out during the year.

Suspicions between the SGB and parents over governance of finances diminished parental trust in the credibility and good faith of the SGB to preside over conditions of teaching and learning at the school. An SGB member explained that misuse of funding is a common point of contention in many schools, but accusations of financial impropriety can also be used (without evidence) to destabilise the SGB.

The role of trust between parents/caregivers and teachers

Teacher beliefs that parents did not care, were uneducated, and could not support the school with homework led to clear distrust from parents, something which educators realised:

> There are some [parents] who really, just a few, some who really trust teachers, who really come if they've got a problem, but they are minimal. (Teacher, School 3)

> Parents experiencing problems with their children in the school tended to go to the principal rather than to the teacher concerned, despite it being school policy to approach the teacher first. (Deputy principal, School 4)

The first quotation implies that a majority of parents/caregivers had low trust in teachers, may have low confidence in the school's capacity or willingness to work with them on jointly improving schooling outcomes, or displace responsibility from themselves onto the school. Educators said that parents regularly assumed teachers held negative intentions, communicated antagonistically, and refused to engage in mutual problem-solving.

The second quotation shows that teachers were unhappy about parents/ caregivers commonly bypassing the standard rule of engagement that requires parents to raise a matter directly with the teacher concerned. Instead, parents would commonly first approach the principal, which teachers considered a sign of disrespect.

Similarly, parents/caregivers would raise matters relating to their individual children publicly at school meetings instead of broaching them in private. Although, in some cases, parents were unaware of the protocols, a picture emerges of parents strategically choosing their point of contact, which could signify a lack of trust, a need to resolve an outstanding issue, or to avoid a one-to-one engagement with teachers.

Dealing with the culture of blame: two instances of school responsiveness

In this final section of analysis we present two strategies used by schools to deal with parent/caregiver involvement and blame. While both helped in the short term, one was certainly not a long-term solution.

Because parents/caregivers were perceived as unable or unwilling to assist with homework, one school decided not to give homework, ensuring learners completed the work at school:

> They [parents] don't support in homework. As a result, in the Foundation Phase, we don't give them [learners] homework. They do it at school. (Head of department, School 3)

At this school, a decision was taken not to give homework to learners in the Foundation Phase because of the lack of parental/caregiver support. The school's decision reflected a view that doing homework at school is necessary, even if it means sacrificing school time allocated to other activities. This tactic was designed to ensure "homework" was completed in a structured environment that avoided the possibility of low parent/caregiver involvement. It was intended to limit perceived parental/caregiver neglect from negatively impacting early learning. This approach temporarily removed the responsibility from parents, who were excluded, and themselves did not benefit from the learning opportunity that they would certainly be required to take up when their children entered the Intermediate Phase.

The second example provides some insight into how schools have taken steps to be proactive. A teacher advanced an approach that she advocated for other educators in the same learning area to adopt:

> Mark your books. If you mark your books, you'll see a problem immediately. You'll pick up the problem immediately. Be prepared; mark your books; be in contact with the parents … and if you need help, ask. (Head of department, School 1)

The head of department emphasised diligent teacher marking to generate early evidence of learner needs. She was prepared to support her unit members in this drive, highlighting the importance of using evidence and liaising with parents. This implied that raising parent/caregiver involvement needs to be a systematic strategy that involves both teachers and parents. This requires teachers to set homework and act on the outcomes of homework. More attention needs to be given to finding out how schools respond to the challenges referred to above and seeking out examples of good practice that can be shared and replicated.

Conclusion

Research in four Gauteng schools confirmed that blame narratives are common amongst teachers and parents/caregivers, and that these are part of the everyday ways that schools operate, without necessarily leading to significant conflict and disruptions. Teachers blamed parents/caregivers for being uneducated, not caring, not assisting with homework or not visiting the school, and for many other things that they observed in learners. However, it is important to note that many teachers were critically aware of the dangers of speaking in generalisations. For example, a teacher demonstrated a clear-headed perspective on the slippage from generalisation into blaming:

> Like I said earlier on, the community that we are dealing with, if I may put this statement, are just saying, 'The parents trust the teachers or [do] not trust the teachers.' It becomes just a sweeping statement – sweeping statements about the situation. (Teacher, School 3)

Teachers were therefore aware of tendencies to slip into generalisations. While the research did not engage with parents/caregivers, it certainly indicated that neither group – parents/caregivers nor teachers – was perfect. In one of the schools, as reported by a teacher, the principal was forced to compel teachers to attend parent meetings, because some teachers were repeatedly absent without reason, leading to parents feeling discouraged.

Rather than trying to get to the bottom of "who is to blame" for school challenges, the literature shows that proposals for collaboration can more productively improve the quality and strength of parent/caregiver participation and eradicate blame. Some of the interventions put forward include: clarifying roles and responsibilities (Sibanda 2021); initiating inclusive and context-friendly programmes (Munje & Mncube 2018); improving communication, information, and knowledge-sharing between parents/caregivers and the school/teachers in an inclusive, welcoming and encouraging manner (Munje and Mncube 2018); implementing parent training programmes for orientation, preparing for the responsibilities of supporting their children's learning progress, and for participating in the affairs of the SGB; and in-service training of teachers in building parent–school–community relationships (Munje & Mncube 2018). An important area for exploration is finding workable approaches towards reconciliation and recovery from blame.

In parallel, we suggest initiatives that build awareness about how blame works and how to counteract blame by implementing sound governance, and coordinated parent–teacher partnerships. We also suggest that taking up the phenomenon of blame in initial teacher education may be useful.

Finally, additional research should be undertaken to understand how to grow trust and accountability to counter the effects of blame and blaming.

Notes

1   Human L, Government criticised for blaming Covid for the country's literacy crisis. *GroundUp*, 23 May 2023. Accessed May 2025, https://groundup.org.za/article/government-criticised-for-blaming-covid-for-the-countrys-literacy-crisis/

2   Molver L, Don't blame Covid-19 for the reading catastrophe revealed by Pirls – blame our education system. *Daily Maverick*, 23 May 2023. Accessed May 2025, https://www.dailymaverick.co.za/opinionista/2023-05-23-dont-blame-covid-19-for-the-reading-catastrophe-revealed-by-pirls-blame-our-education-system/

3   Zeeman K, Poll: Are parents to blame for misbehaviour in schools? *Daily Dispatch*, 25 April 2022. Accessed May 2025, https://www.dispatchlive.co.za/news/2022-04-25-poll-are-parents-to-blame-for-misbehaviour-in-schools/

4   Ntshangase S, Teenage pregnancy rises – blame game between government and parents, *Sunday Tribune*, 26 June 2023. Accessed May 2025, https://iol.co.za/sunday-tribune/news/2023-06-26-teenage-pregnancy-rises-blame-game-between-government-and-parents/

5   Dlamini P (2018) Parents to blame for children's behaviour, says schools federation. *Times Live*, 16 March 2018. Accessed May 2025, https://www.timeslive.co.za/news/south-africa/2018-03-16-parents-to-blame-for-childrens-behaviour-says-schools-federation/

References

Baxter J & Ehren M (2023) Factors contributing to and detracting from relational trust in leadership: The case of primary schools in South Africa. *Frontiers in Education* 8: 1–17

Chisley CE (2014) Teachers' and parents' attitudes and perceptions of parental involvement in a Louisiana school district. Doctoral dissertation, Capella University. Accessed June 2025, https://www.proquest.com/docview/1527094372?sourcetype=Dissertations&Theses

Conradie MS (2020) Pure politicking! Racialised blame games and moral panic in the case of a South African high school. *Society Register* 4(1): 37–60

DGMT (Douglas George Murray Trust) (2018) The noble profession that 'feels like a double-edged sword': Do teachers make the grade? *Human Factor* 1(Nov): 6–35

Ehren MCM & Baxter J (Eds) (2021) *Trust, accountability, and capacity in education system reform: Global perspectives in comparative education.* London: Routledge

Ehren M, Paterson A & Baxter J (2020a) Accountability and trust: Two sides of the same coin? *Journal of Educational Change* 21: 183–213. Accessed May 2025, https://link.springer.com/article/10.1007/s10833-019-09352-4

Ehren M, Paterson A & Baxter J (2020b) *Case study report: Accountability, capacity, and trust to improve learning outcomes in South Africa: A systems approach.* JET Education Services funded by Economic and Social Research Council and the Department for International Development. Accessed May 2025, https://www.jet.org.za/news/case-study-report-trust-capacity-and-accountability-to-improve-learning-outcomes-in-south-africa-a-systems-approach

Hansson S (2018a) Analysing opposition–government blame games: Argument models and strategic manoeuvring. *Critical Discourse Studies* 15(3): 228–246

Hansson S (2018b) The discursive micro-politics of blame avoidance: Unpacking the language of government blame games. *Policy Sciences* 51: 545–564. Accessed May 2025, https://doi.org/10.1007/s11077-018-9335-3

Mitchell CE (1998) 'If I am not to blame, does that mean I don't have to be responsible?' Possible effect of a systems approach on personal accountability within families. *Family Therapy: The Journal of the California Graduate School of Family Psychology* 25(3): 227–230

Munje PN & Mncube V (2018) The lack of parent involvement as hindrance in selected public primary schools in South Africa: The voices of educators. *Perspectives in Education* 36(1): 80–93

Pawlewicz DDA (2022) Teacher blame as the grammar of public school reform. *History of Education Quarterly* 62(3): 291–311

Peterson ER, Rubie-Davies CM, Elley-Brown M, Widdowson DA, Dixon RS & Irving E (2011) Who is to blame? Students', teachers', and parents' views on who is responsible for student achievement. *Research in Education* 86: 1–12

Sibanda R (2021) 'I'm not a teacher': A case of (dys)functional parent–teacher partnerships in a South African township. *South African Journal of Education* 41(3): 1–13

Singh P, Mbokodi SM & Msila VT (2004) Black parental involvement in education. *South African Journal of Education* 24(4): 301–307

South African Council for Educators (2020) *Handbook for teachers' rights, responsibilities, and safety.* LeadAfrika Consulting. Accessed May 2025, https://www.sace.org.za/assets/documents/uploads/sace_90707-2020-01-10-Teachers%20Handbook%20Draft.pdf

8 Black Middle-Class Parents' Involvement in Children's Education: Stories of Trauma and Hope

Thembeka Myende and Phumlani Myende

Introduction

There is a generally accepted view that Black and white middle-class parents, due to their strong cultural capital, are more involved in their children's education than the working class (Golden et al. 2021; Barg 2019; Holloway & Pimlott-Wilson 2013; Msila 2012). While this view exists, Cucchiara and Horvat (2009) and Gupta (2023) argue that middle-class parental involvement is more complex than assumed in scholarship. Furthermore, we have observed that the stories regarding the involvement of these parents are largely told from the schools' perspective, and Western notions dominate the discourse. To this point, there is a lack of understanding of the realities of being a Black middle-class parent involved in their child's education, particularly in a developing country like South Africa. On the one hand, the complexity of adopting the Western notions is exacerbated by the dynamic nature of Global South and South African Black middle-class families (Hunter 2017; Lentz 2020). In his study conducted in South Africa, Hunter's findings (2017) suggest that, unlike the Global North where nuclear families are common, in South Africa, nuclear Black middle-class families are a minority. This necessarily affects family structure and, consequently, parental involvement. Furthermore, regardless of the rise of Black middle-class families in South Africa, it has been found that women still carry more home responsibilities as their husbands (or male partners) are reluctant to accept changes in gender roles (James 2017). This results in the unique dynamics of Black middle-class families and hence the challenge of generalising Global North findings on the phenomenon of parental involvement.

There is, therefore, a need for local studies on the involvement of Black middle-class parents in education. This need is also justified by the fact that recent studies conducted on South African Black parents' involvement generally focus on poor parents (see Langa, Wassermann & Maposa 2021; Mncube 2010; Msila 2012; Munje & Mncube 2018; Okeke 2014). For this reason, in this chapter, we use our own lived and collective experiences to share our stories of hope and trauma associated with being Black middle-class parents who consider themselves involved in our child's education. We ask: *What are our lived and collective experiences of being Black middle-class parents in relation to parental involvement, and what do these experiences teach us about Black middle-class parents' involvement in children's education?* This chapter advances four main arguments suggesting that being Black middle-class parents does not translate into "smooth-sailing" regarding involvement in a child's education. The argument is divided into five parts. First, we show that the school is an extension of a very busy home, which means that, second, we have struggled to provide our child with academic support. To help deal with this struggle, we, third, use our child's agency as a navigational tool, and fourth, rely on support from school aftercare. Finally, we show that this struggle is gendered and does not play out in the same way for each of us.

The context: About us and the research approach

We are a married couple living in an urban area in KwaZulu-Natal, Durban. We identify ourselves as middle-class parents because of our education level and income, both of which are considered middle class. We are both employed as academics at two different South African universities.

Phumlani is an associate professor, and Thembeka works as a lecturer. At the time of writing this chapter, our combined income per capita was above the international poverty line of \$1.90 per day (Sullivan & Hickel 2023; Zizzamia et al. 2016), and we owned two bank-financed properties, one in an urban area and one in a suburban area. Both of us grew up in rural areas, even though our families' profiles and our schooling experiences differ. On the one hand, Phumlani grew up in a rural family on the South Coast of KwaZulu-Natal, raised by his mother while his father worked on a farm harvesting sugarcane, coming home only at the end of the month or when the harvesting season was over. On the other hand, Thembeka was raised by a migrant single parent who worked as a nurse in the United Kingdom. Thembeka would live with her grandmother during school holidays and with her aunt during the school term. Phumlani went to quintile 1 primary and secondary schools, whereas Thembeka attended quintile 5 primary and secondary schools. At the time of writing this chapter, we were living with our child who was in Grade 3, which accounts for our involvement in education as parents. Our child attends a quintile 5 school, which means that parents pay the majority of the school costs.

We use our experiences constructed from our personal collective narratives to present our hopes and traumas about parental involvement. What makes collective personal narratives relevant in this work is that we achieve our aim by drawing from our lived experiences, feelings, and knowledge portrayed through the stories we tell (Daiute 2014; Parnell et al. 2023). In response to research suggesting that being a middle-class parent translates to easy and smooth involvement in children's education, our narratives afforded us an opportunity to define ourselves (not in relation to others but in terms of our own unique experiences), to clarify the continuity in our lives in relation to our involvement in our child's schooling, and to share this with others (Willig 2008). Personal narratives reveal multiple and sometimes conflicting self-expressions (McAdams 1999; Clandinin 2023). We opted to share our lived experiences using personal narratives, aware that, as a research method, this approach is regarded as having questionable validity and reliability (Bold 2011; Clandinin 2023). It is important to share how our narratives emerged, especially the aspects we used in this chapter.

Each of us wrote our stories. On completion, we exchanged our stories and read the story we had not written. In this reading process, the reader was required to identify aspects of the story that were similar to aspects in their own story. From this process, we were able to identify both positive and negative parental involvement experiences. We then grouped the common experiences, looked at the different ones, and selected the experiences that we thought were worth sharing.

Beyond this process, we used a "critical friend" as suggested by Samaras and Roberts (2011), to obtain another perspective on how we interpreted and shared our stories. Phumlani took the stories to a colleague familiar with innovative, non-conventional, and reflexive methodologies. The friend was asked to read our stories and examine how we gave them meaning. After reading the stories, the friend commented on whether our interpretations shared the meaning we wanted to impart. Using the friend's comments, we revisited the stories and themes we generated, revising the themes and then presenting them again to the critical friend to obtain her perspective. After her second commentary, we finalised the themes as shared in the next section. Additionally, this process made sure that we were reflective and critical rather than only considering one aspect of our experiences.

(Black) Middle class: Conceptual clarification

The phenomenon of the middle class has received increasing interest from researchers. Noticeable in the scholarly work is a consensus that the number of Black people falling into the category of middle class has increased, but the issue of what constitutes the middle class still contains fuzzy meanings (Iqani 2015; Kitis, Milani & Levon 2018; Mattes 2015; Ncube, Lufumpa & Kayizzi-Mugerwa 2011; Ndletyana 2014; Tschirley et al. 2015; Zizzamia et al. 2016). According to Pressman (2015), one's income range or level has been a dominant approach in defining the middle class. Within the relative income threshold, a middle-class person is in the middle of the income distribution (Zizzamia et al. 2016). This understanding falls short in many ways. For example, with the fluctuating nature of the South African economy (such as the continually increasing price of fuel, which has led to an increase in food costs), it may be difficult to determine how economic instabilities affect those who enjoy being in the middle of the income distribution. This means one can still be in the middle of the distribution but remain poor due to negative economic changes, although the income distribution remains stable. For example, at the time of writing, payments on two bank-financed properties had increased due to an increase in the repo rate. While this increase in our monthly bond payments occurred at least three times our salaries had not risen to the same extent.

Income based approaches to defining being middle-class are therefore problematic because they do not consider the likelihood of remaining in the middle class or falling into poverty. For this reason, López-Calva & Ortiz-Juarez (2014) construct three categories of middle-class people:

The vulnerable middle class comprises people who are slightly above the international poverty line and remain vulnerable to slipping back into poverty. The lower middle class comprises people who live above the subsistence level, and who can save and consume nonessential goods. The upper middle class comprises people with a purchasing power parity that is way above the international poverty line.

We accept these definitions of the three categories and self-identify as upper middle class. However, as indicated earlier, any notion based on income and expenditure may fail to consider the fluctuating nature of the economy, especially in the current South African context. This may suggest that one's social class is fluid and may be linked to continuous efforts to remain within one's preferred class. Given this, we have considered other factors such as health care, education beyond high school, and ownership of assets as crucial factors in determining one's class (Pressman 2015).

Earlier, we described some of the ownership of assets locating us within the middle-class category. To further self-identify as black middle-class parents, we used the racial stratification used in governmental policies and publications. According to these policies, South Africans are racially divided into Blacks, coloureds, Indians, and whites (Bornman 2010; Coates 2018; Pirtle 2020). Blacks are further categorised using the nine South African official languages, and we fall within the isiZulu-speaking group.

Parental involvement and social class in the literature

The concept of parental involvement started to gain currency in South African literature after the introduction of the South African Schools Act in 1996, which came with, among other things, the decentralisation of decision-making in schools. Though different scholars have written about parental involvement, its meanings are mostly common. The meaning that seems to be common across different contexts is that parental involvement entails all activities parents should undertake to support their children's education within and beyond the school premises (Garcia & De Guzman 2020; Myende & Nhlumayo 2022; Young, Austin & Growe 2013). Under section 1118, the 2002 United States No Child Left Behind Act defines parental involvement as the participation of parents in two-way meaningful communication involving student academic learning and other school activities, assisting their child's learning; being actively involved in their child's education at school; serving as full partners in their child's education; and being included, as appropriate, in decision-making and on advisory committees to assist in the education of their child (Johnson 2015: 78–79). Drawing from the work of Epstein (1995), many scholars have summarised parental involvement activities as being in three categories. These categories are: home-based involvement (such as monitoring schoolwork, providing other enriching activities), school-based involvement (for example, parent–teacher communication, attending and/or volunteering at school events), and academic socialisation (such as communicating expectations, providing encouragement to the child) (Garcia & De Guzman 2020: 344).

The definition and categories of parental involvement assume that parents have time to be involved in such activities. Several questions can be asked in relation to the above:

- *How do parents living in poverty find time and resources to fulfil these roles?*
- *Given the nature and dynamics of being a Black middle-class parent in South Africa, are Black middle-class parents well-positioned to perform these tasks?*

Research confirms parental involvement as dependent on a family's social class (Goldstone, Baker & Barg 2021; Strømme & Helland 2020). The involvement of many poor and working-class Black parents in school or home-based activities has been observed to be lacking. In the struggle for economic survival, these parents become inundated with 'multiple and inflexible working schedules' (Allen & White-Smith 2018: 411). Mncube (2009) adds that these parents lack the know-how of parental involvement, while Msila (2012) notes that lack of resources makes it difficult for poor,

Black working-class parents to participate in school and home-based activities. The involvement of parents in poor, Black working-class families has also been described as gendered. Fathers in these families are said to remain passive with regard to childcare provision and the education of their children due to their long working hours (Henz 2019). The above research questions the relevance of Epstein's (1995) work on parental involvement. The work can be seen as relevant to parents who possess the means to be at school or to be fully involved with a child at home. *How does Epstein's work apply to parents in the Global South, who are continually trying to remain within their class or change it?*

Unlike poor and working-class parents' experience of parental involvement, research suggests a positive relationship between a vested amount of cultural capital and excelling in parental involvement (Aarseth 2018; Andersen & Hansen 2012; Goldstone, Baker & Barg 2021). Cultural capital in middle-class families is understood to be higher than that of poor and working-class families due to their economic standing, which therefore advances their children's social and intellectual development (Stacer & Perrucci 2013). Middle-class parents are distinguished by their occupational status, economic resources, higher education qualifications, lifestyle, dress code, urban living, liberal worldview, family life, and value system (Seekings 2008; Lentz 2020). In addition to having the relevant resources and time, middle-class parents can form a reading culture and cultivate meaningful and fun learning engagements (Horvat, Weininger & Lareau 2003). Flanigan (2018) and Vazquez and Greenfield (2021) believe that middle-class parents possess the "know-how" of involvement, and employ scaffolding, tough questioning techniques, and the internet to search for information for their children. Beyond the parental factors, schools have been identified as designers of programmes more conducive to the involvement of middle-class parents. Parents with economic resources are typically more resourceful and hence more likely to be involved in their children's education than parents without such advantages. Mercer and Lemanski (2020) provide compelling cases depicting the ambivalence of Black Africans to the middle-class classification. It is therefore important to investigate the Black middle class and their involvement, given their ambivalence toward this identity. Much of the research regarding the intersection of the Black middle class and parental involvement is documented in Europe and America (see Cucchiara & Horvat 2009; Leath et al. 2020; Schnell et al. 2015; Stacer & Perrucci 2013; Taysum & Ayanlaja 2020). Unlike some Black African families, some European and American families appreciate being categorised as middle class. Like poor and working-class families, Black middle-class parents in Europe and America describe the great amount of time and labour spent in the workplace so that they can afford and support their children's education (Flanigan 2018). Lack of inter-generational support or wealth transfer in Black middle-class families creates an even larger strain on their financial standing (Hamilton & Darity 2017; Vincent et al. 2012). A similar argument can be made about Black middle-class parents in South Africa, with South African Black middle-class families no exception to the lack of inter-generational support.

Our profiles highlight how quintile 1 to 5 schools are funded in South Africa. The fact that quintile 4 and 5 schools usually charge fees means that parents have to work hard to ensure that they can afford these fees, if they choose to send their children to these schools (Languille 2016). The openness of South Africa's school funding policy has allowed independent and fee-paying schools independence in deciding what school fees to charge (Languille 2016; Mestry 2013), resulting in education at these schools being unaffordable for most people.

Different from the above challenges, Vincent et al. (2012) found, in a study of 62 Caribbean Black middle-class parents, that they were clear about their long-term planning, moving house to get their children into particular schools or perhaps moving when children were small into an area with many "good" school options. The study further found that, beyond ensuring that the family was located in an area where they could access good schools, Black middle-class parents were involved in monitoring their children's schoolwork. They communicated with their children about their school experiences and future aspirations.

Another important aspect is the largely gendered nature of parental involvement in the home and school, even within middle-class families. Women or mothers endure a disproportionate obligation in the provision of childcare and educational involvement compared to their male counterparts (Bonal & González 2020; Harding 2015; Jezierski & Wall 2019). This uneven distribution of labour in terms of childcare and educational involvement became more apparent during the COVID-19 pandemic (Villadsen, Conti & Fitzsimons 2020; Yerkes et al. 2020). Mothers were involved in job and home responsibilities, but fathers focused on their work and personal endeavours (Yerkes et al. 2020).

As indicated earlier, little is known about South African Black middle-class parents and their involvement in their children's schooling, which further propels the need for research with this focus. The South African historical experience of apartheid and the post-apartheid transformation agenda may suggest that Black middle-class parents' perceptions and experiences elsewhere differ from those of Black middle-class parents in South Africa. Southall (2016) postulates the need to understand the Black middle class due to the changes brought on by globalisation and democratisation, and their role in restructuring the South African context. The post-apartheid era has opened economic and social opportunities to the Black middle class (Southall 2018), affording Black middle-class families better work opportunities, social status, and urban living in formerly "white" neighbourhoods (Southall 2016). While some Black parents, as suggested by Southall, enjoy the status of being middle class, less attention has been given to how these parents experience involvement in their children's education. We use our experiences as Black middle-class parents, hoping that our experiences can be the portal for more studies on this topic.

School as an extension of a busy home

In the literature review, we have argued that for many Black families remaining within the middle class is a continuous struggle due to changing economic conditions. This argument is further supported by the work of Vincent et al. (2012), Flanigan (2018), and Hamilton and Darity (2017), who share the view that Black middle-class parents, despite their capital, may still find it difficult to be involved in their children's education because of their busy work schedules. Our experiences coincide with the viewpoint of these scholars. While the school communicates through a detailed term newsletter, we often feel that instead of the home being an extension of what happens in school, the school is an extension of what we do at home. We feel like we are "doing more than the school" because of how much homework we have to complete at home. The narratives provided below illustrate how our academic work, which we perform to maintain or enhance our economic situation and social status, puts us in the difficult position of having to balance working productively at the same time as needing to provide school support for our child.

> I become inundated with my work, house chores, studies, childcare, and homework. My work schedule and the demands of homework time frequently collide. In addition, teachers usually expect parents to engage in the teaching, and should one not understand the work, the child will struggle. (Thembeka)

> Besides being an academic, I am also involved in academic management at work. As a full-time employed academic, I often have to cope with, and adapt to, unpredictable work demands. Despite these demands, we are often met with the statement, 'mom and dad, you should help me with my homework; otherwise my teacher will yell at me'. (Phumlani)

Our narratives suggest that as Black middle-class parents, we have tight and, at times unpredictable, work schedules. Against these work schedules, every day is schoolwork time, and we have to be "supermom" and "superdad" who can juggle work demands while ensuring that our child is supported, especially with homework. As we stated earlier, the amount of schoolwork has made us ask three critical questions: *Between the school and the parents, who should serve as the child's primary educator? What is the significance of homework? Is the homework given to supplement what happens in class or to ensure that families do more and schools supplement what happens at home?* Thembeka has posed some of these questions to one of the teachers, as shown below:

> I asked the teacher the rationale behind holiday homework, to which she responded that it is to help the learners not to forget what they have been taught for the term. Unfortunately, one cannot rebel against this school tradition lest the child is punished for not following the teacher's instructions.

> The holiday homework is usually much; it requires some planning without too much playtime. My child prefers to watch YouTube and use the PlayStation instead, as he knows it is the holidays. I have to monitor that homework is done and the answers are correct, which is a tedious job. (Thembeka)

Our experiences are not new, and the questions we raise, especially around homework's importance, emerge in other studies. For example, the findings of a study conducted in China by Sun et al. (2014) indicate that the homework burden is troubling for parents and children. Similarly, in another study conducted in India by Sridevi and Tomar (2016), which included parents, teachers, and children, parents supported the administering of homework. Still, they raised concerns that the way it was utilised did not contribute to children's academic and cognitive development and was monotonous and burdensome to parents. The experience depicted in Thembeka's narrative above shows a similar concern about homework sometimes interfering with the child's leisure time and becoming too much for parents. The experiences narrated show that both parents experienced challenges with being involved, especially with homework. In addition to the aforementioned experiences, we frequently feel we lack proper pedagogical knowledge, making it difficult for us to provide our child with the best possible support.

Struggling to provide academic support

We use a metaphor of 'buying out' our responsibility of parental involvement to indicate how we use our economic capital to shift some of our responsibilities to aftercare providers. Here we argue that contrary to the dominant narrative that Black middle-class parents find it easy to provide decent support to their children (Kainuwa, Binti & Yusuf 2013), we often experience hurdles due to different factors.

> I have always understood the tasks and instructions from my child's teachers, but I will often struggle with finding grade- and age-appropriate pedagogy. I have often opted for the pedagogical approaches that my teachers used. Often, I have been confronted with a confused face with a response, 'This is not how my teacher explained it. Dad, you are confusing me.' (Phumlani)

> Sometimes, my child does not complete homework at aftercare and has to do it at home. Even though he often does not need my assistance, I have to provide guidance to ensure he is on the right track. I find myself asking him to do the work in the way his teachers have taught him because when I explain the work in my understanding, he will refer to how his teachers had taught him, which means that my interpretation of the instructions and the content is understood differently from the specialised way the teachers prefer. That is why I would rather leave the homework task to the aftercare teachers because they seem to know what they are doing. I interpret the work the same way I was taught or in a way that is most convenient for my understanding without realising that the teachers have a set pedagogy they employ for the type of learners they teach. (Thembeka)

Our embodied cultural capital, including our education level and the knowledge we possess, and the fact that our child is in primary school should make it easy for us to support him with homework (Bourdieu 1986; Ireson & Rushforth 2014). However, the experiences narrated above suggest that our pedagogical knowledge seemed inappropriate for our child, who is in the last year of the Foundation Phase (Grade 3). The inappropriateness of our pedagogical knowledge may challenge the notion that parents with high educational qualifications can foster a child's high level of competence, hence the relevance of the concept of cultural capital in our context. While we may argue that the colonial past has little impact on our child's education experience, our experiences are different in that we went through an education system that was not fully free from the colonial past. This means our past experience in relation to access to various resources may still hinder us from understanding education for Grade 3 learners today.

Research notes that parents across different social classes may intrude in or interfere with their children's home-based school activities instead of supporting them. They do this by providing the solutions to the problems given by the teachers, hindering children's self-regulated learning. Parents may do this either because they are frustrated by not knowing how to support their children or because they are driven to see their children perform well (Cunha et al. 2015; Gonida & Cortina 2014; Grolnick 2009). In a similar vein, we must constantly balance being academics – who understand that our role as parents is to encourage our child to find solutions on his own by creating a supportive environment that will allow his independent thinking and self-regulation – with the challenges we face in trying to support our child. We too have experienced being tempted to just provide solutions because of our frustration that we are not providing helpful instructions. While we struggle to offer support, we have observed that our child has some agency, which enables us to navigate parental involvement more easily.

A child's agency as a navigational tool

> I do not know what I would do if my child did not take time to do his work or remind me that he has homework and complete it without me reminding him. My academic management work has kept me so busy that I have delegated the responsibility of checking my child's school communication book. This happens more often when my wife has travelled afar for her academic work commitments. (Phumlani)

Research literature suggests that well-educated, middle-class parents provide their children with supportive social capital. However, due to our busy academic schedules that regularly mean long hours of work beyond normal working hours, we have realised that we give limited attention to our child's work. Instead of our limited involvement being a limitation, it has allowed our child to develop agency, and we use this as our navigational tool. From this agency, we can establish his level of understanding of the work the teachers have given, and from there, we only provide guidance if there is a need. A person's agency is defined by their ability to be resilient, autonomous, and resourceful, and to engage in long-term strategies and plans for personal or communal survival (Rasulova 2013). While the idea that children are actors and agents who contribute to their families or other social contexts has been accepted theoretically, the children's influence and capacity as agents in different spheres has been neglected (Gurdal & Sorbring 2018). Rather than neglecting our child's capacity to plan time for schoolwork and to initiate the conversation for the need for support from us, we have learned to capitalise on our child's agency.

The excerpt shared earlier shows that our child has developed the ability to know when homework needs to be done and to inform us that the homework has been completed or is being done. A crucial feature of this agency is that it has created space for us as parents just to check that schoolwork has been done and to look for minor errors.

While this agency could be linked to our child feeling neglected and therefore developing ways to deal with homework, the embodied or objectified cultural capital that we have may also have enabled our child to find ways to cope with educational tasks without our intense involvement. Embodied cultural capital consists of attributes of oneself, both consciously and passively inherited, usually from the family or community, through the socialisation of culture and tradition (Hampton-Garland 2015). Hong and Zhao (2015) add that embodied and objectified cultural capital includes the family's educational level, resources, and the extracurricular activities in which the child is involved. Bourdieu (1986) claims that embodied capital takes time to acquire compared to objectified capital, but acquiring this capital may positively impact the child's academic performance. We believe our embodied and objectified capital may have added to our child's ability to independently pursue school tasks. Thembeka's narrative below suggests this to some extent:

> My child would complain that he wants to watch YouTube videos, use the PlayStation, or take a break as the homework takes a toll on him. This requires me to give him some time off; however, monitoring is tedious as I have to remind him to get back to the task. (Thembeka)

While Thembeka sees the watching of YouTube videos as an activity that competes with schoolwork for time, we have observed that our child has developed some vocabulary and creative thinking skills beyond his age. After he had correctly completed a task, we sometimes checked how he had managed, and he would indicate that he had watched a YouTube video related to it. These self-driven enquiries through the internet (in this case, YouTube) are some of the actions that make us describe him as a child with agency. Of course, the ability to see this agentic character can arguably be caused by our level of education, so not all parents may be able to identify this in their children. But it keeps our involvement, especially in explaining home-based school activities, to a minimum. This seems to make our task as parents easier, which raises a question about our earlier argument that parental involvement is complex. The complex task is knowing when to be involved and when not to be, helping to maximise the child's agency.

Support from aftercare

> When my child returns from school, I must ensure his homework is
> completed. The aftercare teachers are responsible for assisting all children
> with homework. Therefore, as a parent, I must make sure that all the work
> has been completed. Although this wasn't the case at the beginning of the
> year, the work is usually finished, and thank God for the aftercare teachers
> who actively invest time and expertise in making sure that all the homework
> is completed. (Thembeka)

Our work schedules are very tight and do not allow us to participate fully
in our child's educational activities. Given the little time we have at our
disposal, we had to opt for after-school care.

Immediately after school, our child goes to aftercare, where he receives
homework support along with other children. The aftercare teachers check
the completion of homework and sign on our behalf. In this way, we are
able to delegate our responsibility for supervising our child's schoolwork
to the aftercare teachers. While aftercare has taken on the homework
responsibility, our child has occasionally used this to manipulate us. At
times the homework has not been completed at aftercare but our child tells
us that it has been. We have realised that we still have to check that the work
has been done, as outlined in Thembeka's narrative.

The question that can be asked here is as follows: *Is the involvement
of aftercare a way of making things work or is it a way of shifting our
responsibilities?* Our experience shows that homework is usually done at
aftercare but raises a question about the nature of middle-class parents'
involvement. In their work, researchers argue that children from families
with high socio-economic status perform better because their parents can
provide support and a conducive educational environment for academic
work (Kainuwa, Binti & Yusuf 2013; Golden et al. 2021). An example of
a conducive educational environment and full support is found in the
Taiwanese context. According to Jheng (2015), Taiwanese middle-class
parents use out-of-school private tutoring to ensure their children obtain
extra support beyond what schools offer. The same practice was identified
by Ireson and Rushforth (2014) in their study that focused on the factors
that accounted for parents' use of private tutoring. Likewise, in our context,
we have used the aftercare service to make things work for us and the child.
*While using aftercare gets things done, can it not be considered a shift of
responsibilities that would otherwise be ours in a normal parental involvement
scenario? Can this be regarded as full parental involvement, especially when
the aftercare teacher checks and even signs the homework? To what extent
can this result in parents losing touch with how their child is coping at school?*
The availability of aftercare can be seen as a beacon of hope regarding the

involvement of middle-class parents. Still, in addition to the questions already asked on this theme, the question remains as to whether what we call "outsourced" involvement can be used to argue that middle-class parents are more involved than the working class. We do not intend to make this comparison. Still, we return to this question later in the conclusion of this chapter because we believe this is an aspect that needs to be considered in the discourse of social class and parental involvement. While aftercare has become our saviour, there are times when our involvement in schoolwork is a must, and it is always clear that involvement roles are gendered and unequal.

Involvement roles as gendered

> Commenting on the support that we give to him, my child will say, 'Wena baba uyamrobha umama, njalo nje yena uhlezi engisiza ngomsebenzi weskole wena wenze owakho' (Dad, you're cheating mum, she's the one who always helps me with schoolwork while you are always busy with your own work). My child has noticed that I hardly support homework completion, but Thembeka does. I am involved in taking him to school and to his soccer practice, and I attend the budget meetings and parents' evenings. Surprisingly, if the school sends a letter about school fees, I will find the letter placed on my study desk unopened. (Phumlani)

> Although my child lives with both his parents, I solely check his message book and monitor his homework tasks daily. In addition, I provide a welcoming and motivating environment for him to thrive in his well-being and ask him to share his school experiences daily. I believe engaging in such conversations is crucial as I can decipher how he's coping socially, emotionally, and physically within the school premises, including the parent/child bond that is being maintained between us.

> The distribution of tasks regarding the child's educational involvement was not previously arranged with my partner; it just happened naturally. I wouldn't say I like attending to such things as homework. However, it is much better than attending meetings, volunteering for school activities, and other kinds of involvement that would require me to attend school. Although the latter engagements with the school are seldom on my side, I rather leave it to my partner to attend to when I'm unavailable and should the need arise. (Thembeka)

We have repeatedly tried to negotiate so that we are equally involved in our child's schoolwork, but Thembeka is more involved. Regardless of whether Phumlani is less busy, he is seldom involved in completing homework, checking the communication book, and following-up on how the child experienced his day at school. Our involvement is not only unequal but, we believe, also unintentionally gendered. We have observed that the school intentionally or unintentionally assigns roles to us in a manner that may be regarded as gendered. We submitted our contact details to the school, but every time school fees are overdue, Phumlani will receive a call from the school finance office. Thembeka has internalised this. When a letter about fees is given to our child, Thembeka will place it on Phumlani's study desk. We have also observed that when the child is not feeling well, Thembeka is contacted by the school rather than Phumlani. The issue of parental involvement being gendered and unequal has been reported in other studies, appearing as an issue across different social class contexts. As reported earlier, parental involvement in poor, Black working-class families has also been described as gendered, with fathers in working-class families said to be passive in the provision of childcare and the education of their children due to their long working hours (Henz 2019). However, this experience is not unique to poor and working-class parents; the literature reviewed in this chapter shows that involvement in the home and school contexts, even in middle-class families, is largely gendered, and women or mothers endure a disproportionate obligation (Bonal & González 2020; Harding 2015; Jezierski & Wall 2019; Yerkes et al. 2020).

Likewise, as noted in our profiles, while we are both academics, Thembeka finds herself with more household responsibilities, including parental involvement roles. In line with the studies reported above, our experiences suggest that schools may perpetuate gendered and unequal parental involvement. We see this as one part of the trauma of parental involvement that parents, especially mothers, can suffer.

Conclusion: Learning from our narratives

We have used personal narratives to examine what our lived and collective experiences mean about being Black middle-class parents in the context of parental involvement. The foremost question in this chapter was: *What do our parental involvement experiences teach us about being a Black middle-class parent and the involvement of people like us in a child's education?* Our narratives expose critical lessons about parental involvement and the middle-class family context. These lessons may not be relevant to other families, but may serve as a starting point for reflecting about the involvement of Black middle-class parents in their children's education.

Our experiences of involvement show that being a Black middle-class parent is complex; however, due to the capital that one possesses, it may be easy to build a child's agency, which in turn helps our child develop self-directed learning skills – one of our hopes. The second aspect that we believe exposes an important narrative about parental involvement is the point about middle-class parents' ability to "outsource" several associated parental involvement responsibilities. We have shared in our stories that being a middle-class parent allows us to pay aftercare to look after our child and ensure that his homework demands are met. While this sometimes works for us, it makes us question the claim that middle-class parents are more involved compared to poor and working-class parents.

While we did not do a comparison in this chapter, we use our experiences to suggest that working-class and middle-class parents may be similar. However, the middle class enjoys the availability of cultural capital. Such capital can be used by middle-class parents to delegate their responsibilities to commercial providers, such as aftercare centres and private tutoring institutions. The argument is that this is another type of involvement. Still, we argue that this is "buying out" or outsourcing parental involvement, which may lead to parents losing connection with how their children are progressing and experiencing school life.

Contrary to other findings shared in this chapter that have suggested that helping children in primary schools is usually easy, we argue that the Foundation Phase is a specialised schooling phase that requires expert knowledge on how children learn and understand instructions. We argue that our experiences tell us that, regardless of education level, you can be a middle-class parent but still find it challenging to explain tasks in a grade- and age-appropriate way. Because we want our child to perform well, we had to achieve a balance between our knowledge that we should not provide our child with solutions and the temptation to do so. The situation was exacerbated by our having to continually juggle our academic work and household responsibilities with supporting our child. Further, from this particular trauma associated with parental involvement, our experiences suggest that some home-based school activities are not set by our child's school to advance children's academic and cognitive development but to ensure that parents have something to do. The amount of work given to children raises a question about whether children should do more at school or at home.

The last lesson from our experiences is that the trauma of parental involvement in the middle-class family context is likely to be experienced more by mothers as they mostly bear the burden of parental involvement responsibilities. Therefore, we argue that parental involvement in education, even in middle-class families, may be gendered, and schools may promote this aspect at times.

While these lessons are critical in driving the debate on this topic, the limitation of this work is that it draws from the experience of one father and one mother in one family, drawing attention to the need for large-scale studies of Black middle-class parents' involvement, especially in developing economies.

Although the findings drawn from our experiences cannot be generalised, they provide a base from which other researchers, especially in South Africa, can further explore the issue of class and parental involvement.

References

Aarseth H (2018) Fear of falling – fear of fading: The emotional dynamics of positional and personalised individualism. *Sociology* 52(5): 1087–1102

Allen Q & White-Smith K (2018) 'That's why I say stay in school': Black mothers' parental involvement, cultural wealth, and exclusion in their son's schooling. *Urban Education* 53(3): 409–435

Andersen PL & Hansen MN (2012) Class and cultural capital: The case of class inequality in educational performance. *European Sociological Review* 28(5): 607–621

Barg K (2019) Why are middle-class parents more involved in school than working-class parents? *Research in Social Stratification and Mobility* 59: 14–24

Bold C (2011) *Using narrative in research*. London: Sage

Bonal X & González S (2020) The impact of lockdown on the learning gap: Family and school divisions in times of crisis. *International Review of Education* 66(5–6): 635–655

Bornman E (2010) Emerging patterns of social identification in post-apartheid South Africa. *Journal of Social Issues* 66(2): 237–254

Bourdieu P (1986) The forms of capital. In J Richardson (Ed.) *Handbook of theory and research for the sociology of education*. Westport, CT: Greenwood

Clandinin DJ (2023) *Engaging in narrative inquiry*. New York and Oxford: Routledge

Coates R (2018) The racial state. In BP Batur and J Feagin (Eds) *Handbook for the sociology of racial and ethnic relations*. New York: Springer

Cucchiara MB & Horvat EM (2009) Perils and promises: Middle-class parental involvement in urban schools. *American Educational Research Journal* 46(4): 974–1004

Cunha J, Rosário P, Macedo L, Nunes AR, Fuentes S, Pinto R & Suárez N (2015) Parents' conceptions of their homework involvement in elementary school. *Psicothema* 27(2): 159–165

Daiute C (2014) Narrative analysis of interactive digital storytelling. Paper presented at 7th International Conference on Interactive Digital Storytelling, Singapore (3–6 November)

Epstein JL (1995) School/family/community partnerships: Caring for the children we share. *Phi Delta Kappan* 76(9): 701–712

Flanigan MG (2018) Black middle-class parental investment in their children's higher education. PhD thesis, Seton Hall University

Garcia AS & De Guzman MRT (2020) The meanings and ways of parental involvement among low-income Filipinos. *Early Childhood Research Quarterly* 53: 343–354

Golden DL, Erdreich L, Stefansen K & Smette I (2021) Class, education and parenting: Cross-cultural perspectives. *British Journal of Sociology of Education* 42(4): 453–459

Goldstone R, Baker W & Barg K (2021) A comparative perspective on social class inequalities in parental involvement in education: Structural dynamics, institutional design, and cultural factors. *Educational Review* 75(5): 976–992

Gonida EN & Cortina KS (2014) Parental involvement in homework: Relations with parent and student achievement-related motivational beliefs and achievement. *British Journal of Educational Psychology* 84(3): 376–396

Grolnick WS (2009) The role of parents in facilitating autonomous self-regulation for education. *Theory and Research in Education* 7(2): 164–173

Gupta A (2023) Revisiting educational advantage and social class: A Bourdieusian analysis of middle-class parents' investment in private schooling and shadow education. *British Journal of Sociology of Education* 44(1): 26–42

Gurdal S & Sorbring E (2018) Children's agency in parent–child, teacher–pupil, and peer relationship contexts. *International Journal of Qualitative Studies on Health and Well-being* 13(Sup1): 1565239

Hamilton D & Darity WA (2017) The political economy of education, financial literacy, and the racial wealth gap. *Federal Reserve Bank of St. Louis Review* 99(1): 59–76

Hampton-Garland P (2015) *The influence of embodied cultural capital on the retention and matriculation adults entering college.* Paper presented at the Adult Education Research Conference, University of Kansas (19–22 May)

Harding JF (2015) Increases in maternal education and low-income children's cognitive and behavioural outcomes. *Developmental Psychology* 51(5): 583–599

Henz U (2019) Fathers' involvement with their children in the United Kingdom: Recent trends and class differences. *Demographic Research* (40): 865–896

Holloway SL & Pimlott-Wilson H (2013) Parental involvement in children's learning: Mothers' fourth shift, social class, and the growth of state intervention in family life. *Canadian Geographies/Géographies canadiennes* 57(3): 327–336

Hong Y & Zhao Y (2015) From capital to habitus: Class differentiation of family educational patterns in urban China. *The Journal of Chinese Sociology* 2: 1–18

Horvat EM, Weininger EB & Lareau A (2003) From social ties to social capital: Class differences in the relations between schools and parent networks. *American Educational Research Journal* 40(2): 319–351

Hunter M (2017) Parental choice without parents: Families, education, and class in a South African township. *Compare: A Journal of Comparative and International Education* 47(1): 2–16

Iqani M (2015) Agency and affordability: Being black and 'middle class' in South Africa in 1989. *Critical Arts* 29(2): 126–145

Ireson J & Rushforth K (2014) Why do parents employ private tutors for their children? Exploring psychological factors that influence demand in England. *Journal for Educational Research Online* 6(1): 12–33

James D (2017) Not marrying in South Africa: Consumption, aspiration, and the new middle class. *Anthropology Southern Africa* 40(1): 1–14

Jezierski S & Wall G (2019) Changing understandings and expectations of parental involvement in education. *Gender and Education* 31(7): 811–826

Jheng YJ (2015) The influence of private tutoring on middle-class students' use of in-class time in formal schools in Taiwan. *International Journal of Educational Development* 40: 1–18

Johnson L (2015) Rethinking parental involvement: A critical review of the literature. *Urban Education Research & Policy Annuals* 3(1): 77–90

Kainuwa A, Binti N & Yusuf M (2013) Influence of socio-economic and educational background of parents on their children's education in Nigeria. *International Journal of Scientific and Research Publications* 3(10): 2250–3153

Kitis E, Milani TM & Levon E (2018) 'Black diamonds', "clever blacks", and other metaphors: Constructing the black middle class in contemporary South African print media. *Discourse & Communication* 12(2): 149–170

Langa M, Wassermann J & Maposa M (2021) Black African parents' narratives on apartheid schooling and school history. *Perspectives in Education* 39(3): 3–16

Languille S (2016) 'Affordable' private schools in South Africa: Affordable for whom? *Oxford Review of Education* 42(5): 528–542

Leath S, Marchand AD, Harrison A, Halawah A, Davis C & Rowley S (2020) A qualitative exploration of Black mothers' gendered constructions of their children and their parental school involvement. *Early Childhood Research Quarterly* 53: 124–135

Lentz C (2020) Doing being middle-class in the global South: Comparative perspectives and conceptual challenges. *Africa* 90(3): 439–469

López-Calva LF & Ortiz-Juarez E (2014) A vulnerability approach to the definition of the middle class. *Journal of Economic Inequality* 12: 23–47

Mattes R (2015) South Africa's emerging black middle class: A harbinger of political change? *Journal of International Development* 27(5): 665–692

McAdams DP (1999) Personal narratives and the life story. In L Pervin & O John (Eds) *Handbook of personality: Theory and research* (2nd edition). New York: Guilford Press

Mercer C & Lemanski C (2020) The lived experiences of the African middle classes. *Africa* 90(3): 429–438

Mestry R (2013) A critical analysis of legislation on the financial management of public schools: A South African perspective. *De Jure* 46(1): 162–177

Mncube V (2009) The perceptions of parents of their role in the democratic governance of schools in South Africa: Are they on board? *South African Journal of Education* 29(1): 83–103

Mncube V (2010) Parental involvement in school activities in South Africa to the mutual benefit of the school and the community. *Education as Change* 14(2): 233–246

Msila V (2012) Black parental involvement in South African rural schools: Will parents ever help in enhancing effective school management? *Journal of Educational and Social Research.* 2(2): 303–313

Munje PN & Mncube V (2018) The lack of parent involvement as hindrance in selected public primary schools in South Africa: The voices of educators. *Perspectives in Education* 36(1): 80–93

Myende PE & Nhlumayo BS (2022) Enhancing parent–teacher collaboration in rural schools: Parents' voices and implications for schools. *International Journal of Leadership in Education* 25(3): 490–514

Ncube M, Lufumpa CL & Kayizzi-Mugerwa S (2011) *Market brief: The middle of the pyramid: Dynamics of the middle class in Africa.* Abidjan: African Development Bank

Ndletyana M (2014) Middle class in South Africa: Significance, role, and impact. Paper presented at the 6th BRICS Academic Forum, Rio de Janeiro, Brazil (17–19 March)

Okeke CI (2014) Effective home–school partnership: Some strategies to help strengthen parental involvement. *South African Journal of Education* 34(3): 1–9

Parnell T, Fiske K, Stastny K, Sewell S & Nott M (2023) Lived experience narratives in health professional education: Educators' perspectives of a co-designed, online mental health education resource. *BMC Medical Education* 23(1): 946

Pirtle WNL (2020) Racial states and re-making race: Exploring coloured racial re- and de-formation in state laws and forms in post-apartheid South Africa. *Sociology of Race and Ethnicity* 7(2): 145–159

Pressman S (2015) *Defining and measuring the middle class.* Working Paper 007. American Institute for Economic Research. Great Barrington, MA: AEIR

Rasulova ST (2013) Child agency and economic circumstances: How does family economic status affect child agency in Kyrgyzstan's post-Soviet culture of transition? PhD thesis, University of Oxford

Samaras A & Roberts L (2011) Flying solo: Teachers take charge of their learning through self-study research. *Learning Forward, the Journal of Staff Development* 32(5): 42–45

Schnell P, Fibbi R, Crul M & Montero-Sieburth M (2015) Family involvement and educational success of the children of immigrants in Europe: Comparative perspectives. *Comparative Migration Studies* 3: 14

Seekings J (2008) *The rise and fall of the Weberian analysis of class in South Africa between 1949 and the early 1970s.* CSSR Working Paper 239. Cape Town: Centre for Social Science Research, University of Cape Town

Southall R (2016) (Ed.) *The new black middle class in South Africa.* Johannesburg: Jacana Media

Southall R (2018) What's missing? Reflections on the debate on middle class(es) in Africa. *Transformation: Critical Perspectiives on Southern Africa* 96(1): 1–24

Sridevi KV & Tomar P (2016) Is homework necessary? *The Primary Teacher* 41(3): 27–35

Stacer MJ & Perrucci R (2013) Parental involvement with children at school, home, and community. *Journal of Family and Economic Issues* 34(3): 340–354

Strømme TB & Helland H (2020) Parents' educational involvement: Types of resources and forms of involvement in four countries. *British Educational Research Journal* 46(5): 993–1011

Sullivan D & Hickel J (2023) Capitalism and extreme poverty: A global analysis of real wages, human height, and mortality since the long 16th century. *World Development* 161: 106026

Sun WQ, Spruyt K, Chen WJ, Jiang YR, Schonfeld D, Adams R & Jiang F (2014) The relation among sleep duration, homework burden, and sleep hygiene in Chinese school-aged children. *Behavioral Sleep Medicine* 12(5): 398–411

Taysum A & Ayanlaja CC (2020) Education success for black children in the public school system: Parent participation and community empowerment. In R Papa (Ed.) *Handbook on promoting social justice in education*. Cham: Springer

Tschirley D, Reardon T, Dolislager M & Snyder J (2015) The rise of a middle class in east and southern Africa: Implications for food system transformation. *Journal of International Development* 27(5): 628–646

Vazquez SR & Greenfield PM (2021) The influence of social class on family participation in children's education: A case study. *Revista Colombiana de Psicología* 30(1): 133–147

Villadsen A, Conti G & Fitzsimons E (2020) *Parental involvement in home schooling and developmental play during lockdown: Initial findings from the COVID-19 survey in five national longitudinal studies*. London: UCL Centre for Longitudinal Studies

Vincent C, Rollock N, Ball S & Gillborn D (2012) Being strategic, being watchful, being determined: Black middle-class parents and schooling. *British Journal of Sociology of Education* 33(3): 337–354

Willig C (2008) *Introducing qualitative research in psychology: Adventures in theory and method* (2nd edition). Maidenhead: Open University Press

Yerkes MA, André SCH, Besamusca JW, Kruyen PM, Remery CLHS, Van der Zwan R, Berkers DGJ & Geurts SAE (2020) 'Intelligent' lockdown, intelligent effects? Results from a survey on gender (in)equality in paid work, the division of childcare and household work, and quality of life among parents in the Netherlands during the COVID-19 lockdown. *PLOS ONE* 15(11): 1–23

Young C, Austin S & Growe R (2013) Defining parental involvement: Perception of school administrators. *Education* 133(3): 291–297

Zizzamia R, Schotte S, Leibbrandt M & Ranchhod V (2016) *Vulnerability and the middle class in South Africa*. SALDRU Working Paper 188 / NIDS Discussion Paper 2016/15. Cape Town: Southern Africa Labour and Development Research Unit, University of Cape Town

Section

Intervening

While Section A has laid out the philosophical, social-justice related issues integral to parent and caregiver involvement in schools and Section B has laid out the particular, intersecting South African contexts that mediate how parity of participation plays out, the final section of this book looks at real-world attempts to promote parent involvement with the purpose of catalysing social justice. Five comprehensive interventions are described, with a range of outcomes and implications for the theoretical social justice issues, which are interpreted in context.

In Chapter 9, Kimberley Porteus, Nicky Roberts, and Nobuntu Mazeka look at an intervention at the heart of intersecting education inequalities involving parents contributing to mathematics homework in one of the country's most underserved regions: the rural Eastern Cape. This chapter highlights a typical South African truism about the difficulties of translating policy and ideas into practice, and how social justice snags often rear their ugly heads in the material challenges of project implementation – in practice rather than theory – underscoring the value of a section dedicated to interventions.

Chapter 10, by Craig Gibbs and Kimberleigh Bodley, also offers insights from a programme in challenged rural and semi-urban communities. The innovative use of parents who are trained as peer educators to teach other parents about key parental involvement issues illustrates that parity of participation need not be an antagonistic "us versus them" type of interaction, but rather that a range of intermediary groups can be created to overcome potential or real divisions in the school ecosystem.

Chapter 11 by Ximena Gonzalez and Khanyisa Mkhabele focuses on the aRe Bapaleng Programme that attempted to support the provision of essential ECD services at a grassroots community level by applying a multi-stakeholder partnership approach between an NGO, a private funder, and a set of community organisations. The programme encouraged parents/caregivers to become active members of the ECD ecosystem to positively support their children's development. The programme demonstrates that parity of participation needs to be understood inter-generationally, in terms of children's involvement in all levels of the education system and the ways in which their parents are given opportunities to participate. But the programme also highlights Fraser's (2005) contention that social justice necessarily involves both access to resources and how institutionalised norms shape participation, as marginalised parents cannot be expected to give of their labour time – even if this forms healthy participation – without potential material benefits.

The issue of universal access to high-quality ECD in South Africa is revisited in Chapter 12, where Magali von Blottnitz and Shelley O'Carroll focus on

Together in My Education (TIME). This intervention comprised a home learning programme for children in Grade R and Grade 1 and their families. The programme had to contend with missed learning opportunities resulting from school closures, rotational timetabling, and the severe disruption of the ECD sector during the COVID-19 pandemic, showing how social justice is mediated by a set of intersecting inequalities that are exacerbated in time of crisis. However, the authors show that by reimagining the educational ecosystem beyond the school walls, and by creating productive partnerships between parents and educators, some of the inequalities highlighted by a social justice perspective may be partially overcome.

In Chapter 13, which covers the last of the five interventions described, Adele Mooi and Abigail Dreyer focus on the Pathways Programme adopted by Little People Preschool and Community Development. The chapter foregrounds a disjuncture or "voice gap" between policymakers and those who are receivers of ECD services, showing how parity of participation is eroded in the way that educational policy is translated into practice. The authors argue that the systematic exclusion of primary caregivers and mothers of young children is often built into policy. The strategies and actions presented to overcome this unjust situation constitute a helpful set of suggestions, pointing to ways in which schools can connect with, engage, and sustain parent/caregiver engagement through collaborative efforts to eradicate social injustice.

The interventions section therefore illuminates the challenges of translating social justice theory into practice in contexts where resources, voice, and parity of participation throw up a set of intersecting problems. These chapters highlight how inequalities built into policy have practical implications, that intervening early in the education lifecycle is imperative, and that taking multiple contexts into account is important. However, they also show that innovative interventions that erode divisions and produce new groups may overcome antagonistic relations between caregivers and educators.

9 Deepening our Understanding of Parental Involvement in Rural South Africa: Parental Support of Grade 2 Mathematics Homework Under COVID-19

Kimberley Porteus, Nicky Roberts, and Nobuntu Mazeka

Dedication

This chapter is dedicated to the rural parents and caregivers who went all out to support early grade maths homework under the challenging cloud of COVID-19. Uloyiso lolwenu, ningabanqoni.

Introduction

Homes and schools are some of the most important spaces in which children navigate their lives. While embracing the importance of parental/caregiver involvement in education, the public and policy discourse in South Africa has been somewhat ambivalent about parental/caregiver support of early grade learning, especially in rural settings. There is little clear policy attention on parental/caregiver involvement – what is appropriate, what is fair, what is possible, and what is viable at system scale.

In the early months of 2020, schooling across the world transformed in response to COVID-19. The United Nations (2020) estimates that the school closures under both the hard and soft lockdowns precipitated by COVID-19 represent the largest disruption to schooling in history. South African schools were completely locked down on 18 March 2020. Children in most rural mainstream schools did not return to school on a full-time basis until February 2022. As such, COVID-19 precipitated two years of massive instability in South African schooling. Studies estimate that children in mainstream schools in South Africa missed an equivalent of one year of learning during this period (Shepard et al. 2021; Spaull et al. 2021).

The response to the emergence of COVID-19 in early 2020 quickly exacerbated the bifurcation of the South African schooling system. While the pandemic brought instability and difficulty to all schools, more privileged schools (to the dismay of many parents and caregivers) were able to pivot to home learning in some form. The pivot to home learning was leveraged largely by a culture of "homework" (even in the early grades) and a culture of teacher–parent communication using available mobile phones. Mainstream schools – no fee, historically neglected, African-language-dominant – on the other hand, were shut, with few resources or traditions through which to pivot to home-based learning.

Since 2010, the Nelson Mandela Institute has developed an educational design collective known as the Magic Classroom Collective (MCC), whereby foundation phase teachers, teacher educators, and senior designers work in iterative cycles of material design and piloting to improve literacy and mathematics in primary, African-language-dominant classrooms. Up to early 2020, the work focused primarily on improving teachers' instructional practice inside classrooms (Ramadiro & Porteus 2017, 2018; Porteus 2022, 2023).

One of the strategic advantages of long-term education design hubs is that they are positioned to respond to unexpected and urgent crises emerging in any given system. With strong research relationships, teachers and designers were able to shift their collective gaze more directly to parents/caregivers, hoping to support home learning in some form, under both the hard and soft lockdowns.[*]

This paper focuses on the MCC's education design study, spanning the year from August 2020 to August 2021 during COVID-19, exploring parents'/caregivers' experiences of supporting Grade 2 mathematics homework praxis during COVID-19. The focus of this chapter is on parents' and caregivers' experiences of supporting formal homework under these trying conditions. The emerging design principles, the form and content of homework booklets, and their patterns of completion are not examined in this chapter. Fast-moving and crisis-responsive intervention research is less neat than traditional research; timeframes, activities, and methods are often less pre-planned and carefully delineated. Nevertheless, the experience provides rich opportunities for learning.

Background

In May 2019, before the pandemic, we administered the Early Grade Mathematics Assessment (EGMA) to MCC learners and compared the results to those of an intervention in an urban cohort, operating in a more highly performing district. Expecting rural schools to perform at a lower level than their urban counterparts, we were excited to see MCC learners

---

[*]　The South African government instituted five lockdown levels, with one being the least severe and five the most severe, to curb the spread of COVID-19 (see Hatefi et al. 2020).

outperform the urban cohort. In May 2021, we re-administered the EGMA to MCC learners. Emerging research suggested that the majority of learners had lost the equivalent of one year of learning by May 2021. Given that we did not assume a linear relationship between parental/caregiver support of homework and learner performance, we did not necessarily expect the MCC cohort to demonstrate significantly different results. While the urban cohort experienced modest losses, the MCC cohort maintained their strength across this period (Porteus, Roberts & Moloi 2022). We repeated the exercise in November 2022 to reconfirm the results.

The results are presented in more detail in an upcoming paper. The learner performance across the period is at least partially explained by teachers' strengths and the MCC materials designed to focus their teaching time on high value concepts and number structure (Porteus 2023). However, when the time lost through both hard and soft lockdowns is combined, learners lost at least 75% of their classroom time in school during this period. When asked how they understand the strong results, even teachers (largely sceptical of the capacity of parents/caregivers to support formal schooling) acknowledged the importance of parental support during this period.

This chapter does not attempt to establish a linear relationship between parental/caregiver involvement in supporting homework on the one hand, and improvements in learner performance on the other. However, the results suggest that parental energies during this period translated into learner performance, and therefore justify investments in further development and testing in the future.

Aims of the study

There were two overall aims of the study:
- The first was to understand rural parents'/caregivers' experiences of supporting homework in the early grades in order to extract design principles to guide the development of parent-friendly homework materials. *What design principles maximise parental agency with respect to homework design?*
- The second aim was to explore parents'/caregivers' experiences of supporting early grade mathematics homework, using homework materials guided by the design principles emerging from the first phase of inquiry.

Literature review

Largely motivated by the promise of improving educational performance of the system, there has been a vast array of research focused on parental/caregiver involvement in schooling in the Global North. Wilder (2014) undertook a meta-synthesis of nine meta-analyses that examined the relationship between parental involvement and education, located largely in the Global North. The meta-synthesis was designed to discern trends in research with the goal of informing policy and practice. The work established a wide range of definitions of parental involvement in the literature, from notions that emphasise parental investment of resources (funding, time, energy, attention) to parental attitudes toward schooling, and parental activities and behaviours, either at home or in school to support educational attainment.

Wilder's analysis (2014) suggests that parental involvement (however defined) does not have a linear or strictly causal relationship to a child's education performance. Nevertheless, the overall finding of the meta-synthesis was that the relationship between parent involvement and learner achievement was positive, across contexts, grades, and definitions of both achievement and parental involvement, and was especially impactful in the early years of schooling. Wilder (2014) established a typology to describe the most important ways that parent involvement is expressed: communication between parents and children regarding school; checking and helping with homework; parental educational expectations and aspirations for their children; and attendance of and participation in school activities.

Wilder's synthesis suggests that the relationship was the least clear when it came to associating parental involvement with homework. It was strongest when involvement was defined as parental expectations for academic success, defined as reflecting 'parents' beliefs and attitudes toward school, teachers, subjects, and education in general'. Wilder argues: 'As children are likely to harbour similar attitudes and beliefs as their parents, having high parental expectations appears vital for academic achievement of children' (2014: 392).

In their ongoing work, Hoover-Dempsey et al. also conclude that while remaining circumspect about issues of causation, there is a large body of multidisciplinary research supporting the proposition that 'parents' attitudes, behaviours. and activities influence students' learning and educational success' (2005: 2). Their work suggests that parental involvement is motivated by a combination of fundamental belief systems and the perception of 'invitation for involvement' (both demand and opportunities from schools, teachers, and children). They point to two fundamental and socially constructed belief systems – one related to the construction of the parental role itself (understandings of what parents are supposed to do in relationship to their child's education), and the other related to a parental sense of efficacy for helping their child succeed in school, framing whether parental energies translate into impact in some way. The third element of their model is an overarching focus on parental life contexts. They focus attention not so much on socio-economic status on its own, but socio-economic status as it relates to resources required for parental involvement, including knowledge, skills, time, and energy. This provides a more nuanced approach that both emphasises the difficulties of parental involvement in lower socio-economic contexts and emphasises the possibility of parental involvement in poor and working-class neighbourhoods when issues of resources are better mediated.

In South Africa and the wider African context, there is a growing body of work focusing on parental/caregiver involvement and education. The vast majority of published research focuses on parental/caregiver involvement in secondary schooling, with an emphasis on participation in school governance (Brown & Duku 2008; Mncube 2010; Sayed et al. 2020).

Motala and Luxomo (2014) explored the relationship between the socio-economic background of parents and their perceptions of schooling in a sample of secondary and primary schools in urban (Gauteng) and rural (Eastern Cape) South Africa. Their work confirms some important starting points. South African parents value schoolgoing highly, investing energy and resources to ensure that their children attend school. Parents view schooling as a conduit to a better life in the context of a changing world. While parents had somewhat different ways of talking about schools across urban and rural settings, none claimed to understand or engage in the learning process inside the classroom. They did not believe they had a claim to understanding curricular issues or issues related to teaching and learning.

Felix, Dornbrack, and Scheckle (2008) undertook a series of detailed case studies about the discourses of principals and teachers when discussing parents and homework in South African primary school settings. They concluded that principals and teachers in schools in more affluent areas ascribed parents more agency, whereas principals and teachers in poorer neighbourhoods framed parents as uninterested and unable to assist their children.

Wolf (2020) undertook a study of parental and teacher perceptions of the role of parents in primary schooling in Ghana. When asked directly, parents indicated that they thought the job of educating their children involved both teachers and parents. After parents were probed, Wolf concluded that they largely defined their role, beyond day-to-day care, as procuring the resources required for children to participate in school. They perceived the domain of teaching and learning largely as the territory of teachers, with teachers communicating with parents only when they had serious concerns about their child.

Ngwaru has undertaken extensive research on parental participation in rural Zimbabwe, Kenya, Uganda, and Tanzania. He focused on home and school literacy practices, finding that across these contexts: (a) parents were not aware of roles they could play at home to support formal literacy, despite relevant "funds of knowledge" in the home environment; (b) teachers were under the impression that parents knew little about literacy development and therefore could not play a role to support literacy, either at home or at school; and (c) both parents and teachers view school-based literacy through a lens of reading and writing for formal school purposes, negating parents' and children's "funds of knowledge" available in the home context (2014: 63–64). The three findings share a common implication of school-based interventions that, in the end, were unable to harness the local resources available in homes. He then piloted alternative suggestions for harnessing parental resources by demonstrating small interventions where parents eagerly engaged in a number of activities to support their children.

The studies in South Africa and the wider African context point to a more fundamental history of alienation between working class and poor parents/caregivers in Africa and institutions of formal schooling. This deep alienation, in which parental role construction does not lay claim to the teaching and learning project within schools, is likely rooted in the shadows of a colonial (or apartheid) past in which colonial education hardened local social stratification, and in which the massive expansion of state public education was too often enacted with limited local claim on the classroom.

The Early Grade Reading Study (EGRS) (Taylor et al. 2018) is arguably the most important recent study grappling with parental/caregiver involvement in early grade learning improvement in South Africa. EGRS is a group of reading studies undertaken to better understand how to intervene in early grade reading. At the heart of the EGRS was a cost-effectiveness evaluation for three intervention models to improve reading in the early grades. Two intervention models focused primarily on developing teachers; one model focused on supporting parental involvement.

The parent involvement model held weekly meetings with parents. A "community reading coach" was recruited from local communities. Coaches received one day of training per month and facilitated weekly meetings with parents, covering 10 topics across 30 sessions in a year. The sessions focused on the importance of reading for their children's future and how to support literacy development in the family context. Low-cost materials and reading games for home play were provided (Taylor et al. 2018).

Of the three models, the parental involvement model had the smallest effect. The report concluded that the impact was small, and that a zero effect could not be ruled out. The study team hypothesised that the impact was especially low due to the relatively low levels of attendance at the weekly meetings.

The result of this study has been to further dampen the appetites of policy-makers for investing in the improvement of parental involvement. The Department of Basic Education and the study team recognised the decisive role families play in the context of educational performance. However, the study concluded that South Africa did not yet have a cost-effective model for stimulating parental involvement in a way that translated into measurable learning gains in the early grades. To the extent that resources are available to invest in early learning, the study suggests that parental involvement models are not likely to be the most efficient.

Framing of ambivalence

A wide body of multidisciplinary research suggests that the nature of the relationship between parents/caregivers and their child's formal schooling influences a child's educational experiences and chances of success. Even so, the system of schooling in South Africa – from national policy down to initiatives by teachers in classrooms – remains ambivalent about whether and how to invest in parental involvement in mainstream primary schooling. Framing parental support through formal systems of homework is further fraught. We identify four sources of ambivalence; we reflect on this ambivalence futher at the end of this chapter.

Firstly, there are a number of essentially philosophical concerns. Children in mainstream schools are not keeping up with curricular norms due to profound weaknesses in the teaching and learning project in mainstream primary schools. *Is it fair, even ethical, to land this failure of the state on the backs of already burdened parents/caregivers?*

Secondly, there are unanswered questions about the role of homework in the lives of early primary school children. The question remains: *Are we sure it is good for children?* There are two embedded questions: *Is homework good for any children? And is it good for children in this context?* Internationally, the jury is still out on whether structured homework (and what form of it) serves foundation phase children in the long run (Kim & Fong 2014; Farrow, Tymms & Henderson 1999). There is even less research on the role of formal homework in the context of rural South Africa. *Does early homework create more eager or more reluctant learners across time? Could homework, and the pressures it brings, bring out the worst of parenting instincts, translating into schoolwork becoming further associated with tension and punitive punishment?*

The third source of ambivalence, held strongly by many teachers, questions whether parents/caregivers in the rural context are *interested* or *able* to support children with homework. The role constructed for parenting across many rural African settings has been alienated from the curricular project of formal schooling; parents have neither felt invited into this space, nor felt that their resources (energy, time, care) have value in this domain. Teachers, in turn, question whether parents have the interest, commitment, or ability to provide valuable support in the context of the formal learning project.

For policy-makers, the source of ambivalence is slightly different. Largely accepting, at least at some level, that parents are an important national asset for primary education, they question whether there is a viable and cost-effective model through which to stimulate parent support of learning in the home. Furthermore, to the extent that there is a cost-effective model, where does investing into parental involvement fit within the pressing priorities of educational reform in South Africa?

Conceptual framework

This study was guided by the research of Motala and Luxomo (2014), Wolf (2020), Felix, Dornbrack & Scheckle (2008), and Ngwaru and Niboye (2020) about facilitating parental involvement in primary schooling in rural Africa. In the light of their research, it is suggested as a starting point that the construction of parental roles across rural Africa has been deeply alienated from the curricular (teaching and learning) project of formal schooling.

The study accepts that parental involvement (however defined) does not have a linear or strictly causal relationship to a child's educational performance (Wilder 2014; Hoover-Dempsey et al. 2005). We evaluate parental involvement experiences through two lenses. First, we ask whether the activity is capable of generating expanding patterns of parental/caregiver involvement. We benefit from the framework proposed by Hoover-Dempsey et al. (2005) that suggests that generating parental involvement reflects four factors: parental role construct, sense of efficacy, sense of invitation (demand and opportunities for involvement), and parental context with an emphasis on resources. Second, we consider the impact of the experience on the relationships among key educational players, especially parents/caregivers, children, and teachers. To what extent does the experience trigger a self-reinforcing cycle between beliefs, expectations, relationships, and activity among and between key educational players (Wilder 2014)?

In adopting a conceptual framework, we add two domains to the framework proposed by Hoover-Dempsey et al. (2005). In assessing the experience of parents, the study focuses on five interrelated indicators: parental role construct, parental self-efficacy, invitations for involvement, educational relationships, and educational expectations.

Research design
Methodology

The exploratory study adopts a case study design, framed by educational design research (EDR). As a case study, it aims to develop an in-depth understanding of a bounded case through the collection of multiple forms of data (Plano Clark & Creswell 2008).

EDR is focused on actively engaging problematics where the existence of a pre-existing "solution" is not assumed. It focuses attention on the work of building validated ideas, tools, and principles via interactions between theory and embedded practice. EDR is 'the systematic study of designing, developing, and evaluating educational interventions' especially for 'educational problems for which no or only a few validated principles are available to structure and support the design and development of activities' (Plomp 2007: 13). EDR takes the form of iterative cycles in which successive approximations of the intervention go hand in hand with successive approximations of design principles.

Bounded case
Schools

The bounded case includes 13 deep rural primary schools in the Eastern Cape in two clusters. All schools serve rural villages. The indicators of rurality are more pronounced in one cluster, with a lower population density, a higher proportion of agricultural households (63% vs 48%), a higher dependency ratio (98% vs 67%), and a lower proportion of amenities such as flush toilets (1% vs 26%) and piped water (2% vs 19%) (Statistics South Africa 2011).

Parents/caregivers

The study focused on parents/caregivers of children who were transitioning from Grade 1 in 2021 to Grade 2 in 2022. There were approximately 600 children in this cohort.

Context

The bounded case focuses on a 12-month period, beginning in September 2020 (see Table 9.1 on page 174). Engagement with parents/caregivers during the COVID-19 lockdown predated the formal start of the study. Schools closed from March 2020 through August 2020, reopening on a rotational basis in September 2020 (see Table 9.1, row A). By May 2020, we resolved with teachers to reprint learner workbooks, previously designed mainly for classroom use. Teachers were invited to find a safe mechanism to distribute the workbooks to children at home. Teachers in Cluster A circulated the books to parents by the end of June. Teachers in Cluster B, with less strong relationships with parents, circulated the books largely in September, when schools reopened on a rotational basis.

The formal study also started in September. Stress and fear permeated the system. Teachers were under pressure, unclear about how to make up for time loss while maintaining sanitised classrooms and other COVID-19 safety measures. Schools stopped meetings, even standard meetings between principals, heads of departments, and teachers. Between October 2020 and January 2021, the rate of COVID-19 deaths increased, taking the lives of at least three teachers in the MCC network itself. While teachers appeared interested in the work with parents, their attention was understandably limited.

Study design

Table 9.1 locates the study design across this complex period. Two schools, one in each cluster, were identified as focus schools among the 13 schools included. There were two periods of enquiry – a baseline and an endline. (Given that the education design hub is ongoing, these constituted the baseline and endline in terms of the current study process.) The baseline was undertaken in October and November 2020. By this time, many parents/caregivers had some experience of attempting to support their children using the workbooks that were rapidly circulated during the hard lockdown. The first enquiry sought to understand parents' experiences of supporting homework in the baseline period, with the goal of establishing design principles to inform the redesign of materials for the subsequent intervention cycle (in 2021).

Guided by these design principles, homework materials were developed in the form of weekly booklets. From the beginning of the school year in 2021, teachers across the 13 schools distributed and collected 6 sets of 8-page homework booklets each term (which is discussed in more detail below).

The endline was conducted after the second term, in July and August 2021. The aim of the endline was to better understand parents'/caregivers' experiences of supporting Grade 2 homework, using the materials based on the parental design principles that emerged from the baseline.

The baseline and endline shared two common tools. During both periods, a printed survey was distributed to all parents/caregivers in the focus schools by teachers, who handed them out to learners. The printed surveys were presented bilingually (in isiXhosa and English). The response rate of the baseline survey was 74% (67 of 90); the rate at which parents/caregivers returned the endline survey was 70% (64 of 91). These are high response rates in comparison with comparable initiatives (Bojuwoye 2009). The endline survey was slightly longer, repeating some questions from the initial survey and asking additional reflective questions.

A small parent/caregiver focus group was convened in both focus schools.[*] From October 2020 to January 2021, the focus groups met three times. The purpose was to inform parents and caregivers of the purpose of the study, to reflect on past experiences, and to analyse different possible exemplars for homework presentation. The focus groups met again at the end of the intervention to reflect on the experience and lessons learned. Bilingual discussions were recorded and transcribed line by line (isiXhosa and English).

Two additional activities were undertaken during the endline period. Semi-structured questionnaires were completed by all teachers from the 13 schools, probing their analysis of the experience. A set of Term 2 homework booklets were collected from schools in each cluster (including the focus schools), which were analysed for completion and understanding. The quality of learner work was coded simply, differentiating between items that were fully correct, partially correct, and fully incorrect.

The analysis of quantitative data, across tools, was undertaken using Excel, drawing on basic descriptive statistics.[†] The qualitative items were coded inductively to identify both common themes and divergent views (Chandra & Shang 2019).

Table 9.1 *Study timeline map: COVID-19 implications and study activities*

	Apr	May	Jun	Jul	Aug	Sep	Oct	Nov	Dec	Jan	Feb	Mar	Apr	May	Jun	Jul	Aug
Study	Pre study					Study period											
Years	2020					2020				2021							
Terms	Term 2			Term 3		Term 4				Term 1			Term 2			Term 1	
	Apr	May	Jun	Jul	Aug	Sep	Oct	Nov	Dec	Jan	Feb	Mar	Apr	May	Jun	Jul	Aug
	Schools Closed					Rotational			School holiday		Rotational schedule						
A		Homework books (rapid)							School holiday		Homework books (design principles)						
B					Plan	Baseline		Redesign					EGMA			Endline	

---

[*] The focus groups were designed to be small (between 5 and 10 parents) and conducive to more intimate communication. In the focus school in one cluster, most parents came to the briefing meeting and had to draw straws to participate. In the focus group in the second cluster, only seven parents came to the meeting. All parents agreed to participate in the focus groups. Participation fluctuated from full attendance to less than 50% attendance.

[†] The surveys included Likert scale items, where parents were asked to indicate whether they strongly agree, agree, disagree or strongly disagree. Our experience with analysing Likert scale items in this context is to accept that most parents (and teachers) have been part of a system that rewards compliance. We have seen that teachers tend to select the answer that they interpret as most appropriate in their view. We find teachers more willing to express their hesitations by choosing pleasing answers but selecting "agree" (or "disagree") rather than "strongly agree" (or "strongly disagree"). We place emphasis on the shift within these answers in the direction of the more pleasing answer during the endline.

Limitations

As a relatively small study conducted in a complex context, the study was intentionally exploratory. Rather than seeking generalisable findings, the study sought to deepen our understanding of the experience of rural parents/caregivers supporting formal homework in order to establish generative ideas and hypotheses for further work in this area.

Findings

The findings focus on the experiences of parents/caregivers, both in the baseline and endline periods. We begin by presenting findings from the baseline. These experiences and analyses framed design principles upon which homework was designed for the subsequent cycle. We briefly present the form of the workbooks and the initial analysis of completion rates. In the final section of the baseline findings, we present the experiences of parents and caregivers working with the newly designed homework booklets with their children across this period.

Baseline findings

Respondents

The relationship between the learners and the survey respondents (who will be referred to as 'parents' although their relationships were varied) is presented in Table 9.2. Respondents are largely mothers and grandmothers. Just over 20% of respondents did not answer the question. Only 6% identified themselves as 'caregiver' or 'guardian'. The average household size was 9.7 people, with two thirds of members under 13 years old, and one third of household members below the age of 10.

Table 9.2 *Respondents' relationship with Grade 2 learners*

Survey	Date	N	Mother	Father	Grand-mother	Grand-father	Sister	Brother	Care-giver	No answer
Baseline	Nov 2020	67	43%	–	30%	–	–	–	6%	21%

Parental relationship with teachers and schooling (prior to COVID-19)

Prior to the pandemic, parents said they had little contact with teachers. Some parents had participated in one-off school-based meetings. Parents did not recall meetings specifically with their child's teacher, either in group or individual formats. There were no phone-based systems of communication. Thirty-five per cent of parents had phones capable of receiving a message in WhatsApp. While 91% of parents indicated that they had a phone capable of receiving SMS messages, they were very concerned about the costs of sending and receiving SMSs.

Parents overwhelmingly associated communication from teachers with children failing. When a child was not going to progress into the next grade, teachers called the parent to inform them.

While hesitant to speak poorly of teachers, parents spoke about school as a place their children went, but one with which they had little relationship. They experienced their relationship with schooling as one primarily focused on resources – the resources required to bathe, feed, and clothe children to go to school. While these schools do not charge school fees, parents continue to associate schools with the pressure of material resources.

The role construction for parents did not encompass issues of curriculum or formal teaching and learning in the classroom. They did not experience their skills as a valuable resource in reference to the formal learning of their children.

Parents appeared somewhat surprised to be asked about their relationship with teachers in the survey. They used largely positive, yet general, words to describe their relationship with teachers. Most parents said that they did not know what the teacher thought of them, but assumed things were fine (see Box 9.1).

> **Box 9.1** *Parents' description of communication with teachers (prior to COVID-19)*
>
> Khange sithethe ngaphambi kweCovid nangona besithetha kunyaka ophelileyo kuba umntwana uyamphinda uGrade1. [There has been no contact before COVID, though we communicated last year because my child is repeating Grade 1.]
>
> Andazi into yokuba umisi undithatha ukuba ndingumzali onjani kodwa intombi leyam iqhuba kakuhle kakhulu. [I don't know what the teacher thinks of me as a parent, but my child is doing so well.]
>
> Utitshalakazi akanasikhalazo kuba uba ebenaso ngaye wandifowunela. [The teacher has no complaints so far, because if there were complaints, she would call me.]

Parents' early experience of supporting homework

Parents in the baseline presented themselves as open and optimistic about the notion of supporting their children to do homework. The proportion of parents who indicated that they would be interested in being a part of a group to talk more about homework and parent–teacher communications was 93%; and 96% of parents in the survey indicated that they felt able to assist their child with early grade maths homework.

The focus groups discussed their initial experiences of supporting children to complete the maths workbooks at home during the pandemic. Parents were not only constructive but enthusiastic about their role in supporting their children with early grade maths homework. In the focus groups, parents wanted to share their experiences and stories with each other in some detail.

We recognise the tendency in such discussions to share positive information more readily than sharing difficulties and challenges. Hence, due credence was given to the few parents who spoke more openly about some of the difficulties. Given the well-known phenomenon of homework contributing to tension within parent–child relationships, we probed this experience. The majority of parents did not associate homework with tension. Two parents discussed the day-to-day difficulties with one parent saying: 'Umnntwana wam akathandi ukubhala nokufunda. Ebendisokolisa athi andinguye utitshala wakhe.' [My child doesn't like to write and read. He was difficult and would tell me that I'm not his teacher.] Interestingly, the few parents who spoke about the difficulties were still optimistic about their role in supporting learning at home.

Parents strongly embraced the form of a workbook. When studying alternative forms of homework, they rejected any format that was not a printed homework book. They specifically did not relate to homework pamphlets with ideas of homework activities. Parents emphasised the importance of structure and clarity. Navigating the pressures in their daily lives, they called for clear and explicit expectations; they wanted to know exactly what was required each day. They were concerned about the length of the workbooks distributed during lockdown. The structure of the workbook did not make daily expectations clear. Some parents encouraged children to write one page a day; others wrote more than four pages. There were a few parents who pushed children to complete the 100-page book within the first two weeks.

They did not see their role as "teaching" and were concerned about concepts that they believed required more teacher input. They did not see themselves as replacing teachers and consistently emphasised the distinction between parents and teachers.

Parents expressed concern about mathematics content that required ongoing interpretation. Instead, they gravitated to mathematics content that was familiar in form to what they had seen in their own schooling, such as lists of "sums". A few parents spoke in detail about mathematical concepts that they hoped teachers would focus more attention on while their children were in class. They noted that children were eager to count forwards but less eager to count backwards. They spoke about children struggling with differentiating between addition and subtraction, and struggling with the notion of zero. They spoke about misunderstanding the words for 'before' and 'after' in isiXhosa due to differences in the way that isiXhosa refers to time. They spoke about some children continuing to reverse some letters and numbers. (These struggles, of course, are well documented in educational literature.)

When speaking about their role in supporting their children, they used the word 'ndimncedisa' to refer to the notion of support in general. They overwhelmingly emphasised their role as overseeing and checking, helping to make sure their children did the work. A few parents spoke about explaining (ndichaze), correcting (ndilungisa), giving clarity (ndicacise), encouraging their child to read the instructions (ndisonyanzelisa ukuba makafunde umyalelo), and counting together (siyabala).

Summary: Homework booklet design and return rates

Homework took the form of printed workbooks. Responding to the parents' call for developing workbooks that were time bound, we developed six booklets (A3 folded into eight pages), each providing work for one week. This design assumes that children complete two pages per day across four days of the learning week. The intention was for to teachers to distribute books to learners, and learners to return them a week later. The structure of the mathematics work, while not limited to lists of sums, was highly consistent across time, minimising new interpretation. Of the six inside pages, the even pages focused on number sense, and additive and multiplicative relations, supporting curricular expectations by building fluency rather than new concepts.. The odd pages presented space and shape work, in forms that minimised instructional interpretation. The back page focused on time, alternating between clocks and calendars. The front page illustrated and summarised two or three home-based "games". Falling outside of the design principles, we retained games, understanding that they would not be used in many homes. We remained interested in understanding whether "stretching" activities would benefit some learners.

Homework booklets were collected from five schools. We reviewed the second booklet from Term 2 in April 2021, when schools were operating on a rotational basis. The return rates (percentage of learners who returned the booklet) are presented in Table 9.3. The overall return rate of this booklet was 58%, with a high variance between schools. As an overall trend, the schools in Cluster A, where teachers have a stronger relationship with local parents, had a higher return rate than schools in Cluster B. The only exception is School 3 in Cluster B, which was a focus school, highly supported in the period. No support was provided to Schools 2, 4, and 5 in this period, beyond printing the homework booklets. Even so, more than 40% of learners returned completed homework booklets in Schools 4 and 5. School 2 stood out with a 72% rate of return.

Table 9.3 *Return rate of homework booklets: Term 2, Book 2: Booklet review (5 schools)*

School	Cluster	Focus school?	Learners		
			Booklets collected	Enrolment	Percentage
School 1	A	Y	53	84	63
School 2	A	N	43	60	72
School 3	B	Y	20	23	87
School 4	B	N	21	46	46
School 5	B	N	16	39	41
Totals			133	229	58

Endline findings

Respondents

There were modest changes in how survey respondents categorised their relationships with learners by the time of the endline survey. There was a modest drop in grandparents, with an increase in siblings. Fewer respondents skipped the question about their relationship with the learner, perhaps indicating greater trust in the research process, especially among child-headed households, as shown in Table 9.4.

Respondents were asked if there was anyone else who supported their child doing homework, beyond themselves. Thirty per cent of parents indicated that a sibling of the child also assisted their child; 11% of parents indicated that a grandparent also assisted their child. Only three parents (5%) indicated that a neighbour helped to support their child. The data suggests that engaging in homework across this period may have mobilised slightly wider resources for learning in the home.

Table 9.4 *Respondents' relationship with Grade 2 learners in endline survey*

Survey	Date	N	Mother	Father	Grand-mother	Grand-father	Sister	Brother	Caregiver	No answer
Baseline	Nov 2020	67	43%	–	30%	–	–	–	6%	21%
Endline	Aug 2021	64	47%	2%	22%	–	6%	5%	9%	11%

Parents' description of homework

At the endline, all parents completing the survey (N=60) indicated that their Grade 2 learner had brought homework books home. Thirty per cent indicated that their children 'brought maths homework' home every day; 60% indicated that their children brought maths homework home once a week. These answers, together, may reflect daily work on weekly workbooks. Ten per cent of parents said children brought homework once a month.

Half (50%) of the parents indicated that their children completed the maths homework all of the time; 35% of parents indicated that their children completed the maths homework most of the time; and 15% of parents indicated that their children only completed the maths homework sometimes. No parents indicated that their children never completed the maths homework. These estimates were somewhat higher (but not too different) from the final completion rate of 58%. Afternoons after school were indicated by 72% of parents as the best time for their child to do homework, while evenings were indicated as the best time by 17% of parents. Less than 10% indicated that they preferred their children to work over weekends.

Parents' perceptions of homework books

Parents in the focus groups were united in their relationship with the homework books. They embraced the clear format and expectations of the booklets, continually using the words 'user friendly' (see Box 9.2).

Forty per cent of parents in the survey indicated that their children found the homework 'very easy'. A further 53% of parents indicated that their children found the homework 'easy'. Only 6% of parents indicated that their children found homework 'difficult'; none of the parents indicated that their children found it 'very difficult'. Some parents spoke about children being 'challenged' by the homework at times but considered the challenge to be productive rather than paralysing.

One parent in Cluster A spoke about struggling with the isiXhosa, indicating that she herself had learned through isiZulu. This is likely a reference to the differences between standard isiXhosa and local isiMpondo (a dialect of isiXhosa with a strong influence from isiZulu). This parent said, 'Nami ngikwazile ukumncedisa nangona bendiye ndicele abanye abantwana abakwamanye amaGrade kuba isiXhosa ngibuye ndingakwazi ukusifunda ngoba ndifunde isiZulu.' [I also managed to assist the child at home with homework, though sometimes I am challenged with isiXhosa since I learned isiZulu.] Further responses from parents are contained in Box 9.2.

> **Box 9.2** *Parents' descriptions of homework booklets*
>
> Iincwadi ezi bezenazo sezibhaliwe ziyasincedisa kuba thina besingeke sikwazi ukuba masibenzise ntoni engumsebenzi wesikolo. Ndirhalela siqhubeke nazo. [The user-friendly workbooks that we are currently receiving are of great help. Without them, I wouldn't know what to do with my child's education or where to start. My wish is to continue getting the booklets.]
>
> Andikaluboni olunye uncedo ndisoneliswa kukuza kwakhe neencwadi ezi thina sithathe ngokuncedisa xa ephendula. [The issuing of workbooks is enough. I am satisfied when he brings ready-made workbooks and for us to guide and show him how and what to do.]
>
> Ndithanda kakhulu le ncwadi yeveki kuba incinci kamandi ne sum zayo zilula futhi iyamkhuthaza umntwana ukuba makaqale ngayo phambi kokuba ayodlala kuba ndiyijonga ngokuhlwa phambi kokuba silale ukuba uyenzile imisetyenzana yezibalo yosuku. [I love the weekly booklet the most because it's small, and the maths sums in it are easy. I encourage my child to start with it before she can go play because I check it in the evening before we sleep to make sure that she has done the maths work of the day.]
>
> Ubemhle kwaye umntwana wenze kakuhle ngoku, andiseva bunzima bungako. Umntwana ubemana enzinyelwa kwezinye iindawo kodwa kuqhubekile. [The work has been very good. My child has been doing good. I'm not stressed as much. The child would feel challenged at times, but the work has been going on.]

Parents' role in homework support

In the parent survey, all parents indicated that they supported their child with homework. In the endline, parents either strongly agreed (49%) or agreed (46%) that their child needed their help to complete their maths homework. In both the endline and baseline surveys, parents responded to the statement about whether they were able to support their child with maths homework (see Figure 9.1): 97% of parents agreed with this statement in the baseline; 98% of parents agreed with this statement at the endline. The number of parents who 'strongly agreed' increased by roughly 10%. Parents also responded to the statement, 'I do not have time to help my child with homework'. The number of parents who agreed with this statement before the intervention decreased after the intervention by roughly 20% (see Figure 9.2).

Figure 9.1 *Parent response regarding their ability to assist children with maths homework*

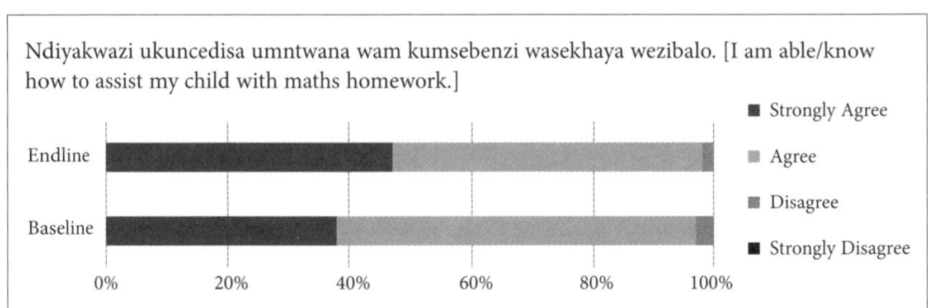

Figure 9.2 *Parent response regarding having time to assist children with homework*

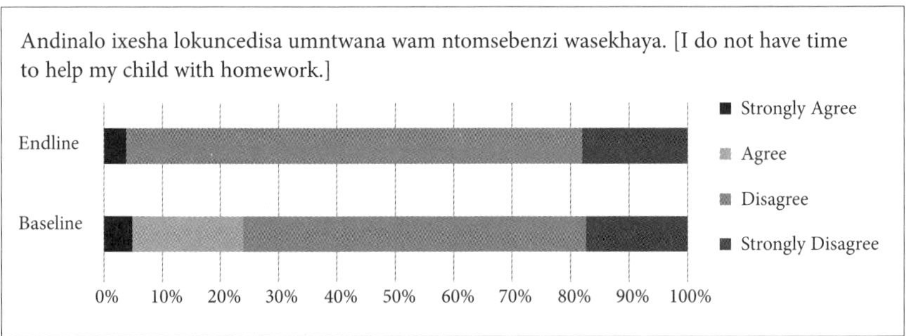

In the endline survey, 80% of those parents who said they supported their children with homework (N=57) indicated that they supported their child every day, 12% indicated that they supported their child more than once a week, and 8% indicated that they supported their child once a week.

The survey asked parents to characterise the way they supported their children with maths homework. They were provided with six ways that parents could support homework from which they were asked to select all the ways that they regularly supported their child. The results of this question are presented in Table 9.5. As shown in this table, the highest number of parents indicated that the role they played with their children was to teach (73%). The next highest roles were encouraging (61%) and overseeing (56%). Only 31% of parents indicated that their role was to discipline. Forty-three per cent of parents indicated that they assisted their children by reading the instructions out loud: 28% of parents indicated that they played maths games with their children.

Table 9.5 *Ways that parents/caregivers can support homework*

How did you support your child? Tick all the ways that you regularly supported your child with maths homework.*	
QAPHELA: Ndiqinisekisa ukuba umntwana wam uyawenza umsebenzi wesikolo. OVERSEE: I make sure my child does homework.	56%
BENDIMKHUTHAZA: Bendimkhuthaza umntwana wam ukwenza umsebenzi wasekhaya. ENCOURAGE: I encourage my child to do homework.	61%
NDIYAMQEQESHA: Ndiyamqeqesha umntwana wam xa engawenzi umsebenzi wasekhaya. DISCIPLINE: I discipline my child when they do not do homework.	31%
NDIYAMFUNDISA: Ndiyamfundisa umntwana wam izibalo xa engazi ukuba makenze ntoni. TEACH: I teach my child when my child does not know what to do.	73%
NDIDLALA IMIDLALO YEZIBALO: Ndidladla imidlalo yezibalo nomntwana wam. PLAY MATHS GAMES: I play maths games with my child.	28%
NDIFUNDA NDIKHWAZA: Nidfunda ndikhwaza imibuzo kwiincwadi zezibalo. READ ALOUD: I read aloud the questions in the maths homework books.	43%

The parents who did not play maths games were asked to explain why they did not play the maths games, choosing among four options.† Eighty per cent of parents (35/44) indicated that they did not understand the games; 9% indicated that they did not have time; and 9% said that their child did not want to play with them.

One set of games in the homework booklet expected parents to cut or tear a page out of the booklets to create "maths cards". There was no evidence that any parents did this.

The endline parent focus groups discussed their experiences of supporting children with homework. Again, they used several verbs to talk about the way they supported children. They continued to use the word 'ndimncedisa' to refer to the notion of support in general. Parents also used the verbs nokumbuza (ask/remind), mabambonise (to show), ndibheke (check), bebebhala bampractizise (give practice in writing), sibala (count together), and ndimkhuthaza (encouraged).

---

*　Six parents did not answer this set of questions. Ten parents only chose one answer: it is possible that these parents did not understand that they could choose more than one answer.

†　The four options were: 1) they did not understand the games; 2) they did not have time to play; 3) they were not used to playing games with their children; and 4) their child did not want to play the games.

In both the baseline and endline, we asked parents to respond to the statement, 'I am not good at maths'. Fifty-five per cent of parents disagreed (or strongly disagreed) with this statement in the baseline, increasing by almost 20% to 74% in the endline.

Figure 9.3 *Parents' perceptions of their maths abilities*

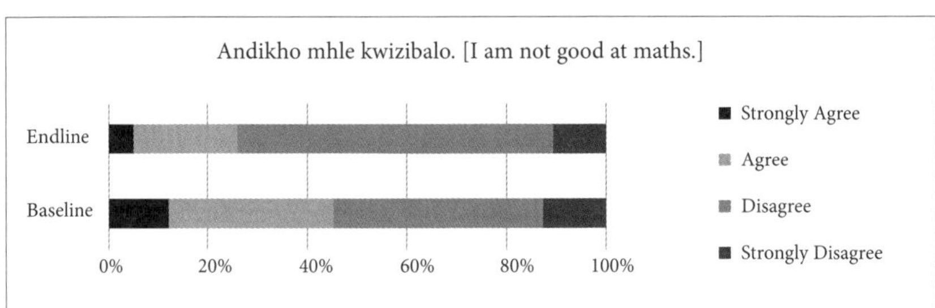

Parents' perceptions of homework and relationship with learners

In the endline survey, parents engaged with statements about the way that working with their child on homework influenced their relationship with their children. Forty-five per cent of parents agreed or strongly agreed that doing homework with children is stressful. (Half of these parents strongly agreed.) One grandmother elaborated on this stress in the focus group (see Box 9.3).

Box 9.3 *A grandmother's perception of supporting homework as being stressful*

Ingxaki ebendisiba nayo xa kufuneka kuncediswe umsebenzi wasekhaya kukuba ndingaboni. Bendincedwa ngumntwana wasebumelwaneni obeyed ngamanye amaxesha sincedise lo mzukulwana wam bebukele ITV's, xa ndinqanda athi akanakungayibukeli ITV's yena, ndiyeke ke kuba ndifuna kuncedakale umntwana wam. [The problem I encountered with homework was when I had to ask a neighbour's child to help my grandchild because I have sight problems. Sometimes they would do homework watching TV. When I comment, she would say she could not afford to miss out watching TV.]

While many parents acknowledged that the activity can be stressful, over 95% of parents agreed that they enjoyed doing maths with their child, of which almost half strongly agreed. Furthermore, 95% of parents agreed that doing homework with their child improved their relationship, of which 60% of these parents strongly agreed (see Figure 9.4). Parents in the focus group spoke extensively about the relationship with their child improving through working with them on their homework (see Box 9.4).

Figure 9.4 *Homework and parent–child relationships*

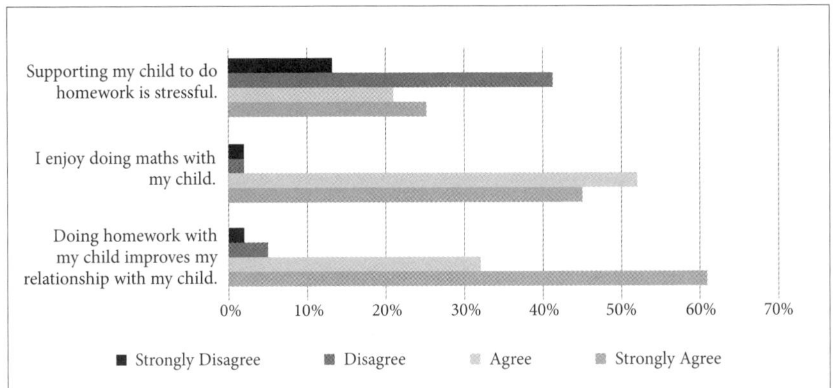

Box 9.4 *Parents' perceptions of how their relationship with their child was affected by doing homework together*

Unxibelelwano nomntwana wam luye lwaphucuka kakhulu. Ubonakalie umdla omkhulu xa sisebenza. [The relationship with my child has improved a lot. He has developed much interest when we were doing homework.]

Ubudlelwane nomntwana wam bukhule kakhulu. Xa ndifika ekhaya emailing ndisuka emsebenzini, ndifika abantwana bam ababini bendilinde phandle. Bathi, 'Yiza, Mama. Masenze umsebenzi wasekhaya kunye.' [It improved so much. When I come home in the afternoon from work, I find my two children waiting for me outside. 'Come, Mama,' they say. 'Let's do homework together.']

Kwelilile kakhulu ukusokolisana xa kufuneka kwenziwe umsebenzi wasekhaya. [I am no longer struggling when encouraging him to do work.]

Parents' perceptions of their child's relationship with maths and the impact of homework

In the parent survey during the baseline and endline periods, we posed statements about parents' perceptions of their child's relationship with maths. In the baseline period, 83% of parents either agreed or strongly agreed that their 'child is good at maths'. In the endline period, the overall number grew modestly to 87%; the numbers of parents who strongly agreed also grew by 5%.

Figure 9.5 *Parents' perceptions of their child's relationship with maths*

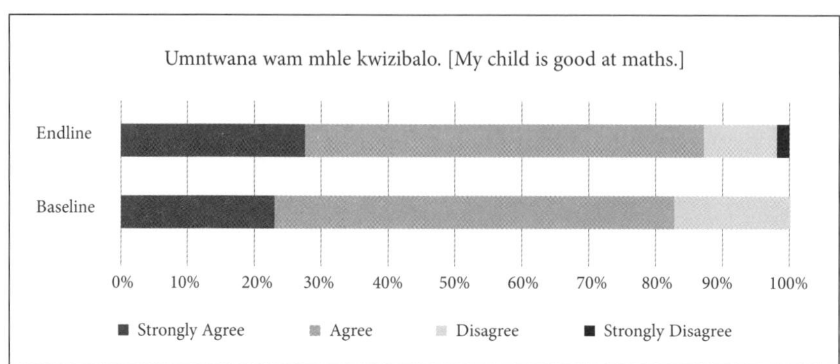

The parents in the focus groups each wanted to share what they saw as the impact of the homework on their child. One grandparent, who could not read, brought her child's report card to show the group the score of 7 (highest possible mark category) that her child had received in maths. Parents saw their children grow in strength and independence and associated this growth with their homework practice.

> **Box 9.5** *Parents' descriptions of the impact of homework*
>
> Umntwana wam uwuthande kakhulu umsebenzi, kakngangokuba ubede afune ukusebenza esavela esikolweni. Ebede akwazi nokuzisebenzela. [My child has enjoyed this work a lot, in so much that he would want to work immediately when he comes back from school. He would even be able to work independently.]
>
> Isebenze kakhulu, kwaye abantwana bebecacelwa, nam kuyacaca. [It worked very well. The child has been understanding, and it has been clear – even to me.]
>
> Ubemhle kwaye umntwana wenze kakuhle ngoku, andiseva bunzima bungako. Umntwana ubemana enzinyelwa kwezinye iindawo kodwa kuqhubekile. [The work has been very good. My child has been doing good. I'm not stressed as much. The child would feel challenged at times, but the work has been going on.]
>
> Ndiziva ndi happy kuba umntwana wam uyancediseka kwayena uyakwazi ngoku ukubuya azenzele ihomework. [I am feeling happy because my child is getting assistance, and she is able to do homework without being pushed behind.]

The parents participating in the focus group also spoke about gaining from their participation in the focus group itself. They spoke about their relationship with their children's schoolwork changing as a function of participating in the focus group. One parent explained this carefully (see Box 9.6).

> **Box 9.6** *A parent's description of the impact of the focus group*
>
> Ndiziva ndonwabe kakhulu mna. Umntana utshintsho alucholeyo ukusukela kunyaka ophelileyo, usahamba kahle kakhulu. Kuye kwatshintsha njengoba benisifundis ezi zinto nizifundisayo, siyayibona ukuba le ndlela yokufundisa yokufunda komzali nomntwana iyancedisa kakhulu kuba umntwana iHomework oyinikiweyo akakwazi ukuyilibala. Kanti ngelaxesha bebezifundela bona bebeyilibala ihomework ngoku uthi efika athi mama kuthiwe undincedise apha nathi singene emsebenzini simncedise. Isincedise kakhulu ke lonto nathi siyababona abantwana bahambela phezulu. [I am feeling extremely happy. I am noticing changes with my child since last year. Her attitude towards schoolwork has improved. The change is the outcome of different interactions we have with you, the mentoring we received on how we can support our children as parents. They never forget to do their homework anymore now that we are assisting them, unlike when they used to do it on their own. My support has been a motivation to my child to ask for assistance with homework.]

Parents' relationships with teachers

In both the surveys and the focus groups, parents indicated that communication with teachers increased because of the homework, and the relationships between parents and teachers may have improved somewhat. During the baseline and endline surveys, parents engaged with the sentence, 'Teachers respect parents'. More than 90% of parents agreed with this statement, with the proportion of parents who more decisively 'strongly agreed' increasing by 17%. That said, the few parents who disagreed grew modestly from 2% to 8%, with one parent disagreeing strongly for the first time. See Figure 9.6.

Figure 9.6 *Parents' perceptions of teachers' respect*

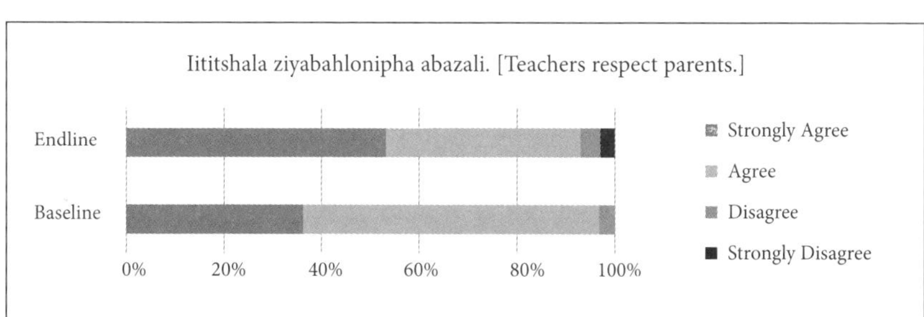

While there was no set mechanism for parents to receive feedback from teachers during this period, some parents sought teachers out. They spoke positively of these interactions in the focus group, valuing the opportunity to work with their children to make corrections. The focus groups discussed how to improve the homework experience, focusing largely on improving systems of feedback from teachers, whereby they could work through corrections with their children (see Box 9.7).

> **Box 9.7** *Parents' descriptions of the impact of homework on communication with teachers*
>
> Umsebenzi wasekhaya uyiphucule indlela nisebenza ngayo umzukulwana wam. Isinike nethuba Lihle lokunxibelelana notitshala. Xa kukho into endingayiqondiyo bendisiya esikolweni, utitshala asidibanise nomntwana outshot kucace. [Homework has improved the performance of my grandchild. It has also given us an opportunity to communicate better with teachers. Whenever I encountered problems in assisting my grandson, I went to school, and the teacher would sit me with my grandson, and she would explain the problem, and we would go home happy.]
>
> Xa zihambile iincwadi, zathathwa ngootitshalakazi mabasicacisele apho singenzanga kakuhle khona, Sicela ulwenza izilungiso. Incwadi mayenziwe ibe nendawo eshiyelwe izilungiso. Masazi ukuba kuqhubeka ntoni. [When the homework booklets have been submitted, we ask for comments from teachers, to explain how the work has been done. We want to know what is going on. We also ask that there should be space provided for corrections in the homework booklet.]

Discussion

Evaluating the experience

As presented in the conceptual framework, we do not hold the quality of parental involvement to be directly accountable for children's educational performance (Wilder 2014; Hoover-Dempsey et al. 2005).

In this chapter, we evaluate the experience through two interrelated lenses. We consider the extent to which parental involvement creates the conditions to expand involvement over time; and we consider whether parental involvement triggers a self-reinforcing cycle between beliefs, expectations, relationships, and activity among and between key educational players. Borrowing and extending the frameworks of Hoover-Dempsey et al. (2005) and Wilder (2014), we focus on five interrelated indicators established in the conceptual framework: parental role construct, parental self-efficacy, educationally oriented relationships, expectations, and invitations for involvement.

Limitations

Before reviewing the findings through these lenses, we take a step back to speak about the limitations of the study. While the patterns of completion arise from a larger experience, the voices of parents in this study were extracted from a relatively small survey (N=60) and two small but intensive focus groups (N=18). The parents participating in the focus group were somewhat self-selected, in that those who participated in all groups were, by definition, parents ready to "step in" to these discussions. We are constantly conscious of the natural "performativity" that results from long-term power imbalances, in which parents, in this case, may emphasise their praise rather than their critique, simply to encourage the long-term engagement. Furthermore, the study took place under the conditions of the pandemic, with children participating in schooling at most on a rotational basis. The eagerness of parents may also reflect the pandemic backdrop, during which parents were especially concerned about their children's access to schooling.

Key indicators

We review the experience through the five key interrelated indicators established in the conceptual framework: parental role construct, parental self-efficacy, educationally oriented relationships, expectations, and invitations for involvement.

Parental role construct: The parents in the survey and focus group appear to have expanded their understanding of their role as parents. They felt needed by their children; at the endline, parents strongly agreed (49%) or agreed (46%) that their children needed their help. At the baseline, parents emphasised that their role should be framed by notions of checking, encouraging, and overseeing. They were particularly clear that it was not their role to 'teach'. By the endline, however, they described their role in much wider terms. The most common verb chosen in the parent survey to describe their role was 'teaching' (73%). They also spoke about reading aloud (43%) and even playing maths games (28%). Their role appeared to expand beyond simply supervising, to seeing themselves in relationship to the curricular project – the content of the classroom. Parents had an accurate analysis of mathematical weaknesses at the grade level. In asking for feedback from teachers, they clearly had begun to locate themselves within the teaching and learning circle surrounding their children.

Parental self-efficacy: By the endline, 98% of parents agreed that they were able/knew how to support their child with homework; of these parents, just shy of 50% strongly agreed. Parents associated their competence with the form of the homework booklets: without them 'I wouldn't know what to do with my children or where to start'. The number of parents who agreed that they did not have time to support children with their homework decreased by 20% by the endline. Ninety-five per cent of parents indicated that they enjoyed working with their children to complete maths homework, with 45% strongly agreeing that they enjoyed the activity. Furthermore, the experience appeared to boost parents' assessment of their own maths skills, with the number of parents who disagreed (or strongly disagreed) in the baseline with the statement 'I am not good at maths' increasing in the endline by almost 20% to 74%.

Educationally oriented relationships: Across the experience, a number of relationships appear to have transformed. The distribution of respondents from the baseline to the endline suggests that engaging in homework across this period may have mobilised slightly wider resources for learning in the home, especially older siblings. Unexpectedly, parents indicated that their relationship with their children improved through working with them on homework. While some parents acknowledged the stress of the experience, 95% of parents agreed that doing homework with their child improved their relationship; of these parents, 60% strongly agreed. Parents in focus groups were keen to speak about how they had felt a sense of common purpose with their children. Direct engagements between parents and teachers had not been woven into the model. Nevertheless, parents' relationships with teachers appeared to strengthen somewhat, with 17% more parents strongly agreeing that teachers respect parents. (There was at least one parent who felt disrespected through the experience.)

Expectations: The percentage of parents who either agreed or strongly agreed that their 'child is good at maths' climbed modestly from 83% to 87%; the number of parents who strongly agreed also grew by 5%. Across the focus groups, the facilitators reflected that, as parents engaged with their children's work, their pride in their children seemed to grow. They spoke less about their expectations of their children in isolation and more about their expectations of their children with their support. They mentioned that their children's maths skills appeared to expand as they supported them.

Invitations for involvement: One of the most striking features of how parents talked about their experiences was their strong association with the printed homework booklets. Parents interpreted the printed homework booklets as a clear invitation, perhaps even a mandate, for involvement. Physicality and structure of the learner workbooks mattered to them. Unlike activities that they would have to initiate on their own with children, the booklets represented a material invitation to support children, accepted by children themselves. For some of the more active parents, the booklets represented not only an invitation to support their children, but an invitation to engage teachers in issues of learning content, with a handful of parents seeking out teachers to engage with content and asking for better systems of teacher feedback.

What have we learned?

A theme that weaves through the experience was the importance of the specific format of the workbooks, reflecting the design principles emerging from the initial baseline exploration. In the early phase of discussions, parents spoke about a 'sweet spot'; if designed carefully and correctly, they experienced homework as empowering; outside of threading this needle, they did not. The experience focuses attention on the homework materials themselves, and how (and for whom) they are designed. The question is not simply whether parental support of homework is possible, but how to design homework to leverage parental and child resources (skills, energies, time) in any given context.

This chapter started by emphasising that while a wide body of multidisciplinary research supports the importance of parental involvement in education, the South African system has remained ambivalent about whether and how to harness parental support for schooling, especially in the early grades. We identified four different sources of ambivalence, rooted in four different kinds of questions: is it fair; does it benefit children; are parents interested and capable; and is there a viable model for investment at scale? This study does not resolve any of these. However, it contributes some insight into each of the key questions that are raised.

The first concern emanates out of questions about fairness. Is it ethical to land the challenges of a struggling school system on already burdened parents in poor rural settings? While arriving at an answer will not be easy, this study experience argues against a simple "no" answer. The experience presented in this paper appears to have triggered a self-reinforcing cycle between beliefs, expectations, relationships, and activity among and between parents, learners, and teachers. Parents' sense of self-efficacy expanded. While investing in teachers remains top priority, the study experience suggests that engaging parents to support carefully designed homework systems may contribute to an upward cycle of relationships and expectations, critical in the long term for a child's educational success.

The second question focuses on whether this type of homework experience is good for children. Wilder's meta-synthesis of studies on parental engagement suggested that parental involvement relating to supporting homework had the least consistent positive relationship with educational performance (2014). This study does not engage this question directly. The study suggests only that parents perceived that their relationships with their children improved, and that they enjoyed working with their children on homework. That said, approximately one third of parents indicated that their role included disciplining their child when their child did not complete their homework. The form and function of this discipline was not explored in the current study; it remains a useful topic for future research.

The third source of ambivalence, most frequently raised by teachers (Felix, Dornbrack & Scheckle 2008), is rooted in a concern that parents are neither interested nor able to support children with homework, especially in rural contexts. The study challenges this concern most directly. While exploratory in nature, the study provides an example whereby a system of homework, designed carefully to meet the needs of rural parents, establishes an opportunity for parents to demonstrate both their interest in and ability to support their children in homework praxis, expanding parents' understanding of their role and contributing to their self-efficacy, while improving educational relationships and expectations.

The final ambivalence is located at a policy level. The conclusion of policy-makers emerging out of the early grade reading study (Taylor et al. 2018) was that the system did not have a cost-effective method of expanding parental support of home-based learning at system scale.

Conclusion

This chapter presented an intervention case study that was guided by education design research and focused on parental support of homework in Grade 2 mathematics during the COVID-19 pandemic. The case focused on 13 rural schools in the Eastern Cape across 12 months, beginning in September 2020. The first phase engaged parents' early experience of homework support in order to develop design principles to guide the redevelopment of homework materials used in the subsequent homework cycle. The second phase focused on understanding the experience of parents in supporting Grade 2 maths homework across the first two terms in 2021.

Accepting that parental involvement (however defined) does not have a linear or strictly causal relationship to a child's education performance, the study benefited from the work of both Wilder (2014) and Hoover-Dempsey et al. (2005) in establishing a new framework for analysing the value of parental involvement through five key interrelated indicators: parental role construct, parental self-efficacy, educationally oriented relationships, educational expectations, and invitations for involvement.

While exploratory in nature, the study experience focuses attention on the sensitive nature of the endeavour, emphasising the importance of the design of homework tools, which should ensure that the form, function, and content leverage interest and activity among parents. The study provides an example of parental support of homework in Grade 2 mathematics that served to widen parents' sense of their role in relationship to formal education, contributed to parents' sense of self-efficacy, and triggered a reinforcing cycle of expanding beliefs, expectations, relationships, and activity among and between key educational players.

References

Bojuwoye O (2009) Home–school partnership: A study of opinions of selected parents and teachers in Kwazulu-Natal Province, South Africa. *Research Papers in Education* 24(4): 461–475

Brown BA & Duku NS (2008) Participation politics: African parents' negotiation of social identities in school governance and its policy implications. *International Journal of Lifelong Education* 27(4): 413–429

Chandra Y & Shang L (2019) *Qualitative research using R: A systematic approach.* Singapore: Springer

Farrow S, Tymms P & Henderson B (1999) Homework and attainment in primary schools. *British Educational Research Journal* 25(3): 323–341

Felix N, Dornbrack J & Scheckle E (2008) Parents, homework, and socio-economic class: Discourses of deficit and disadvantage in the 'new' South Africa. *English Teaching: Practice and Critique* 7(2): 99–112

Hatefi S, Smith F, Abou-El-Hossein K & Alizargar J (2020) COVID-19 in South Africa: Lockdown strategy and its effects on public health and other contagious diseases. Letter to the Editor. *Public Health* 185: 159–160. Accessed June 2025, https://doi.org/10.1016/j.puhe.2020.06.033

Hoover-Dempsey KV, Walker MT, Sandler HM, Whetsel D, Green CL, Wilkins AS & Closson K (2005) Why do parents become involved? Research findings and implications. *The Elementary School Journal* 106(2): 105–130

Kim SW & Fong VL (2014) Homework help, achievement in middle school, and later college attainment in China. *Asia Pacific Education Review* 15: 617–631

Mncube V (2010) Parental involvement in school activities in South Africa to the mutual benefit of the school and community. *Education as Change* 14(2): 233–246

Motala S & Luxomo V (2014) Parental involvement and access to learning: A perspective from Gauteng and the Eastern Cape, South Africa. *Southern African Review of Education* 20(2): 80–96

Ngwaru F & Niboye EP (2020) Local resilience to natural hazards in Zimbabwe: Experiences from Mhondoro-Ngezi rural communities. *Tanzania Journal of Development Studies* 18(1): 116–132

Ngwaru JM (2014) Promoting children's sustainable access to early schooling in Africa: Reflections on the roles of parents in their children's early childhood care and education. *New Directions for Child and Adolescent Development* 2014(146): 61–76

Plano Clark VL & Creswell JW (2008) *The mixed methods reader.* Thousand Oaks: Sage

Plomp T (2007) *An introduction to educational design research.* Netherlands: Institute for Curriculum Development

Porteus K (2022) Improving early grade mathematics: Design principles and patterns of improvement. In Venkat H & Roberts N (Eds) *Early grade mathematics in South Africa.* Cape Town: Oxford University Press

Porteus K (2023) Mapping design principles to instructional realities in early grade mathematics in South Africa: A framework for designing and evaluating learning and teaching support materials (LTSM). *African Journal of Research in Mathematics, Science, and Technology Education* Special Edition: 350–366

Porteus K, Roberts N & Moloi Q (2022) *Grade 3 maths backlogs under Covid: Exploring the form and function of Grade 3 maths backlogs in two interventions in rural and urban South Africa.* Research report for the Zenex Foundation

Ramadiro B & Porteus K (2017) *Foundation Phase matters: Language and learning in South African rural schools.* East London: Magic Classroom Collective Press

Ramadiro B & Porteus K (2018) *Policy brief. Early Grade Literacy and Mathematics: Placing the African-Language-Speaking Child at the Centre.* East London: Magic Classroom Collective Press

Sayed Y, Motala S, Carel D & Ahmed R (2020) School governance and funding policy in South Africa: Towards social justice and equity in education policy. *South African Journal of Education* 40(4): 1–12

Shepard D, Mohohlwane N, Taylor S & Kotzé J (2021) *Changes in education: A reflection on COVID-19 effects over a year.* Wave 4: National Income Dynamics Study (NIDS) – Coronavirus Rapid Mobile Survey (CRAM)

Spaull N, Daniels RC, Ardington C, Benhura M, Bridgman G et al. (2021) *Synthesis report.* Wave 4: National Income Dynamics Study (NIDS) – Coronavirus Rapid Mobile Survey (CRAM)

Statistics South Africa (2011) *Census 2011 Key Results.* Pretoria: Statistics South Africa. Accessed May 2025, https://www.statssa.gov.za/?page_id=3955

Taylor S, Cilliers J, Prinsloo C, Fleisch B & Reddy V (2018) *Improving early grade reading in South Africa.* Grantee Final Report. International Initiative for Impact Evaluation

United Nations (2020) *Policy brief. Education during COVID-19 and Beyond.* United Nations

Wilder S (2014) Effects of parental involvement on academic achievement: A meta-synthesis. *Educational Review* 66(3): 377–397

Wolf S (2020) 'Me I don't really discuss anything with them': Parent and teacher perceptions of early childhood education and parent–teacher relationships in Ghana. *International Journal of Educational Research* 99: 101525

10 Parental Involvement Programme: A Case Study Across Schools and Communities in Rural South Africa

Craig Gibbs and Kimberleigh Bodley

Introduction

This chapter highlights a parental/caregiver involvement programme conducted in three provinces across South Africa in order to explore how schools can engage parents and caregivers and utilise them as a powerful resource for improving literacy and numeracy outcomes in the Foundation Phase. In a number of studies related to education in South Africa, lack of parental participation has been seen as a barrier to improving literacy and numeracy during the early years of development of children living in rural communities (Motshusi, Ngobeni & Sepeng 2024). This chapter begins by outlining a case study of the Alladin Learning Solutions parent involvement programme that aims to improve learners' academic results and community engagement in three provinces in South Africa. The findings highlight barriers to parental/caregiver involvement and how enhanced involvement may improve literacy and numeracy skills in the Foundation Phase. This chapter makes recommendations for a parental/caregiver involvement programme not only to support teachers but also to generate enthusiasm and commitment from parents and caregivers through skills development training and capacitation.

Alladin Learning Solutions parental involvement programme

Alladin Learning Solutions (ALS) is a registered non-profit company working in early childhood development (ECD) that aims to address challenges of insufficient educational resources and low parental involvement in South Africa's education sector. ALS's parental involvement programme operates in three provinces, targeting both rural and semi-urban areas. It began by supplying Foundation Phase classrooms with supplementary teaching materials aligned with the Department of Basic Education's Curriculum and Assessment Policy Statements (CAPS) for numeracy and literacy. The programme was then extended to involve parents/caregivers in assembling and distributing resource packs aimed at enhancing home-based learning and supporting children's numeracy and literacy development. Each term, Reception and Foundation Phase teachers receive a resource pack containing 10–15 curriculum-aligned resources and activities crafted from recycled and low-cost materials. These packs facilitate hands-on teaching and are replicable by teachers. Parents/caregivers who are trained through workshops assist in creating these packs, earning a stipend of R500 per session. This involvement helps parents understand their children's learning processes and connects them with the school environment.

Literacy and numeracy in the Foundation Phase

The need for a programme for parents and caregivers to support the development of their child's literacy and numeracy skills is evident in research in South Africa and other countries (Lehrl, Evangelou & Sammons 2020). Evan and Hares (2021) indicate that less than half of all children in low- and middle-income countries can read by the time they are 10 years old. Similarly, the Progress in International Reading Literacy Study report (Department of Basic Education 2023) also highlights concerns around primary school-level reading literacy in South Africa. Statistics released in 2023 revealed that 81% of 10-year-olds cannot read for meaning in any language (Department of Basic Education 2023). In addition, Chetty (2019), reporting on teachers' experiences of literacy in low-income communities in the Western Cape province of South Africa, found that some of the key factors for literacy under-achievement included lack of resources, parental support, and teacher knowledge; changes in the curriculum; the absence of cognitive activities; and the social complexity of poverty.

Another possible reason for the low literacy and numeracy rates is that teachers may not be aware of the important literacy and numeracy skills that children learn in the Foundation Phase, or how to adapt their teaching to address these skills (Aunio 2019; Aunio et al. 2016). Furthermore, Salminen et al. (2021) suggest clear associations between parental measures, home environments, and young children developing literacy and numeracy skills. To address these issues, Aunio et al. (2016) believe that more adequate educational resources and targeted, evidence-based pedagogical support for numeracy should be aimed specifically at public schools and parents in low socio-economic areas.

Munje and Mncube (2018) advocate for context-sensitive parental involvement strategies, which ALS incorporates by upskilling parents/caregivers through employment opportunities and practical training. In the context of a South African unemployment rate of 33.9% in the second quarter of 2022 and youth unemployment at 61.4%, parents and caregivers were presented with the opportunity for short-term employment and skills development (Statistics South Africa 2022). The programme therefore provides these benefits in addition to supporting educational development. Aunio et al. (2016) highlight the importance of adequate resources and support for teachers to improve literacy and numeracy. Therefore, ALS's initiative directly addresses this need by equipping both teachers and parents/caregivers with effective, practical tools to support early childhood education.

Low-cost resource packs

Considering the concept of Learning through Play, the ALS resource packs intentionally include literacy and numeracy resources in the form of teaching aids that allow children to interact with the resources and learn through using them. Given the rural context in which the resource packs were distributed, it was important to use low-cost materials to show parents and caregivers that resources and materials do not have to be expensive to make and/or that they could develop these themselves. The overall aims of the ALS resource packs for parents/caregivers are to:
- learn about the curriculum, including CAPS Mathematics and Literacy (English First Additional Language) topic areas;
- learn about the different kinds of resources and materials that can be used for teaching Mathematics and Literacy;
- encourage collaboration with Foundation Phase educators;
- understand the importance of interacting with their children in the home environment; and
- create opportunities for collaboration between parents/caregivers and Foundation Phase educators.

Community engagement

The programme encourages community engagement by building relationships between parent-volunteers and schools. Parent-volunteers are involved in assembling resource packs and engaging with educators, thus fostering direct collaboration. Additionally, the community extension programme extends these efforts into the broader community. This comprehensive strategy includes a three-month campaign in which trained parent-volunteers conduct home visits to advocate for parental/caregiver involvement in education. The training sessions feature two videos: one on the concept and value of parental/caregiver involvement, and another on recycling resources to support literacy and numeracy using everyday items. The parental/caregiver involvement training video addresses the following topics: the meaning of parental involvement; the areas of parental involvement; the value of parental involvement; and ways to be an involved parent.

During sessions, parents and caregivers discuss the training content in their home language and conduct mock home visits. To support these efforts, parents and caregivers receive infographics in various home languages to guide discussions about literacy and numeracy development at home. This approach not only engages parents and caregivers in resource assembly but also educates them on enhancing their children's learning experiences.

To monitor the implementation of the programme, parent-volunteers were set up with a paper-based monitoring document that tracked information such as number of households visited, number of children per household, grades of those children, and the name and contact information for parents/caregivers. This household visit form also detailed a personal evaluation of the visit, the topic areas covered or activities conducted, as well as any challenges or successes.

Surveys and interviews helped the researchers understand whether the ALS programme was achieving its intended aims. Surveys evaluated all parents'/caregivers' experiences of participating in the programme, with the result that surveys provided a holistic picture of their experiences. Interviews were used to supplement the surveys and to gain a deeper understanding of these experiences. Programme evaluation helped inform ways to enhance or adapt the programme for future implementation.

The case study aimed to understand the uniqueness of the ALS programme, in all its complexity, with a focus on the experiences of parents-volunteers who were trained and who conducted home visits within the school community. The evaluation also helped understand how the case study provided parents/caregivers with the opportunity to use the resources to support their child's literacy and numeracy development.

A three-point Likert scale was selected to provide sufficient choice without over-complicating the survey, aligning it to the participant's level of understanding. The analysed questions complemented the interview questions, allowing for a more in-depth understanding of the experiences of parents and caregivers.

Results of the surveys and interviews

Parent-volunteer training and capacitation

The surveys looked at whether the training on parental involvement achieved its intended outcome of preparing parent-volunteers to conduct home visits. Over 80% of parent-volunteers felt they had the necessary theoretical knowledge on parental/caregiver involvement and an in-depth understanding to share with parents/caregivers visited during the community extension campaign. This response suggests that parent-volunteers understood the importance of parental/caregiver involvement. The findings that emerged from the interviews are that parents and caregivers learned important lessons, including their role in their child's education, ways to be more involved in the home environment, and that learning takes place both at home and at school.

Part of the surveys evaluated the support strategies and resources shared with parent-volunteers during the initial training. Seventy-one per cent of parent-volunteers felt that using resource packs together with teaching parents/caregivers to develop their own resources was both practical and relevant. These responses indicate that the programme is contextually appropriate. Furthermore, responses from the interviews highlight that parents benefited from the practical nature of the programme and the skills acquired during home visits.

Level of school support

Some survey questions focused on understanding the levels of interest and support from school stakeholders, including principals and Foundation Phase heads of department (HODs), and the impact this would have on parents' and caregivers' implementation of the programme. Seventy-seven per cent of parents reported that the school and principal supported the programme, with less than 4% reporting that the school and principal were not supportive. This high level of support is positive; however, it came through in interviews that parents felt that schools still had a long way to go in improving how they interact with parents and caregivers. It became evident that Foundation Phase HODs demonstrated a significantly less positive belief in the importance of the programme. This reinforces existing research and the feedback from the interview responses (Munje & Mncube 2018). It is important to advocate at the school level and involve relevant stakeholders in order for schools to understand the value and importance of parental/caregiver involvement, and to understand how parents and caregivers can support and reinforce what is being done in school.

Receptiveness of parents/caregivers visited

Some survey questions focused on understanding how home visits were received by parents and caregivers within the school community. It also looked to evaluate the use of home visits as a way of encouraging parental involvement. Parents had mixed responses; however, the responses indicate that parents and caregivers who received a visit were receptive and responsive to the support offered. Parent-volunteers stated that it took time to explain the programme to parents, and for them to understand that the programme was in place to support and provide information rather than judge or criticise parenting practices. It is important to guide parent-volunteers on presenting the information and engaging with parents and caregivers in a positive and productive manner. It became apparent in interviews that parents found the one-on-one approach more effective than previous methods such as attending school meetings; however, some parents indicated in the interviews that they would like to hold small workshop sessions with four to five parents in order to access more parental support within the school community.

The role of resource packs

Part of the evaluation sought to understand the role played by ALS resource packs during home visits. According to the survey responses, children showed the most interest in the resource packs, followed by parents/ caregivers, and then Foundation Phase educators. Only 11% of parent-volunteers felt they did not have enough support materials to engage with other parents during home visits. Parent-volunteers suggested that they receive some materials, such as number and alphabet posters or reading books, that they could leave with parents/caregivers during their home visits so that the latter could be further incentivised to support their children at home.

Perceived impact of home visits

The following section looks at parent-volunteers' personal evaluation of the home visits that they conducted. It is important to consider their personal bias when answering this section of the survey. However, 80.7% of parent-volunteers reported that they believed their household visits made a positive impact in the community. Furthermore, 61.4% of parent-volunteers reported that during follow-up visits, they saw evidence that parents/caregivers were encouraging and supporting their children at home.

Seventy-three per cent of parent-volunteers witnessed a change in other parents' attitudes about parental involvement. This indicates that parent-volunteers could effectively converse about parental/caregiver involvement with the households visited. Interview responses highlight that this change in attitude resulted in changed behaviour in the home environment, such as asking questions about school, checking homework, and making resources to use at home.

The results of the semi-structured interview questions

Six main themes emerged from the semi-structured interviews. The themes were identified based on how frequently parents alluded to a certain point of view and were informed by relevant literature on parental involvement. The six themes described in Table 10.1 were identified.

Table 10.1 *Themes identified in the thematic analysis*

Theme	Criteria
Debunking the myth that learning only takes place in school	Any responses indicating a shift in understanding that learning takes place in both the school and home environment. Key words: • awareness • role • home • learning • supporting
Skills sharing is an essential part of parental/caregiver involvement	Any responses highlighting that the knowledge and skills shared during home visits empowered and capacitated the parents/caregivers visited. Key words: • at home • how to • resources • show/demonstrate
Resource packs made home visits interactive and engaged	Those responses related to the use of resource packs in the home environment. Key words: • resource packs • resources • play • interest/engagement
Household visits are an effective way to reach parents/caregivers	Any response demonstrating how parents/caregivers benefited from direct, one-on-one support. Key words: • information • skills • questions • engagement
Consistency and repetition are important for sustained impact	Responses that demonstrated a shift in the attitudes of parents/caregivers towards parental involvement, or positive changes in their behaviour. Key words: • support/encourage • assist • involved
Schools should revise their approach to parental/caregiver involvement	Any response indicating how parents/caregivers feel that schools could improve parental involvement. Key words: • communication • collaboration • encouragement

Debunking the myth that learning only takes place at school

Many parents/caregivers mistakenly believe that their children's education is entirely in the hands of teachers or the school (Brooks 2019). They assume that by sending their children to school they do enough to support their child's education. This is one of the most important attitudes and mindsets to challenge by showing parents and caregivers the important role that they play in their child's education (Brooks 2023). Once they understand this, it is necessary to demonstrate how they can modify their behaviour to support the education of their children. During interviews, it was found that many parents/caregivers were unaware or did not appreciate the significance of their role in their child's education. Upon learning of their role and practical ways to support their children, parents and caregivers demonstrated a different mindset towards their child's education:

> The fact of the matter is that parents have been made aware of their role in supporting their children at home and have understood that they can contribute a lot towards the improvement of their child. (Parent-volunteer 2)

> Parents appreciated [being] made aware that they could make such a meaningful role in the education of their children. (Parent-volunteer 5)

> These visits helped because some didn't understand that learning also takes place at home. (Parent-volunteer 11)

Skills sharing is an essential part of parental involvement

Sharing knowledge and practical skills is an essential part of the parental/caregiver involvement programme. Skills sharing not only builds capacity but builds confidence (Brooks 2023). An important part of the intervention was ensuring that parents/caregivers had the skills but, more importantly, the confidence to support the education of their children. Building confidence came from showing parents that they could engage with children using materials from the home environment. It was a big lesson for parents/caregivers to understand that they do not have to buy expensive educational materials but rather that they can make them using recycled materials or items from home, as the following comments show:

> It is not true that parents do not care about the education of their children, but our visits have revealed that they do want [to] but they did not know how. (Parent-volunteer 2)

> My visits help[ed] because they are managing to make those resources at home … I showed them how to help the child to read and how to count and also [how to identify] shapes. (Parent-volunteer 1)

It makes a very big impact because some of the parents are still coming to me to ask where they can get [cardboard] boxes and pegs and more stuff like in the resource packet to help their kids at home. (Parent-volunteer 9)

Resource packs made home visits interactive and engaged

Having support materials is an essential part of making home visits an engaging and interactive experience for parents/caregivers and children. Parent-volunteers reported that it was a positive experience seeing parents and children engaging with the materials from the resource packs. The resource packs achieved the intended outcome of helping parents/caregivers gain insight into what children are learning in school. It was also a unique experience in which parents and caregivers had the opportunity to watch their child play and learn at home:

> I did use the resources that were provided. That made it easier and parents actually liked that you had resources and it was not a matter of you doing everything verbally. (Parent-volunteer 8)

> It made the visits easy and simple when we used the resource packs. Parents were very interested when we used the resources in their homes. (Parent-volunteer 12)

> When we go to the homes with the bags, the neighbours come and check in the bags, they also want to play with them. (Parent-volunteer 3)

Household visits are an effective way to reach parents

School-driven parental involvement initiatives often invite parents and caregivers to attend a meeting. Prior to implementing the programme, general feedback from school principals is that these meetings are not well attended and thus the perception of parental involvement is low. As a result of these historical experiences, the programme design opted for one-on-one household visits. One hundred per cent of parent-volunteers indicated in their surveys that they could successfully execute their home visits. However, the challenges encountered by some parent-volunteers included:

- parents/caregivers working late;
- parents' unavailability on weekends;
- schools having the wrong contact information; and
- parents'/caregivers' apprehension that they would be reported to the Department of Education.

Parent-volunteers reported that a one-on-one approach is more effective with parents/caregivers as you can have detailed discussions about parental involvement and listen to parents' challenges at home. According to Munje and Mncube (2018), being considerate of contextual realities and challenges facing parents is an important part of any parental involvement programme. Overall, parent-volunteers found that the practical strategies and methods learned during training helped them to engage more in the home environment:

> Our visits are more impactful than any school meeting because they are helpful and practical. (Parent-volunteer 16)

> When I pass through the street, parents are asking some questions and just smiling, asking when will I come back again and how they can learn more. (Parent-volunteer 3)

> Your approach matters; it mustn't come across like you are questioning or correcting them. You are just sharing information and supporting. (Parent-volunteer 16)

A persistent barrier to successful home visits was that schools did not have the correct contact information and addresses for parents and caregivers. Contact numbers and physical addresses change regularly, so schools need to update this information annually. As highlighted in research by Lehrl, Evangelou and Sammons (2020) regular and open communication between the school and the parent is essential for positive parental involvement.

Consistency and repetition are important for sustained impact

In the programme design, ALS opted for the same households to be visited two to three times to ensure that parents/caregivers were receiving as much support and guidance as possible. This allowed parent-volunteers to conduct initial visits to encourage parental involvement and then to follow up with visits using the resource packs, infographics, and demonstrations of transforming recycling into resources. Parents and caregivers appreciated learning that they could use things found in their home environment to support their children:

> Most parents you could see that they were not involved in the education or the learning or the curriculum or the homework. But after I left the house or certain houses, parents would say now I can see the importance and I would like to be a supportive parent. (Parent-volunteer 4)

> Parents made a promise that the first thing they will ask is how school was so that they could further be involved. They said they would ask what the

children learned in school and see if they could help with homework before children went to play. (Parent-volunteer 7)

Schools should revise their approach to parental involvement

Results from the survey indicated that a large majority of parent-volunteers received a good level of school support from principals as well as Foundation Phase HODs during the programme. It is positive that schools were supportive of the programme; however, parents' general experiences prior to the programme were not typically positive. For many parents and caregivers, being called into school is a negative experience and typically occurs when something is wrong. It was found that schools need to work on making parental involvement a positive experience for parents and caregivers.

> I would give the advice to the HODs to get more involved in such sessions [because] it helps the parents a lot and to do more 1-1 sessions with parents because that's how you can help these kids. (Parent-volunteer 1)

> There needs to be more positive communication between parents and teachers. (Parent-volunteer 6)

> It is the parent's responsibility to come to these things [school meetings] but they need to be supported and encouraged. (Parent-volunteer 9)

> Parents are scared to come and talk to teachers; the teachers should be more welcoming and understanding of parents' problems. (Parent-volunteer 10)

Findings of internal evaluation

The findings of the internal evaluation are drawn from parents' responses to the survey and interview questions conducted during the internal review. These findings suggest that parents/caregivers in rural communities have a willingness and desire to support their children's education despite some of the previous findings on parental involvement in rural communities (Sedibe 2012).

However, prior to the implementation of the programme, a large majority of parents/caregivers felt that they did not have the knowledge, skills, capacity or confidence to be actively involved in their child's education. It was important for parents to learn about the vital role that they play in their child's academic journey. This echoes the findings of Olsen and Fuller (2017): that one of the benefits of parental involvement programmes is that parents can learn about the educational and developmental needs of their children. Considering this research, it is evident that interventions aimed at enhancing parental involvement should prioritise practicality and clearly showcase actionable ways for parents and caregivers to engage both at home and in the school environment. This aligns with the viewpoints of Munje and Mncube (2018), who emphasise the importance of contextual relevance and the consideration of parental challenges when designing parental involvement programmes. Furthermore, case study outcomes reiterate the significance of schools, principals, and educators adapting their approach to parental involvement to foster a more welcoming and positive experience for parents and caregivers. By doing so, schools can create a conducive environment that encourages active parental engagement, ultimately benefiting the overall educational experience of the students.

In making some of these changes, parents and caregivers may feel less intimidated by the school environment, which in turn may result in active participation in school activities and supporting their children at home. Communication is considered to be a crucial aspect of parental involvement. When parents can receive and respond to messages from the school, or when they take the initiative to communicate with the school, positive parental involvement occurs (Moreeng et al. 2024). Therefore, it is also important for schools to have accurate and up-to-date contact information for parents and caregivers so that they can engage and interact with them regularly. Training teachers in how to work with parents should be understood as one of the ways of encouraging positive parental involvement programmes.

The unanimous feedback from parent-volunteers in their survey responses is that the programme should be extended to include more families. In future parental involvement programmes, this can be achieved by extending the number of months during which parent-volunteers conduct household visits. If this is not possible due to time or budget constraints, parents can be taught how to form communities of practice within their neighbourhoods or within the school community. In this way, a group of four to five parents and caregivers can be reached simultaneously. By forming communities of practice within the school community, parents would be engaging with others within the school community and creating spaces for learning and development outside of the school environment.

Recommendations

Based on the findings of the case study, a recommendation for improving parental involvement programmes is to capacitate Foundation Phase educators on how to communicate and engage with parents/caregivers effectively and positively. Collaboration between parents and the school should be proactive rather than reactive. These sentiments are documented in previously conducted research in South Africa and are reinforced by the findings of this research. Parents and schools need to identify mutual priorities, and schools need to recognise the positive contribution parents and caregivers can make.

A further recommendation for improving parental involvement programmes is to increase contact time with parents/caregivers in a way that is practical and engaged. The findings of this research indicate that parents benefited immensely from the practical advice and skills sharing that enabled them to be more involved in their child's education in the home environment.

Parental involvement programmes need to be aligned with contextual realities and should consider the challenges facing parents and caregivers in the school community. Barriers to parental involvement may include parents and caregivers who work away from home, work long hours, or are illiterate, as well as cultural parenting practices. In response to these challenges, the parental involvement programme attempted to make adjustments to better suit the circumstances of the parents/caregivers. For instance, it acknowledged that many children in the community were being raised by illiterate grandparents. To address this, the programme introduced strategies and support mechanisms that accommodated the unique needs of these grandparents, recognising their limitations in terms of literacy and education but still valuing their role in children's lives.

However, as the landscape of education and family dynamics evolves, it is imperative to continually innovate and adapt this and any other parental involvement programmes to meet the needs of parents/caregivers and their circumstances. In the context of parents and caregivers who genuinely desire to be involved in their child's education, there is a clear need for creative solutions. As demonstrated in this case study, these solutions might involve alternative communication methods, resources that cater to different learning styles, or community-based initiatives to ensure that parents and caregivers can actively participate in their child's educational journey. In this way, parental involvement programmes can be truly effective in nurturing a supportive and collaborative educational environment, especially for those parents/caregivers raising children in disadvantaged communities.

Conclusion

The significance of children's relationships with their parents or caregivers, who are a constant presence in their lives, cannot be overstated. While children do spend a significant amount of time at school, their experiences and learning outside of it are often shaped by parental influence, which can have a profound impact on their overall development. Therefore, parents and caregivers play a crucial role in supporting their children's educational journey, making it imperative that they are informed and guided on how they can provide a conducive learning environment outside of the classroom. This case study demonstrated how it is possible to increase parents'/caregivers' knowledge and understanding of how they can support their children and have a positive impact on improving their levels of literacy and numeracy.

References

Aunio P (2019) Early numeracy skills learning and learning difficulties: Evidence-based assessment and interventions. In Geary DC, Berch DB & Koepke KM (Eds) *Cognitive foundations for improving mathematical learning. Cambridge, MA: Academic Press*

Aunio P, Mononen R, Ragpot L & Törmänen M (2016) Early numeracy performance of South African school beginners. *South African Journal of Childhood Education* 6(1): 1–8. Accessed May 2025, https://doi.org/10.4102/sajce.v6i1.496

Brooks A (2019) Experts discuss the importance of positive parental involvement in education. *Rasmussen University*, 18 November. Accessed June 2025, https://www.rasmussen.edu/degrees/education/blog/parental-involvement-in-education/

Brooks RB (2023) The power of parenting. In Goldstein S & Brooks RB (Eds) *Handbook of resilience in children* (3rd edition). Cham: Springer

Chetty R (2019). Literacy teaching in disadvantaged South African schools. *Literacy* 53(4): 245–253

Department of Basic Education (2023) *Progress in International Reading Literacy Study 2021: South African Preliminary Highlights Report*. Pretoria: Department of Basic Education

Evans D & Hares S (2021) Foundational literacy and numeracy skills are important, obviously. but are they more important than all other education investments? *Center for Global Development*, 4 May. Accessed October 2022, https://www.cgdev.org/blog/foundational-literacy-and-numeracy-skills-are-important-obviously-are-they-more-important-all

Lehrl S, Evangelou M & Sammons P (2020) The home learning environment and its role in shaping children's educational development. *School Effectiveness and School Improvement* 31(1): 1–6

Moreng B, Mbatha ZM, Ntsala SA & Motsoeneng TJ (2024) Parental involvement as a convergence of understanding by teachers and parents. *Interdisciplinary Journal of Sociality Studies* 4: 1–10. Accessed May 2025, https://pubs.ufs.ac.za/index.php/ijss/article/view/1043

Motshusi MC, Ngobeni ET & Sepeng P (2024) Lack of parental involvement in the education of their children in the Foundation Phase: Case of selected schools in the Thabazimbi Circuit. *Research in Educational Policy and Management* 6(2): 21–41

Munje PN & Mncube V (2018) The lack of parent involvement as hindrance in selected public primary schools in South Africa: The voices of educators. *Perspectives in Education* 36(1): 80–93

Olsen G & Fuller M (2017) The benefits of parent involvement: What research has to say. In Olsen G & Fuller M (Eds) *Home–school relations: Working successfully with parents and families*. London: Pearson. Accessed June 2025, https://www.paulding.k12.ga.us/cms/lib/GA01903603/Centricity/Domain/211/Research.pdf

Salminen J, Khanolainen D, Koponen T, Torppa M & Lerkkanen MK (2021) Development of numeracy and literacy skills in early childhood: A longitudinal study on the roles of home environment and familial risk for reading and math difficulties. *Frontiers in Education* 6: 1–23. Accessed October 2022, https://www.frontiersin.org/journals/education/articles/10.3389/feduc.2021.725337/full

Sedibe M (2012) Parental involvement in the teaching and learning of their children in disadvantaged schools. *Journal of Social Sciences* 30(2): 153–159

Statistics South Africa (2022) *South Africa's youth continues to bear the burden of unemployment*. Pretoria: Statistics South Africa (1 June). Accessed October 2022, https://www.statssa.gov.za/?p=15407

11 aRe Bapaleng: Working With Caregivers to Create Stronger Local (In-Community) Early Childhood Development Ecosystems

Ximena Gonzalez and Khanyisa Mkhabele

Introduction

In the South African context, there is political support for the concept of children having access to high-quality early childhood development (ECD) services. However, the reality is that many marginalised children do not receive this kind of support. Figure 11.1 illustrates the components that are considered to make up a comprehensive ECD package of support for young children in South Africa.

Figure 11.1 *An essential package for ECD*

From conception

To Grade 1

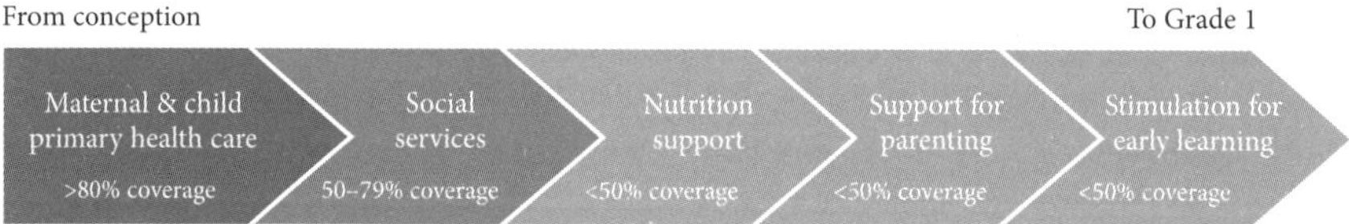

Source: Ilifa Labantwana & Kago Ya Bana (2018: 3)

In addition to these services, young children thrive if they receive nurturing care, essentially an environment created by caregivers that supports the good health and nutrition of the child, protects them from threats, and gives them opportunities for early learning through interactions that are emotionally supportive and responsive.[1]

For most young children in South Africa, many of these components are not available, and despite acknowledgement of its critical role, ECD remains a significantly under-resourced sector in South Africa.

In this chapter, we describe a programme that seeks to support the provision of these essential ECD services at a grassroots community level by applying a multi-stakeholder partnership approach involving a non-governmental organisation (NGO), a private funder, a set of community organisations, and government. The aRe Bapaleng Programme has been running since 2020 and has, to date, reached more than 80 000 parents or caregivers directly, over 80% of whom are youth, with more than 100 000 young children benefiting as a result. With full implementation of the Caregiver Network-ER* aspect of the programme starting in 2022, the mobilisation of around 3 000 National Youth Service (NYS) Caregiver Networker-ERs (also known as ECD Champions†) has resulted in marginalised communities all over South Africa having a hub of higher quality, community ECD support. In addition, NYS Caregiver Network-ERs have volunteered at ECD centres (both formal and informal), providing much-needed additional capacity.

The programme provides face-to-face engagement with the parents/caregivers†† of young children in underserviced communities. The focus is on capacitating parents and caregivers to support the growth and development of their young children by providing relevant and basic information and resources that promote early learning and development. The aim is to ensure that the children of these parents/caregivers do not miss the critical development window that could lead to a chance at better future learning outcomes. The programme seeks to encourage parents/caregivers to become active members of the ECD ecosystem to positively support their children´s development.

The approach to delivering capacity-building support to these parents/caregivers is primarily through delivering a series of Active Learning Workshops (ALWs). These are part of a facilitated training programme whereby parents/caregivers are exposed to skills and knowledge that could enable them to confidently support the development of the children in their care. The approach used is experiential learning, meaning that parents/caregivers are actively involved in the learning process by doing the activities and exercises during the workshops, and then doing them with their children at home or in other settings.

Learning through play is a key element of the programme´s learning approach. aRe Bapaleng is Sesotho for 'let's play'. Learning through play

---

* Caregiver Network-ER is short for Caregiver Network Educator.

† Through the implementation of the NYS, the programme was able to grow its Caregiver Network. However, due to the limited time allocated to the NYS work, these Caregiver Network-ERs have not received enough training to qualify them as fully fledged aRe Bapaleng Caregiver Network-ERs. Instead they are categorised as local ECD Champions, some of whom graduate to become fully fledged aRe Bapaleng Caregiver Network-ERs.

†† For this programme, the term parent/caregiver simply refers to a person who cares, supervises or resides with the child daily; this could be the child's biological or non-biological parent, a grandparent, aunt or uncle, or sibling.

is an important part of the way children develop, especially in their early years, and forms the core of what the programme aims to communicate to parents/caregivers. The programme has shown positive results in terms of parents' individual knowledge about their children, their time management abilities (including prioritising spending more quality time with their children), emotional regulation, and communication skills. Encouraging developments have also been noted at the community level, with increased network support and safety for children, as well as improvements in social cohesion.

The ECD context in South Africa

In South Africa, about 1.5% of gross domestic product is spent on ECD, most of which goes to primary health care for mothers and children. Of the total education budget, only 1 to 2% is directed to early learning programmes (ELPs) or ECD centres (Ilifa Labantwana and Kago Ya Bana 2018: 4). Most of this expenditure on early learning (59%) is directed towards Grade R (five-year-olds attending pre-primary). The balance is spent on grants to fund care for poorer children (under 5 years old) that are at registered ELPs, such as ECD centres, crèches, and nurseries. Only 40% of all ELPs are registered, and of these, only 32.5% receive stipends, according to the 2021 ECD census (Kika-Mistry et al. 2024). The result is that a limited amount of ECD spending supports the provision of ECD services to children in their earliest years.

Access to quality, age-appropriate ECD centres and ELPs is particularly unequal, due to high levels of poverty, amongst other issues, resulting in many children not receiving the benefit of the vital input that would enable them to have better futures. South Africa has about 7 million children under the age of 6 years; of these, nearly 5 million (about two-thirds) live in the poorest 40% of homes (Hall et al. 2024: 12). The experiences of children in poor households in the first five years of their lives highlight the enormous disadvantages they face. For example, poor children are less likely to be able to access quality early health care, nutrition, and early learning support, including ELPs or ECD centres. Children from wealthier households are not only more likely to attend these, but those they attend are also more likely to be of a much better quality (Giese et al. 2022).

For 2021, Statistics South Africa found that many children aged 0 to 4 years did not attend an educational facility and instead were cared for by someone at home, as shown in Figure 11.2. In most circumstances, this was the child's parent or guardian (57.3%), but in other cases, children were cared for by another adult (7.3%). Of the remaining children, 28.5% attended an ECD centre, and 5.6% went to a day mother (Statistics South

Africa 2022: 13). This national picture masks differences at the provincial level that relate particularly to urban versus rural settings. For example, in the rural North West, almost 80% of children in this age group lived at home with a parent, guardian or another adult (Statistics South Africa 2022: 13). Similarly, children aged 0 to 18 years in urban areas were more likely to be living with both parents, while in rural areas more children lived with their mother only (almost half) and almost 30% of children did not live with either of their parents (Statistics South Africa 2022: 11).

Figure 11.2 *Geographic overview of ECD attendance by children between 0–4 years by province*

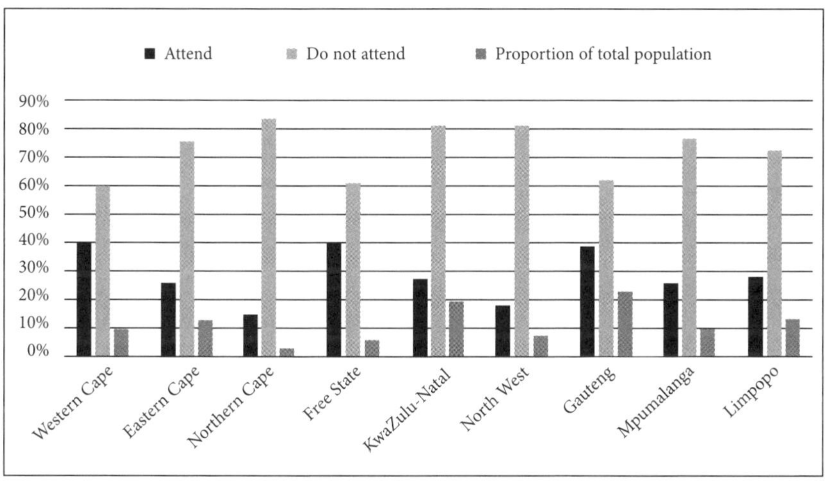

Source: Own calculations using data from Statistics South Africa's General Household Survey 2021 (2022)

The quality of care that children receive in their home environments is critical to their well-being and development. While the 2021 General Household Survey recognised that 'families and households are profoundly important to the developmental, emotional, and cognitive growth of children' (Statistics South Africa 2022: 1), the 2019 South African Early Childhood Development Review highlighted that, for many young children, a critical window for their brain development (from birth to two years of age) was being missed as their caregivers were not stimulating their development (Hall et al. 2019). Dawes et al. (2020) found that caregivers were not engaging in key activities likely to improve early learning outcomes such as reading, telling stories or playing with their children. The study also found that low-income families had very little time available to engage in these activities and lacked resources such as children's books or toys. Similarly, Statistics South Africa (2018) found that caregivers engaged in limited activities that stimulated positive development in young children.

Many of the parents/caregivers in poor communities are often unaware of how important this stage of development is, either lacking the understanding that children's first few years represent a critical window for early learning and development, or not prioritising their children's learning due to competing needs, for example, the need for food. Access to ECD services is not free, and many parents/caregivers are unemployed, which limits their ability to provide their young children with access. In addition, because they must stay at home to look after their children, they cannot seek work, resulting in a vicious cycle of poverty (Spaull et al. 2021). As children grow older, however, access to educational facilities improves. Among five-year-olds nationally, around 20% do not attend an education institution such as a pre-school or primary school. But by the age of six, most children are attending an educational institution, with just under 6% not doing so (Statistics South Africa 2022: 15).

One of the reasons for the increasing level of attendance at a later age is due to the structure of the public schooling system. In South Africa, primary and secondary education is fully subsidised, whereas this is not the case for the pre-primary level. It is estimated that only around 12% of poor children under the age of six have access to partially subsidised ELPs and even then parents are required to pay fees to cover the shortfall between the subsidy and the cost. As Hall et al. state: 'With around two million children aged 0–5 living in households where nobody is employed, universal access to early learning programmes is not achievable with the current funding model and budget' (2019: 38). Fees paid by parents remain the primary source of ELP funding, at 69% (Berry & Slemming 2024: 71).

While affordability remains a key determinant of access to ECD, there are also other factors that determine access. For example, there may be a lack of ECD facilities in the immediate area; in these situations, the impact of transport costs in addition to fees frequently results in children not accessing facilities due to unaffordability. Another key factor, mentioned earlier, is that parents are unaware of the critical importance of early learning for development (Statistics South Africa 2018), often believing that a focus on learning need only begin at school.

Increasing the available supply of ECD services for young children is also complicated by the legislative and regulatory environment. Setting up an ECD centre involves meeting several requirements; this is often difficult to do, particularly for those in informal and low-income communities. When ECD centres are not formalised or registered, communities struggle to access subsidies.[2] In addition, ECD educators need to have a formal qualification, which can also be financially difficult to attain.

On the other hand, while increasing access to ECD and ELPs for young children is critical, so too is ensuring that the accessed ECD is of a high quality, and that attendance is consistent over a long period of time in order for the positive effects on development to be realised (Hall et al. 2019). The 2021 Thrive by Five Index found that only 46% of four- to five-year-old children attending ELPs can do the learning tasks expected of a child their age, which means they are beginning formal schooling at a disadvantage (Hall et al. 2024).

These factors translate into a context where most young children are either at home or attend an informal ECD facility with an educator who is poorly trained. The result is that many young children in South Africa are not receiving the care and development they need. Local and international research shows that this can have an adverse effect on early language as well as cognitive and socio-emotional development[3] (Hannan & Juan 2021; Sénéchal & LeFevre 2002), as well as their self-confidence and self-esteem[4] (Aryani 2021). The home environment is key to supporting the early learning and development of young children, with a particular emphasis on the role played by the parent or caregiver. Stable, caring relationships in the home are critical for the healthy development of a young child (Center on the Developing Child 2007). The well-being of the parent/caregiver themselves also affects the home environment and their ability to be responsive caregivers.[5] In a context like South Africa where parents and caregivers face numerous stressors, including unemployment, parents'/caregivers' own lack of well-being can adversely affect the well-being of children.

Importance of learning through play

Play sparks imagination, enhances creativity and problem-solving capacities, promotes teamwork, and instils empathy. These are critical soft skills that are in demand in today's dynamic world. Using the principles of Learning through Play to engage with and facilitate learning is integral to the aRe Bapaleng approach. There is a large body of research that has proven the effectiveness of such an approach[6] (see Zosh, Hassinger-Das & Laurie 2022). According to Harvard University's Center on the Developing Child,[7] play can support critical aspects of brain development in the early years and it supports three core aspects that enable children and their families to thrive:
- supporting responsive relationships;
- strengthening core life skills, e.g. resilience to hardship; and
- reducing sources of stress.

aRe Bapaleng: A partnership with parents and caregivers

The main component of the programme is a series of Active Learning Workshops (ALWs). During the workshops, the importance of learning through play is emphasised by introducing and doing fun activities with parents/caregivers. These activities include playing with Lego bricks and doing puzzles, which encourage cognitive development and encompass thinking and problem-solving skills. The workshops include other types of play to encourage language development, such as singing, storytelling, and reciting rhymes. In addition, parents/caregivers engage in fun physical activities such as dancing, rope-skipping, and hopscotch, which they are encouraged to do with the children in their care.

Following their successful completion of the workshops, parents/caregivers have a raised awareness and increased knowledge of learning through play, together with other aspects related to supporting the early learning and development of the children in their care, such as health and nutrition, psychosocial support, and encouraging early literacy. They are also given practical tools and approaches that they can implement in their own homes to provide higher quality ECD support to the children in their care.

In 2021, another facet was added to the aRe Bapaleng programme: the Caregiver Network-Educator model. This is a response to the need to increase the sustainability of the initiative and to ensure that there is a stronger, community-based, high-quality ECD capacity that can be used to reach additional parents/caregivers. Through this model, parents/ caregivers who have successfully completed the ALW training are selected to attend additional training so that they become aRe Bapaleng Caregiver Network-ERs who train other parents/caregivers in their community using the ALW methodology.

In 2022, this facet of aRe Bapaleng was scaled up when it became part of a public employment initiative, the revitalised National Youth Service (NYS) programme, which is one of the components of the Presidential Youth Employment Intervention.[*] This introduced the possibility of expanding the aRe Bapaleng Caregiver Network by exposing groups of young parents and caregivers to short-term earning opportunities. The result of this initiative is that a cadre of NYS Caregiver Network-ERs (ECD Champions) are equipped to go into their communities to raise awareness about the importance of providing young children with higher quality ECD support. To ensure that the information given to parents cascades into the community, the programme works through its ECD Champions and partners to implement interventions such as food gardens and reading clubs.

---

[*] The NYS scales up opportunities for young people to contribute to the development of their community by providing specific services that meet priority needs. The initiative aims to unlock the agency of young people and provide opportunities for them to earn an income while contributing to nation-building. The National Youth Development Agency is responsible for the NYS.

Those participating in the initiative are equipped not only with knowledge and tools, but also the hands-on experience that could enable them to work towards a career path in the ECD sector. A number of parents/caregivers have expressed an interest in working in this sector, and the programme is now working towards strengthening other key ECD ecosystem linkages. This includes, for example, increasing the community's capacity to provide high-quality ECD support and assisting parents/caregivers towards an ECD career path. This is turn alleviates the extreme stress of unemployment that exists in these communities.

Social partner network

An indispensable part of the aRe Bapaleng implementation approach is working with a network of social partners, particularly non-profit organisations and community-based organisations. This enables the programme to provide a more comprehensive, holistic set of training modules covering various aspects of ECD, from early literacy to nutrition, mental health, and other areas such as water safety in certain coastal communities. In addition, this approach gives the programme an increased reach and ensures better community ownership of the initiative.

ECD ecosystem

Through the Caregiver Network-ER model and its social partner network approach, aRe Bapaleng can strengthen linkages across the ECD ecosystem and ensure parents/caregivers play an active role in it, as illustrated in Figure 11.3.

Figure 11.3 *aRe Bapaleng and the ECD ecosystem map*

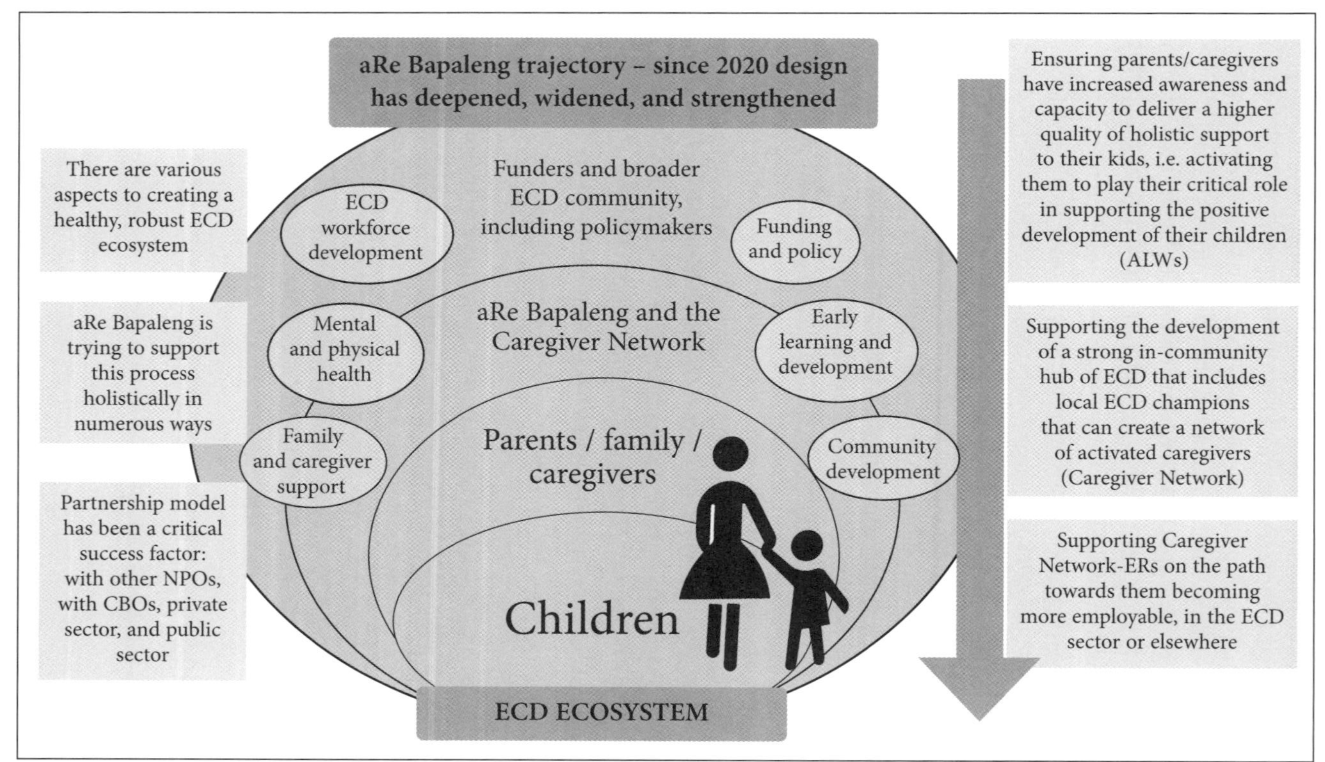

Source: Seriti Institute 2024[8]

Given the nature of the ECD ecosystem, it becomes apparent that much responsibility is placed on those adults who have the most time with young children, generally primary caregivers (such as parents, grandparents, guardians) and other caregivers such as ECD practitioners, childminders, and day mothers (who run play centres or day-care centres). The different components of the aRe Bapaleng Programme work together to enable parents/caregivers in marginalised contexts to play an active role in this ECD ecosystem. The programme helps parents/caregivers to have an appreciation of the importance of early learning support and to be committed to prioritising it, as well as enabling access to this critical support for their young children, both at home and beyond, for example at an ECD centre or by having a day mother. The programme also focuses on unlocking learning opportunities and increasing the skills of parents/caregivers so that they become more employable. This increases the pool of better qualified individuals who can provide higher quality early learning support to young children. See Figure 11.4.

Figure 11.4 *Positive changes recorded by the programme*

CAREGIVERS EXPLAIN HOW THE aRe Bapaleng PROGRAMME HAS CHANGED THE WAY THEY INTERACT WITH THEIR CHILDREN...

1. Caregivers are playing more with their children and allowing them more freedom to explore on their own.
2. They are spending more time with their children and have learned how to engage better with their children.
3. Their ability to communicate with their children has improved and they no longer shout and hit their children to discipline them.
4. They have seen their children's behaviour improve as a result, including listening and sharing more than before, as well as being more playful.
5. Stronger bonds are being formed between the caregivers and their children, with the children now trusting them more.
6. Children have become more independent and want to spend more time playing with their caregivers.
7. Caregivers are showing more love and being more patient with their children.

Source: Seriti Institute 2022[*]

Results associated with the programme

To ascertain what changes the programme brought about, data was gathered from parents/caregivers, primarily in the form of testimonials, as well as through evaluation questionnaires.[†] In this way, parents/caregivers provided

---

[*] Seriti Institute, *A look at 2021: aReBapaleng annual report*, 2 March 2022. Accessed May 2025, https://seriti.org.za/news/are-bapaleng-a-look-at-2021/

[†] aRe Bapaleng collects baseline data for each participant in the programme. This data includes details such as the number of children they care for within their household as well as outside of the household.

feedback related to what they learned through their participation in aRe Bapaleng, as well as the lessons they are applying with their children.

Individual knowledge and attitude changes

Parents reported being more knowledgeable about their children's development, being better able to manage their own time and find opportunities to spend time with their children, and that their emotional regulation and communication skills improved. Parents reported changes in their relationships with their children at different developmental stages. Following their participation in the aRe Bapaleng programme, two mothers from Alexandra explained what they had learned and what they now tried to do.

> I didn't know that building a bond with a child begins when they are still in the womb. I thought it only happens after childbirth, but since I attended training and learnt about the first 1 000 days, I have been communicating with her and feel the kicks whenever I say something, which shows that she's responding! I am glad I was able to learn about this important lesson in building a bond with a child. (Mother 1)

> I got to try out tummy time and saw how my child was able to lift his head and wave his arms and kick freely. I also observed how happy he was, especially when I placed a milk bottle in front of him. He would make an attempt to reach and grab it. I had never tried this before and realised that it is important to give him an opportunity to lie on his tummy as it will help to develop his muscles that will help lift his head or learn to crawl. (Mother 2)

The programme therefore had an impact on mothers' relationships with their unborn children and on caregivers' perceptions of infants learning to crawl.

Parents/caregivers cited time management as a major challenge; they are unable to spend a lot of quality time with their children. During the ALWs, discussions on how to manage their time and instil routines into their children's day were well received. Participants also highlighted how they had learned that quality time with their children could include getting them involved in daily household activities such as cooking or shopping.

A father who participated in the aRe Bapaleng ALWs held in Dobsonville explained that he, like most fathers, had not known how to be actively involved in his son's life because he thought only mothers were responsible for children. This belief changed because of the programme. He now starts his day every morning by brushing his teeth together with his son, who has now become used to the routine. This has improved the amount of time the father gets to spend and interact with his son. Through the workshops, participants came to realise that these are also valuable learning opportunities for their children.

Other parents spoke about the positive impact of the programme on regulating their emotions. In numerous instances, parents/caregivers voiced their appreciation of realising how important it is to communicate with and listen to their children, as opposed to shouting at them or even physically reprimanding them. Parents/caregivers reported positive results when adopting alternative ways of encouraging behavioural change such as through communication and having better, more open relationships with their children. One young mother of two children aged seven and three explained the programme has taught her to communicate with her children. She said, 'I've learned how to keep my emotions intact and how to respond to my kids with empathy.' She indicated how the programme has changed her in so many ways, from knowing that she needs to be her children's role model, through to appreciating and praising her children.

Anger management is a challenge that many parents/caregivers experience. This is often linked to stress due to the challenges they face such as unemployment. As a result, they struggle with remaining patient with, and being kind to, their children when their children's behaviour frustrates them. Many have realised that their "naughty" or "hyperactive" child is merely in need of stimulation and following their instinct to learn and explore. After participating in aRe Bapaleng, parents/caregivers have seen positive changes and feel they are now able to support their children through keeping them busy and learning, thus satisfying the children's appetites for activity and stimulation.

Parents reported that they communicate better with their children, which in turn translates into improved parent/caregiver–child relationships and less tension in the household. More time is spent engaging in playful activities and parents/caregivers have adopted the approach that learning opportunities exist everywhere, even, for example, when doing the shopping. This is resulting in positive changes in development as observed by the parents, for example, children being more confident, able to communicate better, and improved early literacy and numeracy skills such as counting. See Figure 11.5.

Figure 11.5 *Positive changes in parents/caregivers and children*

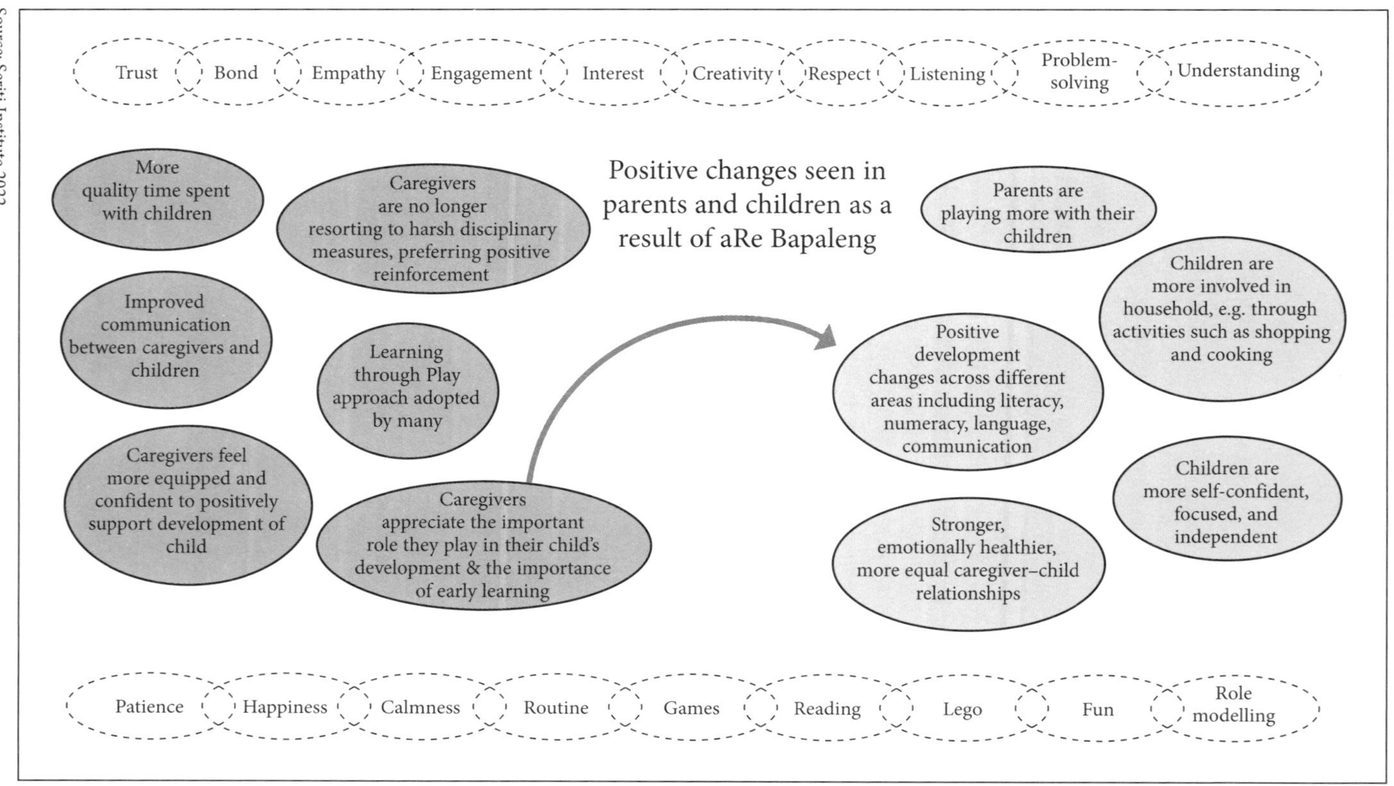

Source: Seriti Institute 2022

Community and local ECD ecosystem changes

Changes were also observed at the community level and at the level of the ECD ecosystem in the marginalised communities where aRe Bapaleng operates. These included improved social cohesion and overall child protection, as well as socio-economic benefits through improved economic well-being and employability. Prior to 2022, the main impact of the programme was on parents/caregivers (and their children) at an individual level, in terms of the quality of interaction, emotional regulation, and time management; since then, however, benefits have subsequently emerged at the broader community level.

During 2022, through the NYS Caregiver Network-ERs, aRe Bapaleng was able to support greater community cohesion, for example, by initiating the creation of parents' forums in ECD centres to facilitate stronger relationships between ECD practitioners and parents. The programme fostered a much stronger network of ECD support as partners from all levels worked together to raise awareness regarding the importance of ECD, and to deliver a higher level of quality ECD in their communities. In NYS partner reports for 2022, NYS partners said that the project had enabled them to connect and enlarge communities where they worked, resulting in a greater impact.[9]

In addition, the programme contributed to valuable training and work experience, with the NYS Caregiver Network-ERs (ECD Champions) benefiting by receiving stipends. These young people explained how being part of NYS aRe Bapaleng provided them with many financial and non-financial benefits. Many spoke of how their participation in aRe Bapaleng has resulted in better mental health as they feel more motivated and confident. This has translated into a positive sense of self as they feel they are making a meaningful contribution to their communities and are more hopeful about their own futures.

An NYS Caregiver Network-ER from Katlehong said:

> It has been an exciting opportunity for me to be finally exposed to a work environment and gain new skills. Being unemployed is stressful and depressing especially if two human beings are fully dependent on you. I must make sure that my sister's school expenses, everyday meals, clothes, and other house essentials are well taken care of.

She had lost hope and felt demotivated about applying for jobs as many of her applications were not shortlisted; however, through her involvement in the programme, she acquired and practised new skills that will make her more employable, such as managing a team, facilitating training, and preparing reports.

Receiving a stipend has relieved financial pressure and enabled the NYS Caregiver Network-ERs to pay for necessities such as food, transport, clothing, medical expenses, and education for household members – even, in some cases, to start a side hustle. That most of the money received was spent on food and education highlights the high levels of food insecurity at household level, which was also evident in the case of parents/caregivers who received ECD services from the Caregiver Network-ERs.

A survey conducted in 2022 by the Seriti Institute of the 3 000 NYS Caregiver Network-ERs confirmed that almost all felt that they had become more employable and better caregivers of young children since participating in the programme.[10]

Summary and conclusion

In South Africa, many children in marginalised areas are growing up without key ECD services. The aRe Bapaleng Programme seeks to change this and to support parents/caregivers with the development of the young children in their care. By 2025, the programme had reached over 80 000 parents/caregivers through its training initiatives, with participant feedback demonstrating the positive impact of both the training sessions and additional activities that were offered. These parents/caregivers provide many examples of how they have positively changed their behaviour, which has in turn positively affected their children. They have more confidence and feel better equipped to take on a more active role in the ECD ecosystem. They highlight how they are supporting their children to explore and learn, and engaging with them in more respectful ways, which is resulting in closer bonds with their children as well as positive development results such as better listening and peer engagement. Most significantly, the programme shows the benefits of combining support for the most urgent socio-economic stresses that parents experience, giving skills and employability training and a stipend, while simultaneously supporting parents in their parenting. This was done while improving social cohesion and bringing together key organisations that impact the lives of young children, enhancing the effects of the programme at both the individual and social levels.

Notes

1   World Health Organization (2018) *Nurturing care for early childhood development: A framework for helping children survive and thrive to transform health and human potential.* Accessed May 2025, https://www.who.int/teams/maternal-newborn-child-adolescent-health-and-ageing/child-health/nurturing-care

2   Why govt needs to review access to early learning, *Bizcommunity*, 8 March 2022. Accessed May 2025, https://www.bizcommunity.com/Article/196/783/225763.html

3   Joyce A, Why it's important to read aloud with your kids, and how to make it count, *The Washington Post*, 16 February 2017; UNICEF (2023) Early childhood

development: UNICEF vision for every child (July). Accessed May 2025, https://www.unicef.org/media/145336/file/Early_Childhood_Development_-_UNICEF_Vision_for_Every_Child.pdf; UNICEF, *Standards for ECD parenting programmes in low-and middle-income countries*. Accessed May 2025, https://www.earlychildhoodworkforce.org/node/1307.

4   Zolten K & Long N, *Parent/child communication*, Center for Effective Parenting. (2006 [1997]). Accessed May 2025, https://parenting-ed.org/wp-content/themes/parenting-ed/files/handouts/communication-parent-to-child.pdf.

5   Van Leer Foundation 2023. *Early Childhood Matters* (132). Accessed May 2025, https://earlychildhoodmatters.online/issues/early-childhood-matters-2023/.

6   Fromberg D, What kindergarten should be: Doris Fromberg at TED[x] Miami University, *YouTube*, 2012. Accessed May 2025, https://www.youtube.com/watch?v=YhpM_jbVopo; Learning through play: What the science says, *Learning Through Play*. Accessed May 2025, https://learningthroughplay.com/explore-the-research/the-scientific-case-for-learning-through-play; Mead S (2016) How do children learn through play? *Whitby School*. Accessed May 2025, https://www.whitbyschool.org/passionforlearning/how-do-children-learn-through-play; Children learn through play, *Great Information*, UC Davis Cancer Center, UC Davis Children's Hospital. Accessed May 2025, https://presidentscircle.childcare.utah.edu/_resources/documents/children-learn-thru-play.pdf.

7   Play in early childhood: The role of play in any setting. *Center on the Developing Child, Harvard University*, 9 August 2019. Accessed June 2025, https://developingchild.harvard.edu/resources/videos/play-in-early-childhood-the-role-of-play-in-any-setting/.

8   Seriti Institute 2024, ECD ecosystem map (aRe Bapaleng Programme 2023 Impact Report). Accessed May 2025, https://seriti.org.za/wp-content/uploads/2024/03/letsplay-booklet-2024.pdf. Adapted from Detroit Early Childhood Development ecosystem map. Executive summary, December 2017. Accessed May 2025, https://detroiteducationcoalition.org/wp-content/uploads/2017/12/ECD-Ecosystem-Map-Executive-Sum-16_1213.pdf.

9   Seriti Institute, aRe Bapaleng NYS survey report of NYS participants (internal document made available to author), 2022.

10   Seriti Institute, aRe Bapaleng NYS survey report of NYS participants (internal document made available to author), 2022.

References

Aryani E (2021) Communication of parents and early childhood to build confidence in the pandemic COVID-19. *Jurnal Pendidikan dan Pemberdayaan Masyarakat* 8(1): 67–7. Accessed May 2025, https://journal.uny.ac.id/index.php/jppm/article/view/35211

Berry L & Slemming W (2024) Mind the policy gap: An overview of progress towards providing universal services for young children in South Africa. In Slemming

W, Biersteker L & Lake L (Eds) *South African child gauge 2024*. Cape Town: Children's Institute, University of Cape Town

Center on the Developing Child (Harvard University) (2007) *InBrief: The Impact of Early Adversity on Child Development. Summary of scientific presentations at the National Symposium on Early Childhood Science and Policy*. Accessed May 2025, https://developingchild.harvard.edu/resources/inbriefs/inbrief-the-impact-of-early-adversity-on-childrens-development/

Dawes A, Biersteker L, Girdwood L, Snelling M & Horler J (2020). *Technical Report. Early Learning Programme Outcomes Study*. Cape Town: Innovation Edge and Ilifa Labantwana. Accessed May 2025, https://datadrive2030.co.za/wp-content/uploads/2022/09/IE-ELPO-Study-Technical-Report-FINAL.pdf

Giese S, Dawes A, Tredoux C, Mattes F, Bridgman G, Van der Berg S, Schenk J & Kotzé J (2022) *Thrive by five index report* (Revised August 2022). Cape Town: Innovation Edge

Hall K, Almeleh C, Giese S, Mphaphuli E, Slemming W, Mathys R, Droomer L, Proudlock P, Kotzé J & Sadan M (2024) *South African early childhood review 2024*. Cape Town: Children's Institute, University of Cape Town and Ilifa Labantwana

Hall K, Sambu W, Almeleh C, Mabaso K, Giese S & Proudlock P (2019) *South African early childhood review 2019*. Cape Town: Children's Institute, University of Cape Town and Ilifa Labantwana

Hannan S & Juan A (2021) *Our first educational building blocks: The role of the home*. HSRC Review 19(2): 23–24

Ilifa Labantwana & Kago Ya Bana (2018) *A Plan to Achieve Universal Coverage of Early Childhood Development Services by 2030*. Accessed May 2025, https://dgmt.co.za/wp-content/uploads/2018/08/ECD-Vision-2018-digital.pdf

Kika-Mistry J, Droomer L, Mohamed Z & Senona E (2024) Strengthening the system: Early childhood development finance. In Slemming W, Biersteker L & Lake L (Eds) *South African child gauge 2024*. Cape Town: Children's Institute, University of Cape Town

Sénéchal M & LeFevre JA (2002) Parental involvement in the development of children's reading skill: A five year longitudinal study. *Child Development* 73(2): 445–460. Accessed May 2025, http://dx.doi.org/10.1111/1467-8624.00417

Spaull N, Daniels RC, Ardington C, Benhura M, Bridgman G et al. (2021) *Synthesis report*. Wave 4: National Income Dynamics Study (NIDS) – Coronavirus Rapid Mobile Survey (CRAM)

Statistics South Africa (2018) *Education series volume VII: Children's education and well-being in South Africa, 2018*. Pretoria: Statistics South Africa. Accessed May 2025, https://www.statssa.gov.za/publications/92-01-07/92-01-072018.pdf

Statistics South Africa (2022) *General household survey 2021*. Pretoria: Statistics South Africa. Accessed May 2025, https://www.statssa.gov.za/publications/P0318/P03182021.pdf

Zosh J, Hassinger-Das B & Laurie M (2022) *White paper. Learning through play and the development of holistic skills across childhood*. Billund: The LEGO Foundation

12 *Do Caregivers Engage With Their Young Children at Home, and Can Teachers Influence Them to Do More? Experiences from the Together in My Education Home Learning Programme*

Magali von Blottnitz and Shelley O'Carroll

Introduction

Early learning, especially emergent literacy, is determined not only by what happens at school but also by what takes place in the home (Crawford & Zygouris-Coe 2006; Mui & Anderson 2008), even before learners enter school. This results in large individual differences in the level of language capability before children start formal schooling (Vasilyeva, Waterfall & Huttenlocher 2008). Research has found that programmes that bridge the gap between home and school and that enhance parental involvement lead to benefits for children, including cognitive gains (Padak & Rasinski 2003; Powell 2004), improved long-term academic development (Levine 2002), and a range of social-emotional benefits (Michael, Wolhuter & Van Wyk 2012; Mqota 2009). In the Global South, positive effects of parental interventions have been found in various African contexts, for example, Ethiopia, Rwanda, Kenya, and South Africa (Bando, Näslund-Hadley & Gertler 2018; Dowd et al. 2016; Pisani 2015).

Yet there is scepticism in South Africa about parental/caregiver programmes related to schooling. Literature confirms the limitations of parental programmes, limitations which are particularly linked to the variable degree of uptake by families, the length of the intervention, and the challenges around monitoring adherence or fidelity (Center on the Developing Child 2016; Mostert, Roberts & Plaatjies 2018; Rao et al. 2014). This chapter asks how teachers and caregivers[*] in different schools interact with material provided in a home learning programme. The chapter aims to contribute to knowledge from interventions that support home learning programmes in order to plan and implement mechanisms and measures

---

[*] In this chapter, the word caregivers refers to significant adults engaging with children at home and supporting informal learning, whether they are biological parents, grandparents, older siblings or others.

that engage teachers and caregivers in a range of schools. This is important for developing home learning interventions delivered at scale.

This chapter shows that in a country like South Africa, with myriad permutations of individual actors contributing to learning outcomes, teacher and caregiver interactions in a particular home learning programme (Together in My Education (TIME)) occur on a continuum. The chapter shows this based on two case studies, each from different schools that participated in the home learning programme. The TIME programme was born as one of the collaborative initiatives of the Western Cape @Homelearning Forum at the height of the COVID-19 pandemic. As school closures forced children to stay at home, representatives of the Western Cape Education Department (WCED) and other education stakeholders gathered to explore possible responses. The unequal presence of learning routines and parental support for children at home had long been on the WCED's radar as an important hurdle to equalising performance among the province's schools, so addressing this would not only help navigate the urgent challenge of school closures but remain relevant post-COVID-19. TIME emerged as one response for Grade R and Grade 1 children, endorsed by the WCED and designed to be deployable at all the schools in the province that could benefit. Each term, activity packs containing daily play-based early literacy or early mathematics activities* give caregivers opportunities to establish interactive learning routines with their children at home.

TIME was designed to be disseminated to many homes (in 2021, more than 50 000 homes) through networks of non-governmental organisations (NGOs)† and, more particularly, schools. The rationale was that the school infrastructure – supported by district officials, and especially by Grade R and Grade 1 teachers with expertise in the developmental needs and ways of learning of very young children – would provide key, pre-existing assets for the scalability of the intervention, if class teachers acted as programme mediators in homes. Teachers were therefore the key intermediary needed to activate parental/caregiver involvement. Their mediation involved

---

*   The activity packs offer a range of concrete resources appropriate for young children. They consist of colour-printed learning materials, currently available in six South African languages, and include early literacy content from Wordworks, early mathematics content from RED INK, and stories from Nal'ibali, African Storybook, and Book Dash. The resources are aligned with the Curriculum and Assessment Policy Statements in order to supplement and reinforce what is being taught during the school day in Grade R and Grade 1. Play-based, interactive activities and questions are presented in familiar contexts that children can relate to in their homes. In addition, multimedia motivational and support messages are available to caregivers and teachers who have access to smartphones. In 2021, these messages were disseminated via the data-free app Moya, with teachers playing a key role in forwarding them to their class's caregivers.

†   Initially, the project relied on Wordworks' existing network of schools and partner NGOs, called WordNetworks. With the WCED's endorsement, a greater number of NGO partners were encouraged to offer TIME to their networks.

physically distributing the resource packs to homes, motivating caregivers, and providing guidance and support to them, in particular by forwarding the Wordworks support messages. Figure 12.1 summarises the three core aspects of the mediating role of teachers.

Figure 12.1 *The three core aspects of teacher mediation in the TIME programme*

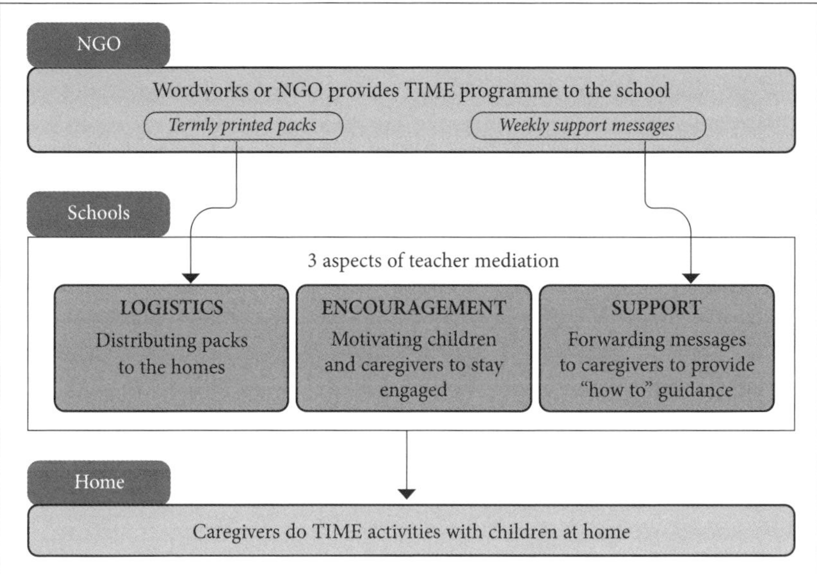

Monitoring data from the TIME programme revealed some variability both in the intensity of teacher mediation and in caregiver engagement with the activities. Two case studies, reflecting varying levels of teacher and caregiver interactions at two different schools, are presented below.

TIME case studies

To illustrate how TIME played out in different contexts, we share the case studies of a teacher and caregiver at two schools on extreme points of the spectrum identified during the intervention. The case studies consider uptake of TIME, which was excellent in School A and modest in School B. Both schools had been part of the 2020 pilot so 2021 was their second year of working with TIME. For each school, we further explore how the teachers reported mediating the TIME programme, and subsequently set out the context of one family, sharing the caregiver's experiences with TIME in their circumstances. The case studies end with a reflection on the factors that influenced engagement with TIME in each case.

TIME in an English-medium, low-fee school in the Metro North district[*]

School A is a low-fee school serving a population of mixed nationalities and home languages. It is an English-medium school, classified as quintile 5,[†] serving families living in the immediate neighbourhood, where 25% of households experience income poverty.[1] The school's fees are less than R1 500 per year. The Grade R class of 28 children is slightly below the prescribed maximum of 30. The area in which School A is located is popular with migrants from other African countries and is therefore linguistically very diverse, with 5% of residents speaking a non-South African language at home.[2]

Teacher Pillay: A journey of teamwork, reflection, and growth with TIME

Ms Pillay, a Grade R teacher, has been involved with TIME since its pilot in 2020 and 'loves'[††] the programme. She finds the materials 'very useful and relevant for use in class' and uses her own pack extensively. She has laminated some of the pictures so that they last longer. She indicated to the interviewer that she 'creates a synergy between her teaching practices, Stellar [a Wordworks-developed classroom programme for Grade R home language teaching] and the TIME materials'.

Asked about the kind of relationship that her school entertains with its community, Ms Pillay admitted that 'before TIME, there was not a lot of communication with parents and caregivers'. However, she has put effort into connecting with them. For example, she indicated that she contacted Somali caregivers and asked them to give her words 'for basic things that we do in class, like colours and shapes', so that she can support Somali-speaking learners in class in the same way as she supports Afrikaans-speaking learners. Overall, she now considers her relationship with caregivers to be 'very good', adding that, 'They cooperate with the school very well'.

Ms Pillay and her colleagues have followed a learning curve in mediating the TIME programme. After the first term of 2021, the team observed confusion among caregivers about how to use the TIME resources. Reflecting on how

---

[*]   Metro North is one of eight education districts in the Western Cape province of South Africa.

[†]   Each South African ordinary public school is categorised into one of five wealth quintiles according to the socio-economic context in which the school is situated. Schools in quintiles 1 to 3 are also classified as no-fee schools. Schools in quintiles 4 and 5 are allowed to charge fees that the school governing body proposes and the parent body agrees to.

[††]   All quotations in this section are from participants in the study, unless a different citation is provided. The names of teachers, children and parents have been changed to protect their privacy.

to address this, they decided to send the materials in weekly chunks rather than the whole term's pack at once. 'Now the TIME work is distributed on a weekly basis, pasted in their books as homework. The weekly distribution works very well.' Another decision taken by the team of School A was to organise a TIME support session at the school for caregivers. 'We did a workshop and took them through all the TIME activities and explained how to work with TIME. Thereafter there was a big improvement in the way they do activities with their kids.'

Following Wordworks' suggestions, Ms Pillay also encouraged caregivers in her class to install the Moya app on their phones so she could send them the TIME messages via Moya. For those who did not have Moya, she still forwarded messages on WhatsApp. She shared all the TIME support messages with the caregivers. She noticed that some activities were initially challenging for caregivers, such as folding little books, but the support provided has paid off. 'They can fold the little books correctly now'.

About a quarter of Ms Pillay's class returns the activity record, a termly sheet that families can use to keep track of the child's progress and feed back to the child's teacher. At the time of the interview at the end of Term 2 in 2021, she estimated that 10 out of 28 caregivers (36%) were doing TIME activities daily with their children. This estimate is based on the children who come to school with evidence of what they did at home the previous day, especially the games they played. Among the remaining 18 children, Ms Pillay believes that roughly equal proportions of them do TIME activities occasionally, rarely or not at all. Ms Pillay had no doubt that the TIME programme has led to improvements in some academic areas for the children who engage with it regularly. 'I have seen an improvement with reading, especially during shared reading', she noted.

Denita and her mother Natasha do TIME activities every day

Denita was a Grade R learner in Ms Pillay's class when we interviewed her mother, Natasha. Natasha lived with her two children (Denita, in Grade R, and a one-month-old baby), her fiancé and both her parents. There was evidence of a warm and nurturing relationship between Denita and her mother, with frequent conversations and engagement in reading and storytelling. The field worker interviewing Natasha experienced the family as stable and supportive. For example, Natasha reported that her mother, and in some cases, the paternal grandparents stepped in to look after Denita when she was at work and had done so especially during the 2020 lockdown when Denita's crèche was closed. At the time of the interview, Natasha was on maternity leave, which allowed for more quality time with Denita. Although the family came from an Afrikaans background, with the grandparents being fluent in Afrikaans, the younger generation tends to speak more English at home, and they deliberately chose an English-medium school for Denita. The interview produced ample evidence of a rich and interactive relationship between Natasha and Denita's teacher. Natasha was unreservedly positive about TIME, and confirmed the great lengths that Ms Pillay went to in order to ensure that caregivers understood how to use the resources at home. Denita's family spends approximately 20 minutes every weekday doing TIME activities with her, as well as some time during weekends. In addition to Natasha, Denita's father also occasionally gets involved, especially with reading stories. They all enjoy the programme very much: usually, Denita wants to do more than one activity per day, which her mother allows. She enjoys all activities, most particularly the activities related to story time, games, and letter and number activities. Natasha feels that the level of the activities is just right for the children, with Denita being challenged, especially when having to think critically. On her side, Natasha finds the questions and instructions very easy to follow. After finishing the activities, they complete the activity record together. Natasha shared the record with the teacher at the end of Term 1. Natasha was receiving the TIME messages on Moya as well as on WhatsApp and found them helpful. She referred to a specific message on how to motivate her child as being one that she found particularly valuable. Even though Natasha had been working with her daughter before the introduction of the TIME programme, she felt that having this resource has helped her to spend quality time with Denita. It has also strengthened the parent–teacher relationship.

Natasha also claimed that her daughter's behaviour had improved: she was more motivated, had better concentration, spoke more, and had developed her vocabulary. She also enjoyed stories, games, and numbers, and was becoming better at following instructions.

Interpretation and reflections

Many aspects of Denita's story illustrate what could be seen as the best-case scenario of TIME implementation at home: daily engagement, involvement of a male caregiver, regular access to the support messages, no challenges with caregivers' understanding, a moderate level of challenge for the child, enjoyment all around, and benefits for the child–parent bond as well as for the child's development. All these elements were made possible by a very proactive, reflective teacher who made sustained efforts to ensure the buy-in of her learners' families.

Given her supportive family context, it is likely that Denita would have reached her developmental milestones even without TIME. Nevertheless, both mother and daughter are receiving an extra boost with the opportunity to use the materials. For the school, it appears that engaging with TIME has helped to create more positive relationships with parents/caregivers, including families of foreign origin.

TIME in an isiXhosa-medium, no-fee school in the Metro East district

School B is a no-fee school serving a very impoverished population in Khayelitsha. It is situated in the Metro East district and classified as quintile 2 and therefore does not charge fees. Like School A, it serves families mostly from the immediate neighbourhood, where income poverty affects 57% of households.[3] In the Foundation Phase, the school's language of learning and teaching is isiXhosa, the home language of 90% of the community.[4] Despite some occasional positive experiences with parent engagement, the teacher we interviewed described the community served by School B as follows: 'Parents of most learners are teenagers and they are not involved in their children's education. Even older parents do not support their kids.'*

Although School B was on Wordworks' list for the TIME pilot in 2020, with activity packs ordered for all Grade R and Grade 1 learners that year, it is not clear whether all teachers mediated the programme in 2020. There are hints that the school only distributed some of the packs received to families. In 2021, however, all the Grade R and Grade 1 teachers at School B were involved in TIME.

Ms Dlongwana: Little evidence of reflection or teamwork and limited communication with caregivers

Ms Dlongwana is a Grade 1 teacher in School B, teaching a class of 45 children. She indicated that she was encouraged by a colleague to get involved with TIME in 2021, but did not otherwise work with her colleagues on the implementation of the programme. She liked the TIME resources, which she believed were pitched at the level of the children. The packs were distributed to caregivers once a term, and Ms Dlongwana would send a WhatsApp message requesting caregivers to support their children with the

---

* All quotations in this section are from participants in the study, unless a different citation is provided.

activities. Letters were also sent home with the learners, but Ms Dlongwana notes that sometimes learners did not deliver the letters to their caregivers.

Unlike School A, at the time of the interview School B had not held any parent meetings to explain to caregivers what TIME was about. Although Ms Dlongwana confirmed receiving the multimedia support messages from Wordworks, she did not forward them to the caregivers, nor did she talk to them about the Moya app.

Ms Dlongwana estimated that more than 75% of families in her class did not use the TIME packs at all. She commented: 'I handed out the Term 1 packs, but at the end of the term I noticed that most packs were still intact in the learners' bags and were never touched'. Despite asking caregivers to send videos or pictures of their engagement with the TIME materials, she did not receive any. There was a small minority of families who did the TIME activities at home, and Ms Dlongwana believed that being supported at home made a difference to those learners. 'They show a lot of interest when they are in class.'

Lukholo and her mother Ntombentsha do some TIME activities two/three times a week

Ntombentsha tries to do TIME regularly with little Lukholo but does not do stories. Lukholo, in Ms Dlongwana's class, is the only child of Ntombentsha, an at-home mother living with an uncle, aunt, and two cousins. Over the past few years, Ntombentsha's attempts to find work have been unsuccessful, so she spends her days at home and has ample time with her son. Lukholo is a sociable child who spends a lot of time playing outdoors with his friends, and his mother made sure that he attended pre-school from the age of two, and that he was enrolled in Grade R at School B. Ntombentsha reported being happy with the school; although she has never personally interacted with her son's teacher, she is satisfied with the WhatsApp communications that she receives from her.

Generally, Ntombentsha and Lukholo's experience with TIME has been good, although a bit more mixed than Natasha and Denita's. Ntombentsha and Lukholo received their first TIME pack in 2020, when Lukholo was in Grade R. Ntombentsha reported that when the improved Grade 1 packs were distributed, she looked at them but only started working with them a bit later. She found that the activities were at the right level, but the instructions sometimes confused her; for example, instructions for the activities that required cutting. She also felt challenged about the stories with questions: she did not understand who should be asked the questions. Ntombentsha described herself as 'an indoor person who does not socialise much', therefore she did not have other people who she could ask when she was unsure what to do.

Ntombentsha reported doing TIME activities two or three times per week for approximately 15 minutes on the days when Lukholo stayed at home because of rotational attendance. She did not complete the activity record.

Parent and child generally enjoyed the TIME activities, and Ntombentsha would definitely recommend it to other caregivers; however, she expressed the wish 'that Lukholo could also enjoy it like me'. They did not engage with the story activities. 'I never did any stories with Lukholo. Whenever we have to do stories, he does not want to sit and concentrate. He always asks to do the letter or number activity instead', she explained, adding that tracing shapes, letters or numbers was Lukholo's preferred activity. (Although Ntombentsha justified the choice to skip story activities by referring to her child's hyperactive personality, the confusion that she reported with instructions may hint at deeper challenges on her part.) Considering that the teacher, Ms Dlongwana, was not forwarding Wordworks' multimedia support messages to her class's parents, it is not surprising that Ntombentsha was unaware of them.

Asked to comment on the benefits for her of doing the TIME programme with her son, Ntombentsha indicated that it helped her to spend quality time with her child and to bond with him. She also felt that it had increased Lukholo's motivation for school and for homework. She claimed that he has become better at following instructions and that his vocabulary was also growing. 'I have noticed that Lukholo likes writing a lot. After playing, he loves to do maths', she remarked.

Interpretation and reflections

Of the 2021 sample, School B was the school that has been most challenged with deriving the full benefits of the TIME programme, more so than other sampled schools in similar environments. In the absence of specific data, it is easy to imagine a myriad of reasons for this, ranging from the shortage of administration staff to teacher exhaustion caused by excessive class sizes, practical difficulties in communicating, parents' own struggles for survival, and other contextual challenges. Apart from the apparent internal miscommunication in 2020 around the pilot version of the programme, Ms Dlongwana's mediation was limited to sending the packs home and posting a WhatsApp message to the families. More pro-active practices like a parent meeting to guide caregivers on the use of the resources or forwarding the support messages might have yielded more uptake. Ntombentsha and Lukholo's story illustrates the kind of difficulties that caregivers can come up against when they are left to their own devices, without access to the support messages or someone to turn to when in doubt. Nevertheless, it also illustrates the pockets of positive outcomes that emerge, even with minimal mediation.

Reflections on factors influencing caregiver involvement, specifically teacher mediation

Contextual factors

The vast contextual disparities between the families, schools, and teachers make it inappropriate to compare the experiences of Denita to those of Lukholo, and those of Ms Dlongwana with those of Ms Pillay.

The cultural and linguistic make-up of Khayelitsha (near School B) is far more homogeneous than that of the area surrounding School A, so Ms Pillay faces the difficulty of having to engage with a greater proportion of caregivers who do not have a good command of English than Ms Dlongwana.

However, School B is in a significantly more deprived socio-economic neighbourhood than School A, as reflected by their different quintiles. School A can raise school fees of R1 500 per year, whereas School B is a no-fee school. The size of Ms Dlongwana's class – 45 learners – indicates a challenging learning environment in School B, and makes communication and relationship-building between teacher and caregivers far more difficult than in School A. Generalising from South Africa's history, it is easy to assume that the parents/caregivers of Ms Dlongwana's learners grew up with vastly different educational experiences from those of School A. This probably affects what they see as a normal pattern of involvement with school matters in adulthood.

Teacher's mediation of the programme

While acknowledging that contextual factors play a fundamental role, we also want to focus on the teacher's agency, and their ability to influence the adoption of new habits and routines through their mediation of the TIME programme.

Although both case-study teachers were positive about TIME, Teacher Pillay engaged with it more actively. She met the expectations of TIME but also adapted the activities to ensure that the outcomes were achieved. The adaptations included sending the required work out once a week instead of once a term, and inviting caregivers to a workshop where activities were explained and clarity was provided about the programme. She also communicated with caregivers more regularly. A quarter of her class returned their activity records. Although Teacher Dlongwana complied with most of the core expectations of the TIME programme, none of the learners returned their activity records.

Applying a theoretical lens to the role of the teacher, then, two levels of mediation emerge, as represented in Figure 12.2 and Table 12.1.

1. The transactional mediation focuses on the physical distribution of the packs and the accompanying communication (that is, support messages) from the school to the caregivers. At this level, the focus is on the dissemination of resources along a pre-determined chain. Both case-study teachers fulfilled that first level of mediation to some degree, although Ms Dlongwana did not comply with the expectation of disseminating the support messages.

2. The second level of mediation can be termed transformational mediation, as it focuses on encouraging behaviour change. This includes providing additional modelling, and customised messages, information, and support to children and caregivers, with the intention of changing caregivers' knowledge, beliefs, and attitudes about their roles and responsibilities. Ms Pillay and her colleagues' practices are an illustration of this transformational mediation, and the case study shows that their efforts could lead to evolving relationships and practices within the education ecosystem.

Whether teachers opt for one or the other model may depend on many factors, including their perceptions of parents and caregivers. Teachers with a deficit view of the parents' contribution may find it difficult to reach out to parents in a spirit of partnership (Jay & Rohl 2005; Longwell-Grice & McIntyre 2006); however, when deliberately equipped to work with parents, their practices may shift (Nutbrown, Hannon & Morgan 2005). This shift ideally also takes place at school-level as a school begins to negotiate the transition from being primarily inward-focused to becoming a 'learning hub for family support' (Eadie 2021: 301). As teachers engage fully with TIME, they make this shift, rethink their own roles as educators, and reshape their social contracts with communities (Eadie 2021: 305).

The case studies suggest that, in areas with an entrenched legacy of disconnect between schools and caregivers, and where multiple practical hurdles impede interactions, the effort required for transformational mediation is more substantial. Shifting patterns of parental/caregiver engagement in these areas will probably take consistent effort and support over a longer period.

Figure 12.2 *TIME implementation flow, reflecting transactional and transformational teacher mediation*

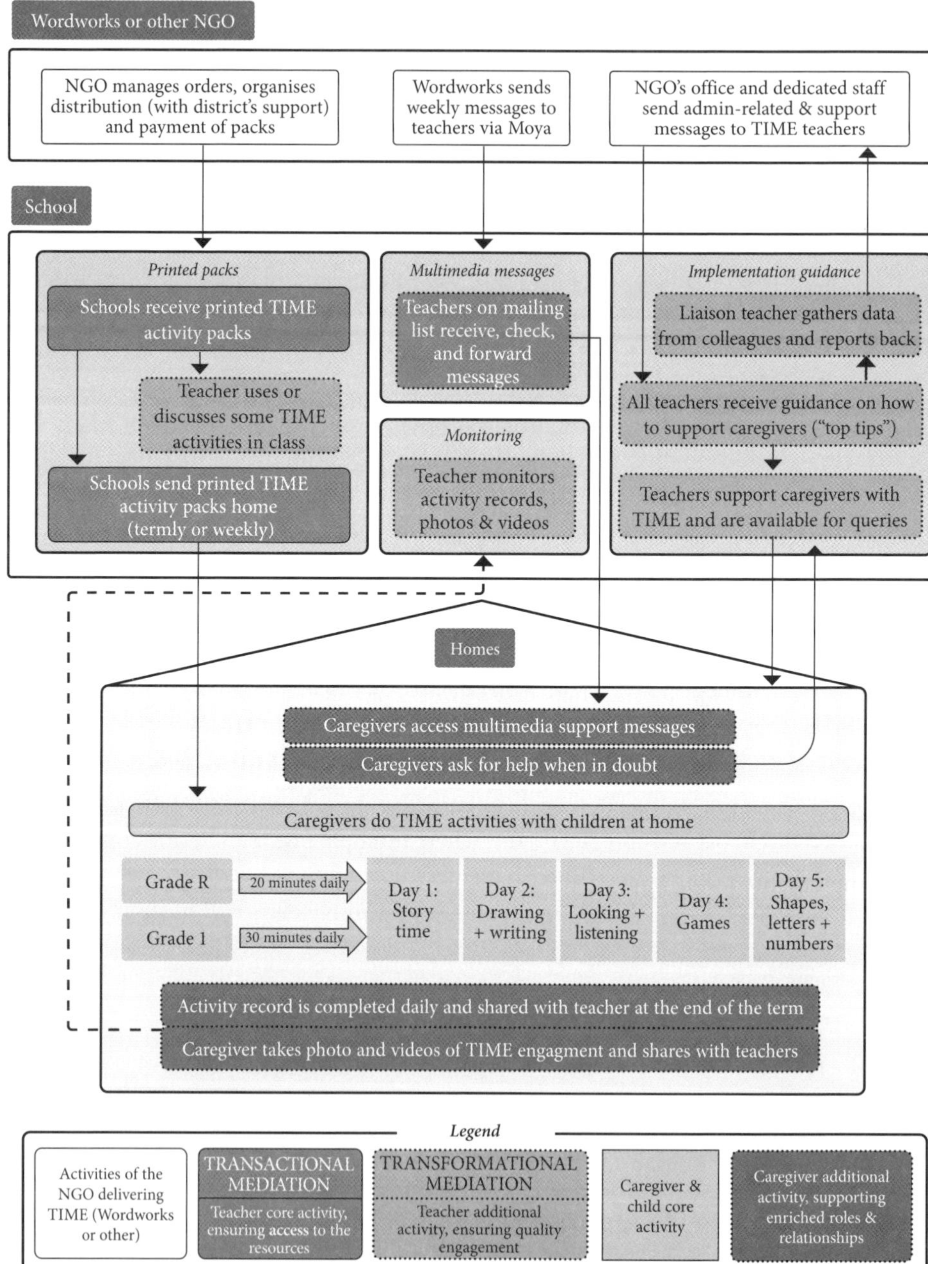

Table 12.1 *Levels of mediation of the TIME programme*

Mediation type	Definition and details	Likely effect
Transactional mediation of the TIME programme	• Mediation focused on the dissemination of printed materials • Includes basic communication (letter and/or WhatsApp message) about the provision of the packs, and a once-off request to return activity registers and share photos and videos	• In schools where the level of caregiver engagement is already high, caregivers are likely to seize the opportunity and spontaneously engage with TIME • In other scenarios, spontaneous engagement is likely to be limited and partial

Transformational mediation of the TIME programme	• Mediation focused on the behaviour of caregivers
	• In addition to the elements of transactional mediation, it involves creating excitement among children as well as multiple engagements with caregivers to create awareness and understanding, providing ongoing support and monitoring uptake
		• When this mediation is sustained, it has the potential to shift perceptions and practices gradually and is likely to result in:
		  ○ more prevalent and sustained uptake at home
		  ○ more generative relationships between home and school

Conclusion

This chapter engages with two case studies related to the TIME home-based learning programme in order to gain an understanding of how the programme played out in different contexts.

TIME was designed as a cost-effective, scalable intervention which, when implemented well, has substantial psycho-social, behavioural, and academic benefits for participating children and their families. It also has benefits for schools, including enhancing their interactions with their communities.

The realisation of these benefits, however, hinges on the engagement of caregivers with TIME activities at home, and programme monitoring has revealed unequal levels of uptake, reflecting real hurdles preventing caregivers from establishing learning routines at home. The case studies presented here illustrate some ways in which the caregivers' involvement is influenced by their context and that of the schools, but also by the quality of teacher mediation.

As the COVID-19 pandemic caused great disruption, followed by intense pressure on teachers to catch up on learning losses, some teachers were more comfortable in a transactional mediation role (ensuring that TIME materials reached homes) than in a transformational one (in which they would partner with caregivers, igniting interest in their children's learning and confidence to establish learning routines at home).

Apart from the schools that have already embarked on the transition from being inward-focused to ecosystem-focused, more time and support will be needed to help schools reshape their social contracts with communities, and to help both teachers and caregivers rethink their own roles as educators. Until then, the testimonies of caregivers and teachers give Wordworks and its partners the energy to continue testing new models of support and communication for schools and caregivers, as well as explore more formal partnerships with aftercare programmes to bring the benefits of the TIME programme to more children, communities, and homes.

Notes

1   Statistics South Africa (2012) *Census 2011*. Accessed via https://youthexplorer.org.za/. Accessed June 2025, https://geo.youthexplorer.org.za/?geo=199015#category-68

2   Statistics South Africa (2012) *Census 2011*. Accessed June 2025, https://geo.youthexplorer.org.za/?geo=199015#category-64

3   Statistics South Africa (2012) *Census 2011*. Accessed June 2025, https://geo.youthexplorer.org.za/?geo=199038#category-40 (for School B: income poverty)

4   Statistics South Africa (2012) *Census 2011*. Accessed June 2025, https://geo.youthexplorer.org.za/?geo=199038#category-36 (for School B: language)

References

Bando R, Näslund-Hadley E & Gertler P (2018) *Inquiry and problem-based pedagogy: Evidence from 10 field experiments*. Inter-American Development Bank Working Paper. Accessed May 2025, https://doi.org/10.18235/0001491

Center on the Developing Child (2016) From best practices to breakthrough impacts: *A science-based approach to building a more promising future for young children and families*. Harvard University. Accessed May 2025, https://developingchild.harvard.edu/resources/report/best-practices-breakthrough-impacts/

Crawford PA & Zygouris-Coe V (2006) All in the family: Connecting home and school with family literacy. *Early Childhood Education Journal* 33(4): 261–267

Dowd AJ, Borisova I, Amente A & Yenew A (2016) Realising capabilities in Ethiopia: Maximising early childhood investment for impact and equity. *Journal of Human Development and Capabilities* 17(4): 477–493

Eadie S (2021) Schools as learning hubs for family support: South Africa. In Reimers F and Opertti R (Eds) *Learning to build back better futures for education: Lessons from educational innovation during the COVID-19 pandemic*. Geneva: UNESCO International Bureau of Education

Jay J & Rohl M (2005) Constructing a family literacy programme: Challenges and successes. *International Journal for Early Childhood* 37(1): 57–78

Levine LA (2002) *Report. Teacher's perceptions of parental involvement: How it effects our children's development in literacy*. US Department of Education. Accessed May 2025, https://files.eric.ed.gov/fulltext/ED465438.pdf

Longwell-Grice H & McIntyre E (2006) Addressing goals of school and community: Lessons from a family literacy programme. *The School Community Journal* 16(2): 115–132

Michael S, Wolhuter CC & Van Wyk N (2012) The management of parental involvement in multicultural schools in South Africa: A case study. *CEPS Journal* 2(1): 57–82

Mostert I, Roberts N & Plaatjies L (2018) *ChildConnect Pilot Evaluation Report: Executive Summary*. Kelello in collaboration with the University of Johannesburg's Centre for Education Practice Research. Accessed May 2025, https://kelello.org/wp-content/uploads/2020/09/2018-07-09-ChildConnect-research-report-Kelello-UJ-CEPR-Executive-Summary.pdf

Mqota V (2009) *Education and democracy: A view from Soweto*. New Jersey: Mqota Publications

Mui S & Anderson J (2008) At home with the Johars: Another look at family literacy. *The Reading Teacher* 62(3): 234–243

Nutbrown C, Hannon P & Morgan A (2005) *Early literacy work with families: Policy, practice and research*. London: Sage Publications

Padak N & Rasinski T (2003) *Family literacy programs: Who benefits?* Ohio Literacy Resource Centre, Kent State University. Accessed May 2025, https://literacy.kent.edu/Oasis/Pubs/WhoBenefits2003.pdf

Pisani L (2015) Rwanda 2015 ELMI Results: Early *Literacy and Math Initiative 2015*. Save the Children, IDELA. Accessed June 2025, https://idela-network.org/resource/rwanda-2015-elmi-results/

Powell DR (2004) Parenting education in family literacy programmes. In Wasik BH (Ed.) *Handbook of family literacy*. New Jersey: Lawrence Erlbaum Associates

Rao N, Sun J, Wong JMS, Weekes B, Ip P et al. (2014) *Early childhood development and cognitive development in developing countries: A rigorous literature review. Report*. Evidence for Policy and Practice, Department for International Development, UK. Accessed May 2025, https://eppi.ioe.ac.uk/cms/Default.aspx?tabid=3465

Statistics South Africa (2012) *Census 2011 Statistical release* - P0301.4. Pretoria: Statistics South Africa

Vasilyeva M, Waterfall H & Huttenlocher J (2008) Emergence of syntax: Commonalities and differences across children. *Developmental Science* 11(1): 84 97

13 *Pathways to Implementing Effective Parental Involvement Programmes in South Africa*

Adele Mooi and Abigail Dreyer

Introduction

Parental/caregiver involvement in early childhood development (ECD) programmes strengthens the bond between parents/caregivers and their children. When parents participate actively, they demonstrate their interest in and commitment to their child's education, which fosters a positive parent–child relationship. This relationship has a significant impact on the child's emotional well-being and overall development. Parents/caregivers know their children best, and by being involved in the ECD programme, they can collaborate with teachers to ensure that their children's specific needs are met, leading to better outcomes. Involving parents in ECD programmes empowers them to take an active role in their child's development. It provides them with knowledge and skills to support their child's learning and development, making them more confident and capable caregivers. This empowerment can have long-term benefits for both child and family. Parental/caregiver involvement in ECD programmes also promotes community engagement. When parents/caregivers are involved, they become part of a larger community of caregivers, educators, and professionals working towards the same goal of supporting children's development. This collaboration strengthens the overall ECD system and creates a supportive network for families.

Despite the numerous benefits of parental/caregiver involvement in ECD programmes, limited parental/caregiver engagement in many early childhood education settings is significant. This lack of involvement poses a challenge to the holistic development and overall success of children in ECD programmes. One of the primary reasons for limited parental/caregiver involvement is a lack of awareness about the importance and benefits of active participation in ECD programmes.

Many parents and caregivers may not fully understand the impact they can have on their child's development, or may not be aware of the opportunities available for involvement. Busy schedules and competing priorities often hinder them from actively participating in ECD programmes.

Work commitments, household responsibilities, and other obligations can limit the time parents and caregivers have available to engage in their child's education, leading to reduced involvement. Similarly, language and cultural differences can create barriers to parental involvement in ECD programmes. Parents/caregivers who do not speak the language of instruction or come from different cultural backgrounds may feel less confident in engaging with a programme or may face challenges in understanding the curriculum and expectations. Some parents/caregivers may lack the necessary resources and support to participate actively in ECD programmes. Financial constraints, lack of transportation, or limited access to information and resources can hinder their ability to engage effectively with their child's education. Inadequate or ineffective communication between ECD programmes and parents/caregivers can also contribute to limited involvement. If parents and caregivers are not regularly informed about their child's progress, activities, and opportunities for involvement, they may feel disconnected and less motivated to engage with the programme. Negative past experiences with education systems or lack of positive role models in their upbringing can also impact parental involvement. Parents/caregivers who have had negative experiences during their own education may be less inclined to participate actively in their child's ECD programme.

When considering these possible reasons for limited parental/caregiver involvement, the following questions were explored by the Little People Preschool (LPPS) and Community Development Centre: *What can be done to encourage parental/caregiver involvement? What opportunities can encourage parental/caregiver involvement? How can an ECD programme facilitate parental/caregiver involvement?*

Methodology

The findings on these questions made use of qualitative feedback from parents/caregivers using an open-ended questionnaire. This questionnaire allowed participants to provide detailed and subjective responses, enabling a deeper understanding of their perspectives and experiences. The participants were selected through a purposive sampling technique, ensuring a diverse range of individuals who have relevant experiences or knowledge related to parental/caregiver involvement. The purpose of the data collection, the voluntary nature of respondent participation, and their right to withdraw at any time without consequences were explained to potential participants, and their informed consent was obtained.

The questionnaire was developed and consists of of a series of open-ended questions that allowed participants to express their thoughts, opinions, and experiences freely. It was also designed to encourage participants to provide detailed and comprehensive responses. The responses were analysed using thematic analysis, which involved identifying patterns, themes, and categories within the data to gain a comprehensive understanding of the participants' feedback. It is recognised that the findings may be limited by the self-reporting nature of the questionnaire, as participants' responses may have been influenced by their own biases or subjective interpretations. The sample size may also affect the generalisability of the findings, as the investigation relied on purposive sampling rather than a random selection process.

Description of the ECD centre

Although the Little People school had started off in a church hall, the dream had always been to build proper premises that would be more conducive for children to learn, grow, and develop. LPPS was established in 1985 in Coronationville, Gauteng, after a primary school teacher recognised a need in the community to equip children with the skills and knowledge required for school readiness and, ultimately, lifelong learning. The history of Little People is a rich tapestry, woven by many difficulties over the years. In 1993, the ceiling in the passage at the church collapsed, so the ECD centre moved to St Joseph's Home, an orphanage in Sophiatown that assisted with accommodation and transport to express its appreciation to the centre for sponsoring several children from the orphanage. In January 1994, the centre relocated to the Coronationville Recreation Centre. In September of that year, a petrol bomb was thrown into the rooms during a political community demonstration. Once again, the ECD centre relocated, this time to an old Catholic church building that was occupied by a teacher's organisation.

After acquiring property in Riverlea Ext. 2, by obtaining a loan, raising funds, and receiving donations, construction began, and the ECD centre was finally able to move into the building in January 1995, 10 years after its start. LPPS is currently a registered non-profit organisation with a functioning governance structure, holds annual general meetings, and, for the past three years, has received some funding from the Department of Social Development.

Parental/caregiver profile

The ECD centre began with families from Coronationville who knew each other from attending the same school, attending the same religious institution, or belonging to the same sports club. Later, it extended to parents and caregivers from the surrounding areas of Newclare, Westbury,

Bosmont, and then the area of Fleurhof. Family composition and size varied, with the majority of parents/caregivers working outside of the community and dropping children off en route to work. During the early years of the ECD centre's existence, parent involvement was successful as most parents and caregivers knew each other. They willingly raised funds and organised social events, including activities like fun walks, sports days, and dances, and worked with staff to organise children's concerts.

When the ECD centre moved to Riverlea Ext. 2, parents and caregivers from the immediate surrounding area enrolled their children. Once again, enrolment expanded to other extensions nearby, including areas like Noordgesig and Pennyville.

The enrolment now comprises diverse working-class families who have expertise that ranges from working in corporate organisations, teaching, and nursing, to owning small businesses. Parents and caregivers are encouraged to volunteer in ways that are not demanding but meaningful. They are invited to participate in events that are hosted at the pre-school, and workshops have been organised to support parenting skills. Parents/caregivers are also invited to be part of the centre's governance through a parent representation committee, and they participate in board decision-making. They have input into school policies and rules. Staff and parents/caregivers work together in the interest of the children.

Beliefs and ethos of the centre

LPPS operates from the foundational ethos that the years of ECD are the most important years of the human life cycle, when children learn about themselves, relationships, the environment, and the world as they are prepared for primary school and lifelong learning. LPPS achieves this by creating an environment where nature and nurture are harnessed to unlock the potential of the children who attend. With support from its staff and parents/caregivers, LPPS provides a developmental space to play, learn, live, and work. For these reasons, LPPS believes that parental involvement brings multiple benefits for the learners, such as improved academic achievements, improved attitudes towards learning, increased security and emotional stability, improved behaviour and better school attendance, and decreased dropout rates, to name just a few (Barge & Loges 2003; De Carvalho 2001; Mahuro & Hungi 2016). LPPS defines parental involvement as parents/caregivers and school staff working together to support and improve the learning development and health of children (Hornby 1990; Abdullahi 2024). For the parents/caregivers, increased self-esteem, improved skills in teaching their children, and fewer feelings of isolation occur because of the engagement (Hilado, Kallemeyn & Phillips 2013; Rattenborg et al. 2019). For teachers and the school, their benefits lie in improved relationships with parents/caregivers, since knowledge of the child's home situation can have a positive influence on education (Hornby & Lafaele 2011; Eden, Chisom & Adeniyi 2024; Appiah-kubi & Amoako 2020). Parental/caregiver involvement can also result in a lighter workload for the teacher and an increased commitment to teaching.

Discussion

The centre has experienced parental/caregiver involvement in different ways, matching the six types of parental involvement proposed by Joyce Epstein (Epstein & Connors 1992; Epstein 2010, 2018): communicating; parenting support; providing a variety of volunteering opportunities; learning at home; decision-making; and collaborating with community. They are elaborated upon below as potential pathways for other ECD centres to consider using in support of parental/caregiver involvement.

Pathway 1: Communicating

Over time, the ECD centre has designed effective forms of communication between the teaching staff and parents/caregivers that promote effective school-to-home and home-to-school communication about school programmes and children's progress. The centre sends out regular newsletters to parents/caregivers and staff members to keep them informed about upcoming programmes, events, and initiatives. These newsletters are distributed via email and/or printed copies, which allows for direct and targeted communication.

The example below illustrates the open email communication between a parent/caregiver and the school principal.

The centre encourages information about programmes and initiatives to be displayed on noticeboards and posters in a prominent area at the entrance to ensure that the information is easily accessible to all members of the school community.

One parent proposed daily communication in order for parents/caregivers to better respond at home.

> My suggestion is for communication to be done on a daily basis. For example, if the kid has been in the office during the day, why has he been there? So that we as parents can deal with it at home as well, especially when the communication of the child is not yet 100% accurate.[*]

---

[*] All quotations in the remainder of the chapter are from research participants, unless a different citation is provided.

Another parent clearly communicated her understanding of her parental duty and did not need the centre to intervene in communicating the need for her involvement.

> As a committed parent, I would not need to be pushed, reminded, or asked to be involved in my child's education or early development, as I see it as my parental duty to be involved from the onset in all the aspects that involve my child's early development and his education.

These sentiments were shared by another parent/caregiver:

> The interview held with the principal was informative in making the decision on whether to continue with the application. As parents who are fully involved with the development of our son, it was delightful to hear the insights the principal has in childhood development by means of reference to books she has read. Also, the participation has confirmed that the pre-school offers services in line with our vision for development and safety of our son.

A proactive request for plans was made by another parent/caregiver, indicating her interest in information for which she needed to plan:

> As we reach the end of the year, a year plan for next year would be highly appreciated, if possible.

The centre plans to make better use of social media platforms such as Facebook, X (formerly Twitter), and Instagram to share updates and information about programmes and initiatives. This will allow for quick and easy communication with a wider audience. There are also plans to create dedicated sections on the centre's website that will include details about goals, benefits, and how parents and caregivers can become involved.

Parent–teacher conferences provide an opportunity for parents/caregivers and teachers to discuss a student's progress as well as any programmes or initiatives that may be relevant to their child.

This face-to-face communication allows for a more personal and detailed discussion. Parents and teachers communicate directly with each other via telephone, email or WhatsApp to arrange these appointments.

The centre organises workshops or information sessions to provide parents/caregivers and students with an opportunity to learn more about specific programmes and initiatives. Developing the different skills that parents have to offer allows for organisational growth and community building. These events include presentations, question-and-answer sessions, and interactive activities. They provide an opportunity for in-depth discussions, brainstorming, and collaboration with relevant stakeholders.

Surveys and feedback forms are used to gather input and suggestions from parents/caregivers, students, and staff members. This allows for two-way communication and helps to provide immediate feedback.

Responses from parents and caregivers for this chapter about their involvement included the following responses to the question of why they were involved:

> We are involved in order for us to educate ourselves with regard to the development of our kids. We always learn every day with our kids; what better way to do it with teachers and other parents?

> I feel that it is of utmost importance for me as a parent to be involved in the Parents' Committee to be in a position to assist the pre-school as and when needed for the growth and prosperity of the school.

> I would like to be involved in my son's early childhood development as well as learning and giving my input as I learn from other parents and their children.

> Our interest in Little People Pre-school was piqued by the excellent feedback from a family friend and observation of their son's development while at Little People Pre-school.

The pathway proposed by Epstein contributes to methods of communication in the South African context that parents/caregivers appreciate and engage in. We need to recognise efforts to sustain this form of communication and the additional time needed to ensure that the communication remains robust.

Pathway 2: Parenting support

The development of practices that help families to establish home environments that will support children is crucial for a child's overall development and well-being. At LPPS, these practices aim to create a nurturing and supportive atmosphere at home, which can positively impact on the child's physical, emotional, cognitive, and social development. LPPS encourages families to establish supportive home environments for children by establishing routines like the routines at school. Setting consistent daily routines for activities such as meals, bedtime, and homework can provide children with a sense of structure and predictability. Routines help children feel secure and develop self-discipline. Parents and caregivers are supported to ensure that their home environment is safe, clean, and free from hazards. They are also encouraged to provide age-appropriate toys, books, and educational materials that can be accessed from LPPS to stimulate their children's curiosity and promote learning. Establishing clear expectations and boundaries helps children understand what is expected of them and promotes responsible behaviour. Consistent enforcement of rules and consequences helps children develop self-control and understand the importance of accountability.

Parents/caregivers are encouraged to create a home environment where children feel comfortable expressing their thoughts, feelings, and concerns. Open and honest communication helps build trust and strengthens the parent–child bond. Healthy habits such as regular exercise, balanced nutrition, and sufficient sleep are essential for children's physical and mental well-being. Parents/caregivers can lead by example and involve children in activities that promote a healthy lifestyle.

Creating a supportive and nurturing environment involves acknowledging and validating children's emotions. Parents/caregivers can offer comfort, empathy, and guidance during challenging times, helping children develop emotional resilience and coping skills. Allowing children to take on age-appropriate responsibilities and encouraging independence fosters their self-confidence and self-esteem. Giving them opportunities to make decisions and solve problems helps develop their critical thinking and decision-making skills. This means that spending quality time together as a family strengthens relationships and creates a sense of belonging.

Engaging in activities such as family meals, game nights, or outings promotes bonding and creates lasting memories. Parents/caregivers can actively support their children's education by showing interest in their schoolwork, attending parent–teacher meetings, and providing a conducive environment for studying. Encouraging a love for learning and providing resources for educational enrichment can enhance children's academic success. Parents/caregivers can benefit from seeking support and resources within their community, such as parenting classes, support groups, or counselling services. These resources can provide guidance, advice, and a network of support for parents in creating a supportive home environment.

LPPS has developed a system that links families to community services, resources, activities, and events. The local clinic is included in this system, and parents/caregivers are responsible for ensuring that their children receive the required immunisations on time. However, if there are any outbreaks of disease, such as measles, the Department of Health and Wellness runs campaigns, and staff from the local clinics visit the ECD centre to immunise children again. During October 2022, ECD centres were visited by clinic staff to check for immunisations that were due and to conduct optimal health checks. Immunisations are not administered without indemnity forms being signed by parents. Once parents/caregivers returned consent forms, some children received their outstanding vaccinations, some received vitamin A drops, and some received deworming treatment.

Those who did not return consent forms or the original clinic cards were requested to take their children to a clinic for their immunisations.

Workshops on parenting skills have also been held. Sometimes workshops are held as fundraising events, for example, breast cancer awareness or HeartPrints (a programme that highlights the acceptance of family members as individuals). Furthermore, parents/caregivers are invited to meet with the teachers, so they can receive feedback on their children's progress, view children's individual portfolios, and ask questions. The quotation below shows a parent's request for more workshops.

> Arrange more parental workshops to create awareness of the different stages of children's growth and development and the activities to do at home to promote their stimulation during the different stages.

For instance, parents/caregivers preferred that the kindergarten and Grade R teachers focus more on nurturing teacher–student interaction as a way to foster family engagement and less on providing parents/caregivers with practical ways to assist. The Grade R children were invited to participate in the City of Johannesburg Kiddies Games, which includes two categories: the regional Kiddies Games and the city-wide Kiddies Games. All the centres received a certificate of participation and a trophy. Region B children won a trip to the Johannesburg Zoo as a prize awarded at the city-wide Kiddies Games. In October 2022, members from the South African Hockey Association and the In-Touch Community Support held a workshop with the staff on Fundamental Movement Skills, which can be adapted for most sport codes. Hockey was introduced to the children as an activity in 2023. Theatrical shows, relating to themes in the learning programme, are booked to reinforce learning for the children. Regular service providers include Spellbound Puppets and Eduvet Kids.

As part of the annual registration process, parents/caregivers need to complete a re-registration form at the end of each year if their child is returning the following year. It is an opportunity for records to be updated, if necessary, as parents do not always provide the information during the year. Acceptance is not automatic. Parents are called to the office for a discussion about parent involvement if their involvement is not satisfactory. Better involvement is discussed, and obstacles are addressed to support their future involvement. This exercise improves relationships between staff and parents.

The pathway proposed by Epstein highlights the extent to which parenting support is needed in the South African context. The demographic profile of parents/caregivers and the high number of households headed by single parents/caregivers add to the need to support parents/caregivers and continuously review their needs within our dynamic, fast-changing context.

Pathway 3: Providing a variety of volunteer opportunities

Involving parents and caregivers as volunteers can enrich and improve the environment for students and contribute to good functionality at the school. Parents are encouraged to volunteer in ways that are meaningful but not demanding. They are invited to volunteer at school activities and participate in recognition events or community events that are hosted at the school. They are also invited to provide training to staff in their areas of expertise. Parents/caregivers volunteer or are elected to serve on the Parent Representative Committee at the annual general meeting. Other areas of involvement include donating paper for the paper bank collection and for recycling, which the children use for creative activities. Retail loyalty programmes (for example, Woolworths, Makro) allow parents/caregivers to fundraise while shopping, when they sign up to the organisation's reward system. Parent/caregiver responses regarding their involvement at the centre included the following:

> Being involved assists me in actively engaging with my children and learning from them what it is that makes school fun and/or enjoyable.

> Little People Pre-School is currently being very active in keeping parents informed of all events that take place or are to take place, therefore I do not think there is need for any further implementation regarding being informed.

> Knowing how to measure all the development of my kids and knowing when to start questioning when something is not achieved.

> I have read articles in which it provides that a parent's involvement in their child's schooling career and development increases the child's potential to grow and have a successful school career/experience.

> We have to measure that it takes so much less to be part of it all. But it means so much more to my son. So, there I was thinking my involvement was for him when it was actually for me. In the end I was learning by giving my input. I was learning from other parents and their children. Learning so much more.

> Volunteering has allowed me to interact with the staff and children differently since observing the daily operations of the facility.

Recently, a former parent, now a grandparent of one of the children attending LPPS, offered her assistance with office administration. Her experience was captured as:

> Working in the office has given me a bigger picture as to what it involves and takes to invest in our children's lives and future. There is a lot to be

done into getting systems in place to manage the office efficiently. When communication is sent out, parents need to respond on time in order for admin to run smoothly.

The pathway proposed by Epstein recognises the multiple ways in which volunteering opportunities can be supported and encouraged in the South African context. Attention must be given to not over-burdening parents/ caregivers as they are faced with multiple other demands.

Pathway 4: Learning at home

Home and family are where children first learn about themselves, relationships, the environment, and the world. This learning is reinforced through access to a quality learning programme at an ECD facility where children learn, develop skills and acquire knowledge that prepares them for school and ultimately lifelong learning (Hornby 1990). We cannot frame ECD in isolation, as such development falls within the timeframe of the human life cycle. Likewise, parent and caregiver involvement cannot be defined in isolation, as such involvement falls within the human environment, which includes parents, family, friends, community, and the educational institution. Parents, together with family, are the primary caregivers, and most parents and families care about their children's education.

During the ECD years, children learn, develop skills and acquire knowledge. Following birth, the Department of Health uses the Road to Health Chart, commonly known as the clinic card, to monitor milestones that occur during the first few years of life. These milestones include growth and development in movement, learning, speech, behaviour, and play. The chart provides a guideline for the changes that we tend to associate with ECD, such as the age at which children start to sit, to crawl, to stand, to walk, to talk, and to respond to adults, among other activities, and when their behaviour tends to change from being passive to having tantrums, and from complaining to being cooperative.

Children learn through their senses, and a good quality ECD programme with age-appropriate routines and activities that promote stimulation should be complemented in the home environment.

The pathway proposed by Epstein highlights the value of learning at home combined with learning in the ECD environment. Our ECD programmes need to allow for what is learned at home to be better incorporated into the programmes. In the South African context, many social ills are experienced in the home environment, such as violence and substance abuse, and ECD programmes need to adapt and incorporate this learning into our curriculum.

Pathway 5: Decision-making

Parents and caregivers become involved in school decisions and develop as parent leaders and representatives by participating in boards and committees. They are invited to be part of the Board and the Parent Committee and participate in decision-making. Thus, they have input into school policies and rules.

One school staff member is appointed as a parent liaison to be the point of contact for parents and caregivers in the school. As part of in-service training, the Grade R teacher joined the principal during the interviews for 2023 applications. This experience was positive for the teacher.

> Being in an interview was interesting as there were open-ended questions, which helped parents to gain a better understanding of the pre-school. It also gave parents the chance to ask questions which stood out the most as it gave parents a chance to think and participate.

> The questions included the learning programme, security throughout the day, the menu, opening and closing times, the general communication at the pre-school, challenges that are faced, school holidays, what happens when children are sick, the need for the change of clothes that is sent, the number of children in each age group and what transport offers are in place. At the end of the interview, parents look forward to completing the application and cannot wait for an acceptance email.

The proposed pathway by Epstein supports the inclusion of parents in the decision-making processes, and while this is not common practice in our South African context, we support the involvement of parents and caregivers through this inclusion.

Pathway 6: Collaborating with the community

The integration of community resources and agencies with school programmes fosters shared responsibility for children (Epstein 2010, 2018). LPPS dreams of building proper premises that are more conducive for children to grow, learn, and develop through the early development phase and into adolescence. There is space at the current location to expand and build an additional building that could serve as a learning centre for older children. The plan is that this additional building (to be called the Udaana Centre) will serve the community as a resource hub and provide space for older children to do homework. Due to the lack of facilities in the area, the premises have been used for different activities over the years, such as Ratepayers' Association meetings, community meetings, and as a voter registration and voting station.

Requests were also received from parents and community members to provide services such as aftercare, adult education, literacy classes, arts and crafts, and holiday programmes. Events held in the outdoor area have been affected by bad weather conditions, hence the idea to build a multipurpose centre.

In August 2017, a fundraiser arranged by staff and community members was held to launch the project to build this centre. The note below was received from one of the attendees.

> What I experience regarding the gathering … Celebrating Humanity of Little People and their supporters, I feel inserted in humanity. I feel a part of humanity, an active member of it. I have a sense of belonging. I feel at home. I feel familiarity – common ground, common experience, common destiny. I experience togetherness, warmth, sameness. I feel rich, expansion, embrace. Joy wells up in me. My face muscles relax. There is a sense of relief, relaxation – home, at home? A feeling of being understood, acceptance, recognition of sameness, oneness, harmony, unity, community. It's a piece of heaven.

The proposed pathway by Epstein recognises the value of collaborating with the community, which is a trusted practice in our South African context, and further fosters the involvement of parents and caregivers by this inclusion, harnessing ubuntu as part of our heritage.

Conclusion

It is important to bring a child's family members into the schoolhouse in a trusting and positive relationship environment in order to establish an effective partnership with school staff. The findings of the investigation suggest that clarifying differences and similarities in teacher and parent/caregiver expectations may facilitate more effective parent/caregiver engagement. These findings have practical promise given that parent–teacher communication, school climate, and role expectations are more easily altered than structural barriers. The strategies and actions presented above provide a framework for how schools can connect and engage with parents/caregivers, and sustain their engagement in preschool activities. Parents/caregivers, schools, and communities all need to work together to create an environment that facilitates the healthy development of children.

Programmes encouraging parent/caregiver involvement or family engagement presently make important contributions to children's lives and have the potential to have an even greater impact. This impact is one that may extend beyond the traditional school setting. Those individuals researching and developing parent involvement/family engagement programmes are urged to continue to move the knowledge base forward for the benefit of all families and their children – regardless of economic status.

References

Abdullahi A (2024) Examining the impact of parental involvement on preschooler's early learning: A case study at the ECCE Demonstration Centre in Jigawa State College of Education and Legal Studies Ringim. *British Journal of Multidisciplinary and Advanced Studies* 5(4):1–11

Appiah-kubi J & Amoako E (2020) Parental participation in children's education: Experiences of parents and teachers in Ghana. *Journal of Theoretical Educational Science* 13(3): 456–473

Barge JK & Loges WE (2003) Parent, student, and teacher perceptions of parental involvement. *Journal of Applied Communication Research* 31(2): 140–163

De Carvalho ME (2001) *Rethinking family–school relations: A critique of parental involvement in schooling.* New York: Routledge

Eden CA, Chisom ON & Adeniyi IS (2024) Parent and community involvement in education: Strengthening partnerships for social Improvement. *International Journal of Applied Research in Social Sciences* 6(3): 372–382

Epstein JL (2010) School/family/community partnerships: Caring for the children we share. *Phi Delta Kappan* 92(3): 81–96. Accessed May 2025, https://doi.org/10.1177/003172171009200326

Epstein JL (2018) School, family, and community partnerships in teachers' professional work. *Journal of Education for Teaching* 44(3): 397–406

Epstein JL & Connors LJ (1992) School and family partnerships. *Practitioner* 18(4): 4–14

Hilado AV, Kallemeyn L & Phillips L (2013) Examining understandings of parent involvement in early childhood programs. *Early Childhood Research & Practice* 15(2): 2

Hornby G (1990) The organisation of parent involvement. *School Organisation* 10(2–3): 247–252

Hornby G & Lafaele R (2011) Barriers to parental involvement in education: An explanatory model. *Educational Review* 63(1): 37–52

Mahuro GM & Hungi N (2016) Parental participation improves student academic achievement: A case of Iganga and Mayuge districts in Uganda. *Cogent Education* 3(1): 1–12

Rattenborg K, MacPhee D, Walker AK & Miller-Heyl J (2019) Pathways to parental engagement: Contributions of parents, teachers, and schools in cultural context. *Early Education and Development* 30(3): 315–336

Conclusion: Systemic Collaboration as an Approach to Parental Involvement

Colleen Magner and Mpinane Mahlatji

Introduction

The chapter is written through the lens of collaboration practices required for addressing parental and caregiver involvement in education. Firstly, it will outline a particular way of approaching complex, system-wide challenges to addressing parental and caregiver involvement in education. The chapter will then summarise the three sections of the book. Using the Systemic Collaboration approach, the chapter ends by proposing seven practices for accelerating systemic collaboration in the parental and caregiver ecosystem, while examining how they apply throughout the book to enable parents, caregivers, and schools to change with speed, scale, and justice.

This book is a critical contribution to understanding and improving parental and caregiver involvement in education in South Africa. Each chapter presents a compelling case that parental or caregiver involvement in children's learning and development, whether at home or at school, plays a catalytic role in improved educational outcomes. When primary caregivers and the school collaborate, they have greater potential to support children's learning and development. Benefits include strengthened relations between the school and parents/caregivers; positive parental/caregiver attitudes towards teachers and the school; improved learner performance in adaptive and social skills; an improved school climate; increased parental/caregiver satisfaction with the school; and overall school improvement.

Unfortunately, the issue of parental or caregiver involvement in children's education is commonly viewed as a stand-alone issue, disconnected from other structural and systemic issues these parents/caregivers and their children may be facing, such as poverty, unemployment, nutritional deficits, sexual and gender-based violence, and the intersection of race since many lower-income parents are Black.

The framing section of the book (Section A) sets out that systemic challenges beyond the education system hinder parental and caregiver involvement. Socio-economic and other barriers (such as language differences) can limit the time available for, and hinder, school involvement, thereby impeding social justice related to parental/caregiver participation. The context section (Section

B) unpacks the South African reality of parental/caregiver involvement as not homogeneous. Without tailored interventions, the relationship between caregivers, their children's learning and development, and the school cannot be adequately addressed. This is particularly the case for parents/caregivers from lower socio-economic backgrounds. Finally, the interventions section (Section C) provides insights into the challenges and opportunities for enhancing parental and caregiver involvement, and advocates for more holistic approaches (involving the whole system surrounding the child) that bridge the gap between home and school to ensure the optimal growth and success of children in South Africa.

A different approach to collaboration

In the face of competing constraints, it is very difficult to allocate time and resources to collaborative efforts as a priority; collaboration also often needs to happen with people who don't understand, trust or agree with each other. Collaboration is particularly important with regard to parent/caregiver involvement. For reasons clearly set out throughout the book, involving parent/caregivers has historical, structural, economic, and social constraints. These barriers to collaboration fragment experiences and perceptions. And the problem with fragmentation is that we all develop different assessments of what is taking place. From this assessment, we derive different conclusions as to what should be done – creating a collaboration gap. To address the issue of parental and caregiver involvement in a holistic, integrated manner that builds trust among the schools, parents/caregivers, governance structures, communities, and support programmes, collaboration is critical.

But we will not be able to solve any of these problems if we do not learn to collaborate better to address this shared and complex challenge. So, how do we become more intentional about learning across the ecosystems in which we work, in order to find faster, more just, and more scalable ways to meet this challenge? As a starting point, a different understanding and approach to addressing complexity is required. Reos Partners, a social impact company designing and facilitating innovative, adaptive strategies, applies a collaborative, systemic, and experimental response to addressing a shared complex challenge, explained below:

- **Collaborative:** The most resilient and sustainable solutions are those that are created and owned by the people (parents, teachers, education activists, schools, governments, and so on) who need to be involved in bringing these solutions to life, embedded from the beginning in collaborative delivery partnerships.
- **Systemic:** A whole systems perspective reflects the diversity of people affected by, and involved in, addressing the obstacles of supporting

children in their education. This enables more creativity and avoids the risk of imposing top-down solutions, which rarely take advantage of the full range of knowledge that can be brought to bear on the problem.

- **Experimental:** There are no preconceived answers to developing an effective and appropriate response to any complex challenge. Trust is required of participants; their answers will emerge through appropriate design and facilitation, and with their full engagement in the process. These intended processes enable participants to apply their collective creativity to developing, prototyping, and testing a portfolio of ideas that can evolve into resilient solutions. Through rapid iterations of trial and error, groups discover what works and can then grow the solution with confidence.

To address the collaboration gap, Reos Partners uses an approach called Systemic Collaboration[1] which is outlined in more detail at the end of this chapter.

The relevance of collaboration to each chapter

Section A: Framing

In the realm of education, the involvement of parents and caregivers plays a pivotal role in shaping the learning outcomes of learners. This involvement, however, is far from uniform and is deeply entwined with socio-economic factors. The framing chapters shed light on the multifaceted dimensions of parental and caregiver involvement through a social justice lens, exploring complexities and addressing the silencing of marginalised voices. These differences in parental and caregiver involvement are fuelled particularly by inequality, and will require a collaborative approach to address, because this power imbalance can make parents and caregivers feel ill-equipped to engage with teachers and school management regarding their children's performance and overall school matters.

Chapter 1 (by McDonald, Mthembu-Salter, and Xaba) underscores the significance of addressing parental/caregiver involvement in education from a social justice perspective. While policy recognises the unequal distribution of income among parents and caregivers, it often falls short in acknowledging the profound impact of that unequal distribution on participation in the educational process. This omission hampers the development of effective remedies and targeted interventions. Parents/caregivers who engage in their children's education convey the value of learning, instilling a sense of importance in their children's endeavours. For parents/caregivers to meaningfully engage, collaboration with the schooling system is required.

Chapter 2 (by Mputle) addresses the dynamics among families, schools, and societies that shape parental involvement in education. Historically, the definition of parental involvement emerged without significant input from parents/caregivers themselves. As education bureaucratised and teaching professionalised in the early 1900s, standards were established that often excluded parents' perspectives on what constituted acceptable support for schools and their children. The chapter encourages us to view schools' interactions with parents and caregivers within broader socio-cultural contexts. The chapter emphasises that parental and caregiver involvement is not a monolithic concept but is heavily influenced by socio-economic class, teachers' perceptions, and geographical factors. These different perceptions need to be shared and understood by the different stakeholders involved. Recognising this diversity is crucial for reforming education to promote parental and caregiver involvement for marginalised individuals who have historically been failed by the system.

Chapter 3 (by Plaatjies) highlights the persistent disparities in access to quality early education, especially among marginalised children living in poverty. The absence of comprehensive parenting/caregiving support programmes further restricts opportunities for vulnerable families. The chapter explores gatekeeping theory, illustrating how powerful stakeholders influence policy decisions and implementation. It identifies a "voice gap", where the voices of citizens are differently heard in policy-making, with powerful gatekeepers holding significant sway. To address these issues, the chapter advocates for open, inclusive, and transparent policy-making processes, requiring collaboration. Diverse voices should be actively sought out and their perspectives considered, while mechanisms for public participation should be strengthened and made accessible to all citizens.

Section B: Contexts

This section explores aspects of parental and caregiver involvement in education, looking into the unique contexts and challenges faced by different stakeholders. From the role of South African parents/caregivers to creating inclusive early childhood care and education environments, and the experiences of school principals and middle-class parents/caregivers, these chapters shed light on the multiple complexities of educational involvement.

Chapter 4 (by De Kock and Cooper) explores the South African educational landscape, emphasising the impact of decentralisation on parental/caregiver involvement. Decentralisation has shifted the power to shape educational policies away from executive or national levels of government to local governments and school governing bodies, where parents/caregivers form a majority. However, this has led to a variety of types of schools and fee policies, impacting parents'/caregivers' interactions with educators on either side of the economic spectrum. The chapter highlights that involvement is heavily conditioned by parents'/caregivers' identity and their ability to navigate school governance structures effectively, which require both the school governance system and parents/caregivers to engage each other.

Chapter 5 (by Mahadew) explores the concept of inclusive early childhood care and education environments (ECCE), and the importance of fostering a sense of belonging for families and communities within ECCE centres. It acknowledges the diversity of family structures in South Africa and the involvement of extended family members and older siblings in caregiving roles. The chapter delves into the concept of ubuntu, which promotes mutual inter-dependence and cooperation within communities. In situations where parents/caregivers are absent or unable to fulfil their roles, extended family members step in collectively for the well-being of children. The chapter also considers Epstein's typology of parental involvement, which includes organising workshops, establishing communication channels, encouraging parent volunteering, extending learning to the home, and involving parents in policy-making – all requiring forms of collaboration.

Chapter 6 (by Mkhize and Govender) focuses on the experiences of school principals in low-income communities regarding parental/caregiver involvement. Despite policies aimed at increasing parental involvement, the study conducted by the authors reveals a low level of parental/caregiver involvement in such schools. The chapter also highlights the impact of the 2021 "July riots", which led to a negative shift in the culture of parental/caregiver involvement. Principals in the study shared both positive and negative experiences, including trauma and wellness issues. Moreover, principals' experiences were found to influence their attitudes toward parental/caregiver involvement. Some developed negative attitudes due to perceived interference from parents/caregivers, poor parental/caregiver attitudes, and a lack of trust. However, despite these challenges, some principals were striving to change the culture of involvement. The three main collaboration strategies employed by principals to promote and sustain parental/caregiver involvement included: frequent communication with parents/caregivers, creating a welcoming environment, and building the leadership capacities of school governing body members.

Chapter 7 (by Paterson, Ehren, and Vally) looks at the complex issue of blame and blaming within the South African education system, focusing on four primary schools. The authors differentiate between the national-level "discourse of blame" surrounding education system performance and the localised "narratives of blame" that emerge among school participants, particularly parents/caregivers and teachers. Blame interacts with trust and accountability, creating feedback loops that can impact learner achievement. The chapter shows how the cycle of blame can lead to fear and cover-ups, and can hinder productive conversations. These feedback loops, if part of a collaborative approach, could be critical to shifting the discourse of blame.

Chapter 8 (by Myende and Myende) explores parental involvement among Black middle-class parents. Despite their substantial economic resources, these parents face unique challenges. Using their own experiences, the authors examine their ability to build their child's agency, the outsourcing of parental responsibilities, and the potentially gendered nature of parental involvement, with mothers often bearing primary responsibility. How Black middle-class parents navigate these challenges will require structured collaborative efforts.

In conclusion, these chapters in Section B collectively provide a comprehensive overview of the unique contexts and challenges surrounding parental and caregiver involvement in education in South Africa, shedding light on the nuanced dynamics that shape these interactions and their impact on educational outcomes.

Section C: Intervening

The five chapters in this section examine the critical topic of intervening in parental and caregiver involvement in education, particularly in the context of South and southern Africa. These chapters shed light on various aspects including the importance of parental and caregiver involvement, strategies to enhance engagement, and the impact of programmes designed to bridge the gap between home and school.

Chapter 9 (by Porteus, Roberts, and Mazeka) discusses a case study of an intervention conducted in rural South Africa that explores parental/caregiver involvement in Grade 2 mathematics homework during the COVID-19 pandemic. The research aimed to understand parents'/caregivers' experiences in supporting homework, extract design principles for parent-friendly homework materials, and explore how parents/caregivers supported early grade mathematics homework. The study identified five key interrelated indicators for evaluating parental involvement: parental role construct; parental self-efficacy; invitations for involvement; educational expectations; and relationships. The findings reveal that parents/caregivers expanded their understanding of their role, felt needed by their children, and developed self-efficacy in supporting homework. Parents' relationships with their children and teachers improved, and their expectations for their children's performance increased. Overall, the findings indicate that engaging parents collaboratively in supporting homework, especially in rural settings, could lead to a self-reinforcing cycle of improved relationships, expectations, and parental self-efficacy, ultimately benefiting children's education.

Chapter 10 (by Gibbs and Bodley) looks at the significance of parental involvement in education, particularly during a child's early years. The chapter discusses common challenges faced by rural primary schools in South Africa including limited parental/caregiver involvement and access to educational resources, as well as literacy and numeracy skill gaps among children. As with previous chapters, this chapter emphasises the multifaceted nature of parental involvement, encompassing support at home, engagement with the school, and effective communication between parents/caregivers and teachers. One of the key barriers identified in the chapter is the misconception among parents and caregivers that their children's education is solely the schools' responsibility. To address this mindset, the authors highlight the importance of demonstrating to parents through active engagement the pivotal role they play in their children's education. Recommendations include capacitating teachers to effectively engage with parents, increasing practical contact time, and tailoring parental involvement programmes to the specific challenges parents and caregivers face such as work commitments and literacy levels.

Chapter 11 (by Gonzalez and Mkhabele) focuses on the critical role of parents and caregivers in early childhood development (ECD) ecosystems. The chapter underscores the idea that a child's environment during the early years significantly impacts the child's development, covering factors like nutrition, safety, nurturing, and stimulating interactions. Parents and caregivers are positioned as essential actors in shaping a child's developmental path. The chapter introduces the aRe Bapaleng Programme. Designed to support parents/caregivers in marginalised communities, the programme emphasises the holistic approach, addressing various aspects of the ECD ecosystem including capacity-building and employment opportunities for caregivers. The programme's capacity to offer employment opportunities further underscores its importance. Collaboration with social partners, including non-profit organisations and community-based organisations, is highlighted as a strategy to extend the reach of ECD training and support initiatives.

Chapter 12 (by Von Blottnitz and O'Carroll) introduces the Together in My Education (TIME) Home Learning Programme, a response to the educational challenges posed by the COVID-19 pandemic. TIME is designed to engage Grade R and Grade 1 children (and their families) in interactive learning routines at home. The programme addresses the role of parents and caregivers in supporting missed learning opportunities due to school disruptions, and presents research from various African contexts that emphasises the positive effects of parental interventions. However, the chapter acknowledges the scepticism and limitations associated with parental/caregiver programmes including variable uptake and challenges in monitoring adherence.

Chapter 13 (by Mooi and Dreyer) discusses pathways to implement effective parental/caregiver involvement programmes in South and southern Africa. It emphasises the need to address barriers to parental/caregiver engagement in early childhood education programmes to create a more inclusive and supportive environment. The chapter introduces six pathways for effective parental/caregiver involvement:

1. **Communicating:** Establishing effective communication between schools and parents/caregivers through various channels, including social media, parent–teacher conferences, workshops, surveys, and feedback forms.

2. **Parenting support:** Encouraging families to establish supportive home environments by implementing consistent daily routines, and linking families to community services and resources.

3. **Volunteer opportunities:** Involving parents and caregivers as volunteers to enrich the learning environment for students.

4. **Learning at home:** Recognising the home as the primary place for children to learn and develop, and promoting educational activities at home.

5. **Decision-making:** Involving parents/caregivers in school decisions and governance to develop parent leaders and representatives.

6. **Collaborating with the community:** Integrating community resources and agencies into school programmes, fostering shared responsibility for children's development.

The chapter highlights the importance of these pathways in overcoming the limitations to parental/caregiver involvement in early childhood education programmes.

A final note: Applying the practices of Systemic Collaboration

As a final note, the authors have outlined the seven leadership practices for Systemic Collaboration. These practices form a framework that education stakeholders may employ to work together to move forward with speed, scale, and justice.

The parental or caregiver involvement challenge facing the South African education sector is substantial and requires a collective response. Across the region and globally, we are seeing people outside the formal education systems stepping forward to act together in big and small ways. This includes numerous different kinds of multi-stakeholder education collaborations, coalitions, campaigns, and partnerships. Some of these collaborations are producing extraordinary results in the sector, but, in the face of increasing socio-economic headwinds, they are not yet big enough or fast enough, even combined, to achieve the societal transformations in education necessary for a just future for children, particularly in South Africa. More than ever, the time to upgrade our capacity to combine resources and to work together is now.

Systemic Collaboration is a pragmatic and proven approach to working together across differences. While Systemic Collaboration is not new (many people are already using it), many more people must now learn to use it quickly. For some, this will be a familiar and easy process, while others will find it more unfamiliar and challenging.

Practice 1: Play your role

Firstly, when exploring collaboration, it is important to decide how your collaboration will play its specific role in the education sector and how you will play your individual role within this collaboration, using your head (your strategic and systemic assessment), your heart (your passion and commitment), and your hands (your learning – from your own experiences and those of others – about what works in practice). The message is: Don't ignore the inter-dependencies with what others are doing. Unite when you can and differentiate when you must. Understanding your strengths and weaknesses as well as those of your fellow collaborators will help leaders to know who to lean on as you move through the practices. Be creative and test multiple solutions: the realm of radical imagination involves finding more creative ways to resolve stuck situations that are not working optimally. Hard evidence shows that creativity yields more effective outputs, and the birthplace of creativity is our collective imagination.[2]

Chapter 6, as an example of playing your role, builds an understanding of, and appreciation for, the unique role principals play in the education ecosystem. We see the development of the three main strategies to promote and sustain parental/caregiver involvement, and can develop an appreciation that the principal's lens is invaluable and, when used correctly, can help the system see itself from the inside out.

Practice 2: Discover necessary allies

To overcome the many inevitable obstacles along the way, actors must collaborate with people who share the same goal and have diverse and complementary capacities. This includes people who are living with and understand the problem you're trying to solve, and who have the will, energy, and capacity to deliver solutions. Leveraging the wisdom of others allows us to innovate and come up with solutions beyond the models we are accustomed to. Amis and Janz write about innovation during the times of COVID-19, but that successful innovation requires the ability to harness the collective insights of a group, and a willingness to engage rapidly with new ideas (Amis & Janz 2020).

The aRe Bapaleng programme in Chapter 11 actively supports parents/caregivers as necessary allies in marginalised communities, and is a product of a holistic approach that addresses various aspects of the ECD ecosystem, including capacity-building and employment for parents/caregivers. The programme's capacity to offer employment opportunities further underscores its importance. Parents/caregivers are not seen simply as missing in the system; they are at the centre of the solution and, when supported, can enable the transformative shift sought.

Practice 3: Build collective power

A collaboration needs collective power to play its role in effecting systemic transformation. This requires recognising and bringing together the different types of assets that each actor can contribute – authority, money, technologies, ideas, followers – to grow your individual and collective capacities. Exercising power together, fairly, is required for speed and scale.

Chapter 13 discusses pathways to implement effective parental/caregiver involvement programmes in South and southern Africa by building collective power. One of the pathways is "collaborating with the community", which suggests the importance of integrating community resources and agencies into school programmes, thus fostering shared responsibility for children's development. This is a successful example of how building collective power amongst stakeholders enables shared leadership and accountability across the ecosystem.

Practice 4: Work your differences

The primary reason for collaborators getting stuck and not achieving change is that they are unable to work productively with their differences and disagreements. Collaborators face different realities, opportunities, and constraints, and so have different positions, perspectives, and powers. This diversity can help you to see more clearly and navigate better through complex and confusing terrain.

In Chapter 5, socio-cultural differences are identified as barriers to family partnerships, emphasising the need for educators to work their differences, and be culturally sensitive and open to learning from parents/caregivers. Appreciating contexts and the concept of ubuntu, which promotes mutual inter-dependence and cooperation within communities, are critical to multi-stakeholder collaborations, even if collaborators do not agree with one another.

Practice 5: Discover ways forward

In playing your role within the complex ecosystem, the way forward will rarely be clear or straightforward. It is not a highway: you cannot clear away the obstacles and make a straight road before you start. The only way to advance with speed, scale, and justice in education is through rapid, disciplined, and iterative experimentation.

> In Chapter 2, we see evidence of the impact of decentralisation on parental/caregiver involvement. As mapped out in the chapter, this has led to a variety of types of schools and fee policies, illustrating that in reality the way forward is not linear. The gap between policy intentions and realities persists, so thinking about the way forward must be done in an agile, adaptable way to set conditions that develop fit-for-purpose solutions.

Practice 6: Share hopeful stories

People more willingly move forward together with compelling stories of realistic hope. Multi-stakeholder groups need narratives and maps about where they are, where they are trying to get to, and why it is important that they move out of the status quo.

> Chapter 12 describes how the TIME Home Learning Programme engages Grade R and Grade 1 children and their families in interactive learning routines at home. TIME's significant outcome is the strengthened bond between parents/caregivers and children. This improvement is attributed to increased time spent together, the fun factor, and opportunities for deeper conversations. This is the kind of narrative that helps to provide perspective and, more than anything else, hope.

Practice 7: Care for yourselves

A healthy movement towards a healthy future requires healthy people, both physically and mentally. You will not be able to move with speed, scale, and justice if you do not take care of yourself and your companions, and acknowledge that we all need support, particularly in difficult social contexts. This seventh practice enables the other six – and it is also the most neglected.

> There is little reference to this practice in the book, which might be useful data of a potential blind spot in the education and parental/caregiver ecosystem. In Chapter 6, there was a real opportunity for this practice to significantly alter the outcomes of principal engagement by paying attention to the care and wellness of principals.

Conclusion

Engaging in Systemic Collaboration requires a willingness to learn about and start applying the seven practices. You do not need a fully aligned team to begin. To get started, we often suggest that engagement is more important than buy-in at this stage of a collaborative partnership. Asking others involved in this shared challenge if they are willing to simply explore other ways of working together is enough to start the effort. With their engagement secured, stakeholders can move into action where teams learn about the seven practices and discuss how they impact the work of the collaboration.

The best way to prepare for the process is to apply Practice 1: Play Your Role. Systems mapping and listening to diverse perspectives are often helpful tools. Look around and assess the best role that you can play in helping the collaboration to learn about and apply the practices. The willingness to listen and to learn from others are important factors in the success of systemic collaborations. Without this willingness, it is hard to apply the practices honestly and sincerely.

To collaborate in contexts that are complex, conflicting, and where we do not have control, we need to stretch beyond what is habitual and comfortable. When ready, collaborations that consistently apply these principles are more likely to produce an inclusive, cooperative, and responsive collaboration. Failing to do so increases the risks of producing a collaboration that is insular, competitive, and rigid, and for which there is no space in the education sector.

Notes

1   Radical Climate Collaboration. Website. Accessed July 2025, https://radicalclimatecollaboration.reospartners.com/.

2   Magner C (2020) Facing down crises with radical imagination and experimentation. *Acumen* (33): 54–57. Accessed May 2025, https://www.acumenmagazine.co.za/articles/facing-down-crises-with-radical-imagination-and-experimentation-11202.html

References

Amis JM & Janz BD (2020) Leading change in response to COVID-19. *The Journal of Applied Behavioral Science* 56(3): 272–278. Accessed May 2025, https://journals.sagepub.com/doi/pdf/10.1177/0021886320936703

About the Authors

Kimberleigh Bodley holds a Bachelor of Social Sciences and a master's degree in psychology, with a dissertation focused on the role of parents in early childhood development in disadvantaged communities in South Africa, from the University of KwaZulu-Natal. She is the founding director of Alladin Learning Solutions (ALS), which designs and implements contextually appropriate early childhood development and education programmes in disadvantaged communities across the country. ALS programmes have been successfully implemented in collaboration with prominent corporate companies such as the Mr Price Foundation, Anglo American South Africa, and Growthpoint Properties.

Adam Cooper is a chief research specialist focused on equitable education and economies at the Human Sciences Research Council. He is also a research associate with the Chair in Youth Unemployment, Employability, and Empowerment at Nelson Mandela University. Adam works at the intersection of the sociologies of youth and education, looking at the practices and policies that empower young people to realise their aspirations. He is the author of *Dialogue in Places of Learning: Youth Amplified in South Africa* (2016) and a co-editor of the *Oxford Handbook of Global South Youth Studies* (2021). Recently, his work has focused on the complex ways young people navigate the worlds of education and work, and the relationships between them.

Tarryn de Kock works as a researcher within the fields of basic and higher education, contributing to reporting, research and programme design, data analysis, and evaluation. She previously worked at the Human Sciences Research Council as a senior researcher, contributing to the official evaluation of the Public Schools Partnership in the Western Cape (South Africa), as well as The Imprint of Education longitudinal study of the Mastercard Foundation Scholars' Programme. Her current work focuses on political economy and governance issues in the making of public education in the Global South.

Abigail Ruth Dreyer is Head of LINK (Learning, Influence, Networking, and Knowledge) at Paediatric–Adolescent Treatment Africa in Cape Town. Prior to this, she was a full-time lecturer in the Department of Family Medicine, Division of Rural Health, at the University of the Witwatersrand. She served as the chairperson of the faculty committee for Community-Based Health Science Education. She is joint faculty for the Sub-Saharan African FAIMER Regional Institute, which supports medical education. Abigail holds a Consortium for Advanced Research Training in Africa fellowship and a fellowship with the sub-Saharan FAIMER Regional Institute. She has more than 25 years of experience working in rural and under-served communities in the Western Cape, Free State, Gauteng, North West, Mpumalanga, Lesotho, and Swaziland. Her teaching is centred on faculty development, and undergraduate and postgraduate programmes in the faculty. She maintains and fosters learning opportunities in communities for students to apply their skills to contribute to community citizenship. Her research interests include curriculum design, innovations in medical and health professions education, community-engaged teaching, collaborative practice, inter-professional teaching, and research that contributes to improving the quality of health care in rural and under-served areas. Her PhD explored the use of decentralised training platforms in the undergraduate training of medical students. As part of her academic citizenship, she served on the board of Little People Preschool as the chairperson from 2020–2024. Currently, she is an extraordinary lecturer at the University of Stellenbosch and an ex-officio member on the current board of Little People Preschool.

Melanie Ehren is a professor in educational governance at the Vrije Universiteit Amsterdam, with previous roles at University College London and visiting professorships at Harvard and Columbia universities. She combines a strong disciplinary background in educational and school effectiveness with a comparative approach to understanding outcomes of education systems. She is a member of the board of ICSEI, the International Congress for School Effectiveness and Improvement, and has worked with various international organisations, including the OECD, UNESCO, and the European Union.

Craig Gibbs holds a master of science degree in research (with distinction) from the University of Portsmouth and is currently a doctoral candidate. His doctoral research explores the impact of e-learning on teacher development. With 25 years of experience as an educator in South Africa and England, including over a decade as a school principal, he brings deep insight into educational leadership and innovation. He has played a central role in conceptualising, designing, implementing, and managing large-scale education projects across South Africa through his work with JET Education Services, including initiatives for the Anglo American South Africa and the Mr Price Foundation. He has been instrumental in the development and delivery of JET's e-learning, artificial intelligence and EdTech programmes, particularly in resource-constrained schools. Additionally, he has led the implementation of leadership, teacher development, learner support, and community engagement programmes across all provinces. A significant focus of his work is on the innovative design and management of research projects that generate actionable insights, with the potential to inform and influence both educational practice and policy. He has written concept papers and many successful competitive proposal and tender documents that won the opportunity to implement a variety of intervention programmes.

Ximena Gonzalez is an independent economist with more than 20 years' experience in the development sector in South Africa. She has worked in a range of areas from trade and industrial policy through to community development, public employment, and early learning programmes. For several years, Ximena headed up Trade and Industrial Policy Strategies, a think tank that provides key policy research and insights to the South African government. Currently, Ximena is part of the team that has created and continues to implement Seriti's aRe Bapaleng Programme, which works with parents and caregivers in marginalised communities to ensure they are able to provide early learning support to the young children in their care. She is passionate about making a difference and catalysing social change through innovative approaches.

Kerishka Govender is a young primary-school educator working in a low-income community since 2018, after graduating in 2017 with her BEd degree from the University of KwaZulu-Natal. While working, Kerishka then went on to pursue her honours in education specialising in educational leadership, management, and administration before returning to the University of KwaZulu-Natal to complete her master's degree specialising in educational leadership, management, and policy part-time. She is currently pursuing her PhD specialising in educational leadership, management, and policy. As a fourth-generation South African educator working in a low-income community, Kerishka became aware of the contextual realities plaguing under-privileged communities from an early age. This sparked her interest in researching parental involvement and teacher job satisfaction in low-income communities.

Colleen Magner is a co-founder of Reos Partners and Director of Innovation and Practice for the Reos Africa office. Since joining Reos in 2007, Colleen has led and managed multi-stakeholder projects in more than 20 countries across a range of issues including food security, land reform, peace and justice transformation, health care, education, mining safety, climate change, and support for orphans and vulnerable children. Colleen is a scenario-planning expert, and has facilitated scenario processes across sectors since 2003. Colleen is also a writer and an adjunct faculty member at the Gordon Institute of Business Science (GIBS). At GIBS, Colleen teaches on social entrepreneurship, systems thinking for organisations, transformative scenario planning, participative practices for social change, and using dialogue for tough problems. Prior to joining GIBS, Colleen worked at the headquarters of PricewaterhouseCoopers in New York from 1997–1999. Colleen graduated with a BCom (Law) from Nelson Mandela University in 1995 and an MCom in organisational change (cum laude) from the University of KwaZulu-Natal in 2004. She has attended the following executive programmes: 'Leadership for systems change' at Harvard Kennedy School, and 'Making markets work' and 'Teaching the practice of management', both offered by Harvard Business School.

Ashnie Mahadew is an academic from the School of Education at the University of KwaZulu-Natal. She holds teaching qualifications and an honours degree in psychology. She completed her master's and PhD degrees at the University of KwaZulu-Natal. She had spent 20 years as a foundation phase teacher before joining the university where she currently lectures to Bachelor of Education students. Mahadew also supervises postgraduate students, and her research focuses on community-based action research in the early childhood care and education sector. She is a mother of two children and enjoys spending quality time with her family.

Mpinane Mahlatji brings with her purpose-driven, socially conscious communications skills rooted in addressing some of the world's most complex social challenges. She is a team player with an agile organisational and learning mindset. Her role involves process facilitation, hosting, participating, and managing client project work and consulting communications. This includes project and stakeholder relations management, conducting client dialogue interviews, producing reports, including synthesising qualitative information, and coaching. Mpinane works with large groups of people in a variety of institutional contexts including education, climate, energy, economic inclusion, health and equity, land and food, and peace and democracy. Her background as a journalist brings aspects of communicative intuition to her work that she often leverages when collaborating with people.

Nobuntu Mazeka was born and bred in rural Mbizana, Eastern Cape, and has been a community activist since her earliest days. For the past 20 years she has worked with the Nelson Mandela Institute for Education and Rural Development, University of Fort Hare. She entered education as a parent activist, coordinating local community education fora in the Mbizana area – a mechanism to increase the participation of parents in local schools. This experience motivated her to study education, in which she received an honours degree in 2020. Nobuntu currently supports teachers to improve their teaching through classroom-based coaching in literacy and mathematics. She is especially interested in how to transform mathematics teaching and learning in the context of rural South Africa. She is currently studying toward her master's degree. She participates in a plethora of community organisations, sitting on the board of Sustaining Wild Coast, and on the project steering committee for Meje Health Care Centre.

Zahraa McDonald is an associate professor in the Department of Religion Studies at the University of Johannesburg, South Africa. She is a sociologist who focuses on the intersection between education, citizenship, and religion. After her PhD, which examined the intersection of Islamic education and post-secular citizenship, she completed post-doctoral fellowships at Stellenbosch University, the University of Cape Town, Cape Peninsula University of Technology, and University of Johannesburg. She has published on the intersections of education and religion.

Khanyisa Mkhabele is a senior evaluation officer at the Department of Planning, Monitoring, and Evaluation in the South African government. She works at the evaluation chief directorate, which is responsible for managing evaluations in the National Evaluation Plan, as well as managing the capacity development sphere per the National Evaluation Policy Framework (2019). She has experience in designing, monitoring, and undertaking evaluations of public programmes, projects, and policies. Khanyisa is passionate about problem-solving, primarily issues addressing unemployment, poverty, and inequalities. Previously, she worked for the Seriti Institute as a monitoring and evaluation officer and as a junior researcher at the Human Sciences Research Council. Academically, she is an honours graduate in economics from the University of Johannesburg, while holding a BSc in Agricultural Economics from the University of Limpopo.

Bongani Nhlanhla Mkhize is a senior lecturer at the University of Johannesburg in the Department of Education Leadership and Management. He has experience as a teacher and a middle manager in secondary schools from 1994 to 2014. Bongani holds a PhD degree specialising in educational leadership and Management. His research interest is in school and district leadership, with a special focus on leading education for sustainable futures. He has published peer-reviewed journal articles and book chapters in his research area and presented papers at both local and international conferences.

Adele Mooi is a passionate advocate for early childhood development, bringing nearly 40 years of experience and dedication to her work. As one of the four founders of Little People Preschool in 1985, she recognised a critical need in her community to prepare young children for school readiness and lifelong learning. What began as a job creation effort has evolved into a thriving institution, now a registered non-profit organisation with a dedicated team and a strong governance framework. The journey of Little People Preschool has been one of resilience and growth. Originally housed in a church hall in Coronationville, the preschool faced various challenges, including relocating multiple times before establishing a permanent home in Riverlea Ext. 2. Under Adele's leadership, the centre has transformed into a beacon for quality ECD, supported by government funding and a commitment to serving the community. As director of ECD at the Dr

CL Smith Foundation, Adele leads initiatives such as article writing for ECD mentorship on the Zibuza platform, organising book fairs to provide children with access to books, and collaborating on training programmes for ECD practitioners. Her work aligns deeply with the foundation's focus on education, contributing to the solid foundation essential for lifelong learning. Inspired by the metaphor of a seedling (*isithombo in isiZulu*), Adele founded Isithombo to support the universalisation of ECD. Isithombo represents the fragile yet promising nature of childhood, a period that requires nurturing, protection, and guidance. Through Isithombo, she offers training and resources that foster the holistic development of young children. Adele is also an accomplished author, having written ten storybooks focused on life skills. Her books cover topics such as 'Who am I?', 'Healthy Living', and 'Your Rights and Needs', designed to engage young readers and teach essential life skills in an enjoyable way. Adele's storytelling is a resource for children's language development, helping them learn about themselves, relationships, and their environment.

Bakang Mputle is currently pursuing a PhD in geography and environmental studies at Stellenbosch University, focusing on climate justice, political ecology, and the just energy transition. He holds multiple degrees from the University of the Witwatersrand: a bachelor of education, an honours in geography and environmental science, and a master's in geography education. His master's research analysed how in-service geography educators interpret and teach education for sustainable development. As a lecturer in geography and environmental education, Bakang continues to influence the field through teaching and research. Inspired by his late grandfather, a passionate geographer and educator, Bakang developed an early interest in environmental issues. He integrates his passion for fine art and photography into his academic work, using these media to communicate environmental themes and engage broader audiences. Through his interdisciplinary approach, Bakang exemplifies a commitment to fostering sustainable development and environmental awareness in South Africa.

Lungelo Mthembu-Salter is currently studying a master's degree in development studies at the University of the Witwatersrand. His dissertation looks at the ways in which the life histories of teachers and principals influence their mindsets to either embrace or reject an AI gamified maths programme. Such socially oriented research has been informed by his honours in history at the university of Cape Town (which looked at how community and creolisation helped South African slaves to survive) as well as his undergraduate degree in history and anthropology, also from UCT. Lungelo is also currently a sessional lecturer in game design at the University of the Witwatersrand, as part of the Digital Arts Department, where he hopes to contribute towards research that looks at the roles that digital games (as related to his master's) and games in general can play in everyday life. Away from his studies, his commitment towards social development also includes working as a researcher for JET Education Services, an organisation committed towards improving education in the southern hemisphere, as well as authoring and illustrating a book that looks at South Africa and the earliest humans, hunter gatherers, before the advent of pastoralism, so that South Africa, as well as humanity, can increase their appreciation of their shared legacy in an accessible manner.

Phumlani Myende is an associate professor of educational leadership, management, and policy in the School of Education at the University of KwaZulu-Natal. He teaches modules in educational leadership and management at both honours and master's level. He has supervised numerous postgraduate students at master's and PhD level to completion. His broad research interests include leadership in the context of deprivation and rurality. He has published papers and book chapters on school–community partnership, parental involvement, asset-based leadership, school financial management, and leadership for teaching and learning in deprived school contexts.

Thembeka Myende is a lecturer in the Department of Educational Foundations, College of Education, University of South Africa. Her research interests are focused on gender inequalities in education and the sexualities of young people.

Shelley O'Carroll started her career as a remedial teacher and educational psychologist with a special interest in reading difficulties. She has a PhD from the University of London and was the founding director of Wordworks, a leading early literacy NGO. She has written content for early language and literacy programmes, and been involved in research exploring the impact of early interventions.

Andrew Paterson is a research associate with JET Education Services He has teaching experience in sociology and history of education, and education and development programmes in higher education faculties, mainly in South Africa. He has worked in full-time research positions at the Human Sciences Research Council, at the Development Bank of Southern Africa, and more recently at JET Education Services. His work has centred mainly on addressing the challenges of national human resource development, and on exploring the relationships between education and training, employment, and economic development. His research spans skills formation in economic sectors; private sector workplace training; public sector skills development; and TVET systems and their links to the labour market. His recent research includes skills recognition and certification for labour mobility of migrants, refugees, and marginalised youth across several African countries; trust and accountability in school systems; and values education in the TVET curriculum.

Lydia-Anne Plaatjies holds a master's degree in journalism and media studies and a PhD in education. She combines her educational and practical experiences of working in the ECD sector as a community worker, trainer, curriculum developer, facilitator, and researcher, with a deep understanding and empathy for the environments in which children are raised. Lydia-Anne understands the ECD policy environment and the complexity of trying to offer integrated ECD services, and continuously advocates for the use of social media, radio, television, and SMS to communicate cost-effectively with the marginalised public.

Kimberley A. Porteus, PhD, is the executive director of the Nelson Mandela Institute for Education and Rural Development, founded by the late President Nelson Mandela at his alma mater, the University of Fort Hare. Her early work focused on education policy transformation following the first democratic elections in South Africa in 1994. In 2004, she moved to the Eastern Cape, interested in gazing up at national policy from the perspective of rural primary classrooms. Working with her primary collaborator, Dr Brian Ramadiro, Kimberley developed an education design hub located within, and accountable to, the exigencies of rural primary-school classrooms. Concerned that the knowledge project in South Africa is not accountable to the majority of its children, she and Brian Porteus have been working with primary school teachers at the chalkface of their classrooms to develop knowledge, tools, and theory to improve teaching and learning at system scale. While Ramadiro's work focuses on literacies, Porteus's work focuses on mathematics education.

Nicky Roberts is director of Kelello Consulting and an extraordinary associate professor at Stellenbosch University. Her education research encompasses both qualitative and quantitative methods, and extensive evaluation experience (in South Africa and internationally). Her teams bring particular expertise in mathematics, languages, technology-enhanced learning, and assessment. The Kelello team offers monitoring, evaluation, and strategic research, frequently acting as technical assistants for large entities such as governments or corporates investing in improving education outcomes. Nicky is widely published in peer-reviewed academic journals, and has written book chapters. She has served on the executive of the Southern African Association for Research in Mathematics, Science, and Technology Education and is a trustee for the International Group for the Psychology of Mathematics Education. She has co-edited two books: *The Pedagogy of Mathematics in South Africa* (with Paul Webb, 2017) and *Early Grade Mathematics in South Africa* (with Hamsa Venkat, 2022).

Zaahedah Vally is a researcher at JET Education Services. After being a fellow on the ASRI Future Leaders Programme, Zaahedah joined JET Education Services in late 2017 as a research intern. Zaahedah is and has been involved in several local and international education interventions focused on the research as well as monitoring and evaluation. Zaahedah is enrolled for a master's degree at the Wits School of Governance, specialising in governance (management: development and economics) and has a keen interest in innovative financing in education.

Magali von Blottnitz holds degrees from French and German universities and a PhD from the University of Cape Town. She worked as a researcher in economics and finance before taking a career turn to the education sector in 2007. She has specialised in monitoring and evaluation since 2016 and now works as a monitoring, evaluation, research, and learning consultant for organisations in the early literacy sector, including Wordworks.

Noxolo Xaba is an academic advisor at the South African College of Applied Psychology in Johannesburg. She graduated from the University of Johannesburg with a Bachelor of Humanities in psychology and a Bachelor of Honours in sociology. She has educational experience in academic support roles and has worked as an Early Learning Outcomes Measure assessor with younger children aged between four and seven. She is raising her own son who is currently three years old. Noxolo worked at JET Education Services in the Research and Data Ecosystems Division where she worked closely on the development of the chapters of this book and co-authored the first chapter. Topics regarding parental and caregiver involvement in education are close to her heart as she has been involved in the school affairs of her younger sibling and her nieces.

Index